Chelsea School Resear~~ ~~
Vol

Graham McFee (ed.)

Dance, Education and Philosophy

Meyer & Meyer Sport

British Library Cataloguing in Publication Data
A catalogue record for this book is available from the British Library

Dance, Education and Philosophy /
Graham McFee (ed.).
– Oxford : Meyer & Meyer Sport (UK) Ltd., 1999
(Chelsea School Research Centre Edition ; Vol. 7)
ISBN 1-84126-008-8

© 1999 by Meyer & Meyer Sport (UK) Ltd
Oxford, Aachen, Olten (CH), Vienna,
Québec, Lansing/ Michigan, Adelaide, Auckland, Johannesburg
Cover design: Walter J. Neumann, N&N Design-Studio, Aachen
Cover exposure: frw, Reiner Wahlen, Aachen
Typesetting: Myrene L. McFee
Printed and bound in Germany by
Firma Mennicken, Aachen
e-mail: verlag@meyer-meyer-sports.com
ISBN 1-84126-008-8

Contents

About the Contributors vii

Chapter 1   Introduction: Thinking Through Dance Studies
             Graham McFee 1

Chapter 2   Dance, Imitation and Representation
             Noël Carroll and Sally Banes 13

Chapter 3   The Historical Character of Dances
             Bonnie Rowell 33

Chapter 4   Productions, Performances, and Their Evaluation
             Aaron Meskin 45

Chapter 5   On Knowing What Dancing Is
             Francis Sparshott 63

Chapter 6   Do Rabbits Dance? A Problem Concerning the
             Identification of Dance
             Sue Jones 85

Chapter 7   Dance Before You Think
             David Best 101

Chapter 8   Further Reflections on Practical Knowledge and
             Dance a Decade On
             David Carr 123

Chapter 9   Dancing Bodies: Can the Art of Dance Be Restored
             to Dance Studies?
             Chris Challis 143

Chapter 10   Technicality, Philosophy and Dance-Study
             Graham McFee 155

Index   189

ABOUT THE CONTRIBUTORS

SALLY BANES is the Marian Hannah Winter Professor of Theatre and Dance Studies at University of Wisconsin-Madison, where from 1992-96 she was chair of the Dance Program. She is the author of *Greenwich Village 1963: Avant- Garde Performance and the Effervescent Body*; *Writing Dancing in the Age of Postmodernism*; *Terpsichore in Sneakers: Post-Modern Dance*; and *Democracy's Body: Judson Dance Theater 1962-1964* and contributed the chapter on breakdancing to *Fresh: Hip Hop Don't Stop*. Her most recent books are *Dancing Women: Female Bodies on Stage* and *Subversive Expectations: Performance Art and Paratheater in New York 1976-85*. She has twice been president of the Dance Critics Association, was on the board of directors of Congress on Research in Dance, and is currently the president of the Society of Dance History Scholars.

DAVID BEST is Professor of Philosophy, Department of Philosophy, University of Wales; Senior Academic Fellow and Honorary Professor, De Montfort University; Visiting Professor Sibelius Academy, Helsinki; and Visiting Professor, International Centre for the Study of Drama in Education. Formerly he was Consultant to Bretton Hall College of the Arts and Visiting Professor, School of Theatre, Manchester Metropolitan University. He is an invited member of the International Association of leading academics and artists, dedicated to supporting culture and the arts, based in The Hermitage, St Petersburg, Russia; and consultant on policy for the arts to Ministries of Education and Culture in Portugal, Chile, and New Zealand. He is consultant for West Midlands Arts, an Appointed Member of the Midlands Carts Centre, and was formerly a member of the Arts Council of Wales, and Honorary Vice President, Dance Council for Wales. He has written four books, and numerous articles. His latest book, *The*

Rationality of Feeling, won the Standing Conference for Studies on Education main prize as the best academic book of 1993. He speaks frequently at international and national conferences, and lectures internationally. His philosophical interests are wide, but he is best known for his work in philosophy of the arts, and the arts in education.

DAVID CARR is Reader in the Faculty of Education at the University of Edinburgh. He is the author of *Educating the Virtues* (Routledge 1991) as well as numerous philosophical and educational articles in scholarly journals and edited collections, and he has also lectured internationally on diverse aspects of philosophy and education. He has very wide ranging interests in philosophy and education and is currently involved in editing two collections of educational philosophical essays — both for Routledge. The first of these is an international collection of essays on educational epistemology to be entitled *Knowledge, Truth and Education*, and the second — coedited with Jan Steutel of the Free University of Amsterdam — is a collection of philosophical papers on the virtue approach to moral education, to be called *Virtue Ethics and Moral Education*. In addition, he is also writing a book on Ethics and Teaching for the Routledge Professional Ethics Series.

NOËL CARROLL is Monroe C. Beardsley Professor of the Philosophy of Art at the University of Wisconsin-Madison. He is the author of *Philosophical Problems of Classical Film Theory* (Princeton University Press); *Mystifying Movies* (Columbia University Press); *The Philosophy of Horror* (Routledge); and *Theorizing the Moving Image* (Cambridge University Press). He as also co-edited *Post-Theory* (University of Wisconsin Press) with David Bordwell. He has published widely in the philosophy of the arts and is currently president-elect of the American Society for Aesthetics. His two most recent books are: *A Philosophy of Mass Art* (Oxford University Press) and *Interpreting the Moving Image* (Cambridge University Press). Presently he is working on a book entitled *An Introduction to the Philosophy of Art* for Routledge.

CHRIS CHALLIS is presently Senior Lecturer in the Dance Department of the Roehampton Institute, London. She left the dance world in the seventies, and returned to university to study philosophy; and thereafter has combined the demands of dance and philosophy into her professional work. Having taught at several universities, and been Head of Dance at Nonington College, Kent, she opened her own professional dance school, which she ran for ten years, in which she was keen to ensure the development of the academic background of her dancers-in-training. She has lectured throughout Europe and North America, and has presented papers at international conferences and major arts festivals. She continues to be actively interested in the interface between the professional dance world and academia by writing and teaching distance learning programmes for dancers and teachers in the professional and private sector.

SUE JONES is a senior lecturer at the Crewe and Alsager faculty of the Manchester Metropolitan University where she teaches dance and philosophical issues in sport to students within the Department of Exercise and Sports Science. She graduated from Chelsea College of Physical Education in 1976 and taught Dance and Physical Education in schools until 1994. Sue was seconded for a year in 1986 to the University of Guildford to take an MA in Dance Studies where she studied Dance Education, Choreography and Dance Criticism and Analysis and presented a dissertation on Wittgenstein's notion of rules in relation to choreography.

GRAHAM McFEE is Professor of Philosophy at University of Brighton. He has delivered papers and made conference presentations — both nationally and internationally — on his major research interests, which include the philosophy of Wittgenstein, and the problem of freewill, as well as aesthetics (especially the aesthetics of dance). A recent concern with the nature of the philosophical enterprise was made public in his inaugural lecture, 'A Nasty Accident With One's Flies; or, Life in Philosophy'. Related interests include educational theory, especially arts education, physical education and dance education, on all of which he has written. His principal publications include 'The Surface Grammar of Dreaming' (*Proceedings of the Aristotelian Society*, 1994) as well as *Understanding Dance* (Routledge) and *The Concept of Dance Education* (Routledge). He is an active member of the British Society of Aesthetics and has served on its Executive Committee.

AARON MESKIN is finishing his Ph.D. dissertation, 'Aesthetic Relevance,' at the Rutgers University Philosophy Department, where he was a fellow at the Center for the Critical Analysis of Contemporary Culture (1997-1998). His presentations to conferences and colloquia in the US and UK include: 'The Aesthetic Relevance of Outsider Art' (American Society for Aesthetics 1997 Annual Meeting; 'The Sorrows of the Imagination: Fiction, Emotions, and Cognitive Science' (13th Annual International Conference in Literature, the Visual Arts, and/or Cinema); and 'Aesthetics as Meta-Criticism' (British Society of Aesthetics national conference 1998). He has published book reviews in the *British Journal of Aesthetics*, and the *Journal of Aesthetics and Art Criticism*; and has studied modern dance, dance improvisation, and ballet for two years.

BONNIE ROWELL teaches dance analysis and choreography in the dance department of Roehampton Institute London. She is engaged in doctoral research on postmodernism and its critical analysis, which initially prompted her interest in and enthusiasm for dance and philosophy. She is currently preparing a book on the Dance Umbrella Festivals to celebrate the 21st anniversary of that organisation and its continuing support of postmodern dance in the United Kingdom.

FRANCIS SPARSHOTT is University Professor Emeritus, University of Toronto. He is author of numerous books of poetry and philosophy, including *The Structure of Aesthetics* (University of Toronto Press), *The Theory of the Arts* (Princeton University Press), *Taking Life Seriously: A Study of the Argument of the Nicomachean Ethics* (University of Toronto Press), and *The Future of Aesthetics* (University of Toronto Press). A seminal figure in the development of a philosophical understanding of dance, he is the author of a two volume study of the aesthetics of dance, *Off the Ground: First Steps to a Philosophical Consideration of the Dance* (Princeton university Press) and *A Measured Pace: Towards a Philosophical Understanding of the Arts of Dance* (University of Toronto Press).

INTRODUCTION:
THINKING THROUGH DANCE STUDIES

Graham Mcfee

Although dance is uncontentiously an artform (a fine art), it has not received the degree of attention from contemporary philosophy that has been lavished on other artforms. So there is no *established* (philosophical) aesthetics of dance. Of course, some contemporary philosophers have taken an interest in dance, writing books and articles, speaking at conferences and the like (and many who have are represented in this text). And articles on the aesthetics of dance appear in recent encyclopedias of philosophy or aesthetics[1]. But there is still nothing like the *volume* of philosophical material on dance that there is on, for instance, music, painting or literature, even if one attends to what is being written (or, better, published) today. At one time, one might, say, have been invited to speak at a conference in philosophical aesthetics on the grounds that dance was a major art not represented — only to find that, since dance topics did not loom large in the conference-goers' consciousnesses, there was no real audience for papers on the aesthetics of dance. (I write from personal experience.) If that situation has improved, it is still true that the audience remains a relatively specialised (and small) one.

In addition, dance studies is something of a 'Jenny-come-lately' at the academic feast (McFee, 1997: p. 104): again, there is nothing like the degree of consensus as to the content for *dance studies* programmes in higher education (university education) that there is for, say, musicology (without implying that there is, or should be, only one syllabus in musicology either). But this has meant that those wishing to study dance have not automatically been introduced to the philosophical aesthetics of dance; and, even when they have, the nature and direction of those introductions have been so diffuse that students have sometimes

1

thought — as one said to me — that different writers (or teachers) were engaged in entirely different subjects, or even working within different disciplines. So, briefly, dance has not been widely discussed as a topic of philosophical concern — with some honourable exceptions — and the precise nature of a reputable *dance studies* in higher education (and of philosophy's place, if any, within such studies) remains obscure: or, at least, not a topic of general consensus.

This volume, linking themes in philosophy with issues in dance and including work by major scholars in the United Kingdom and North America, addresses both of these 'facts' — or, perhaps, they will turn out to be one such 'fact' on investigation, with the relative neglect of dance by theorists connecting to relatively untheorised programmes. Thus some of the chapters here are most easily seen as contributions to the (philosophical) aesthetics of dance and others are more smoothly classified as contributions to the delineation of dance studies. But one strength of this volume — a consequence of the interpenetration of issues identified initially — is that most of the chapters could readily be seen as contributions to either (or, better, to both) topics. In this vein, of course, the organisation of the volume is slightly arbitrary: as we might expect, when philosophers discuss issues in the aesthetics of dance the artform (as, say, Noël Carroll and Sally Banes [Chapter Two] do or Aaron Meskin [Chapter Four] does), they simultaneously practice what *others* — including others in the volume — are preaching. So that, if one wanted to characterise the nature of an honourable *dance studies*, one might as well appeal to the honourable *practice* of such study: as John Wisdom (1965: p. 102) noted, "… at the bar of reason, always the final appeal is to cases".

Moreover, some of the central philosophical issues — those concerning the nature of the value of dance — are both crucial to our characterisation of dance (for instance, in our recognition of it *as* a fine art: something lacking that value would not be fine art) and fundamental to any argument for the educational value of dance. Or so one might think. Thus the title of this volume encompasses not only dance and philosophy but education too.

As the 'eye' of philosophy has at last (and increasingly) begun to turn onto dance, a re-evaluation from some of the established practitioners in the (philo-sophical) aesthetics of dance seemed timely — and also sometimes a re-evaluation of the work of those practitioners! Throughout this volume, we see some writers who have contributed to the development of an aesthetics of dance (in particular, in its educational context) offering thoughts which either *reflect* (and instantiate) their current positions or *discuss* those positions and their development over the past few years (or, of course, both). For example, the contributions by both David Best (Chapter Seven) and David Carr (Chapter Eight) include reflections on past writings of their own. Further, the volume sees the engagement of some new contributors to debates in the aesthetics of dance (and contributions from some — I would single out Chris Challis — best known for their teaching and practice).

In fact, the process of arriving at this volume is revealing in itself; and I describe it below. But there was an earlier stage in the evolution of the project.

The symposium

With financial support (here gratefully acknowledged) from the Chelsea School of the University of Brighton, I invited a small group of scholars to a week-end gathering at the University of Brighton's site in Eastbourne. This group included dance teachers in higher education, dancers, students of aesthetics, general aestheticians, and aestheticians of dance. (There was sufficient overlap among these categories for them to be instantiated in a group small enough to facilitate lively and sustained discussion.) The resulting event was an innovative symposium on dance and philosophy, arranged around six presentations, with ample time for discussion, with participation from such 'founding fathers' of the UK dance/philosophy field as David Best[2] and David Carr.

The symposium was held in Trevin Towers, a site which seemed to me suitable for the discussion of philosophy since Trevin Towers had been the family home of the grandfather of the British philosopher A. J. Ayer (see Ayer, 1977: pp. 64-65). Of course, the symposium was not in the main house, but in an adjacent building which — although I am sure the Ayer family would have thought it the stables — the University of Brighton calls "the Annex". It seemed somehow appropriate to have been discussing philosophy in relation to dance in the Annex to the philosopher's house — participating in what I sometimes think of as an Annex to Philosophy's House!

If that were the right metaphor, certainly our business at the symposium (and in this text) was exploring that Annex, going carefully from room to room, or learning a lot more about some particular room, or perhaps — with luck — finding that *we* are in the main building, the rest is the Annex! For, if the accounts of reasoning, of understanding and of expression sometimes given in philosophy generally will not fit cases from the aesthetics of dance, that may offer a basis for rethinking those accounts.

On a personal note, it gave me great pleasure at the symposium to see old friends and (if I may) new friends, joined in discussion of (roughly) the place of philosophy in dance-studies, a discussion sometimes to be conducted by example — by talking, in the style of philosophy, about the meaning, value or appreciation of dance — and sometimes in a kind of 'meta'-fashion, by directly addressing the place of philosophy in any legitimate study of dance: asking what it has to offer, and how it offers it, and (in passing?) commenting on others' mistakes in the addressing of these issues.

Of course, not everyone could be at the symposium. It was important to have a group small enough to sustain close discussions; and financial constraints (as well as constraints of time) limited my inviting speakers, especially from outside the United Kingdom. Still, the symposium represented a hard core of material for consideration for this volume[3].

The volume

So the contents of the volume began from those at the symposium: further, Noël Carroll and Sally Banes agreed to offer something, as did Francis Sparshott. Attracting interest from such major 'players' in the field of dance aesthetics was gratifying, as were the excellent chapters they submitted.

Someone might think that — since the contents are based on my invitations — they could represent a narrowness of interest or position. Such worries can be dispelled by reading the chapters in the volume, with their diversity of topic, style and position. Nor was the 'family' here especially harmonious. To illustrate, consider the treatment meted-out to my ideas. For instance, my own paper responds in part to some published criticisms by David Carr (1997): in case I had thought them dealt with (and me 'victorious'), Carr here raises a set of related criticisms. And, if one of my positions in dance aesthetics is implicitly endorsed by Bonnie Rowell, who looks at its implications in a specific context, another is forcibly contested by Aaron Meskin and yet another by Sue Jones. But disagreement among the contributors to the volume may, of course, prove profitable; and it is predicated on our mutual commitments to the *value* of the dance/philosophy mix, even when we differ both about how that mix should be achieved and what it should achieve.

Again, a confluence of ideas should not be (mis-)taken for agreement. For example, David Best and I both make use of a quotation from Goethe much beloved of Wittgenstein: "In the beginning was the deed". But our purposes are so radically different that no conclusion should be drawn from this.

Neither is there *one* view of the project of philosophy here — as the chapters by Francis Sparshott and Sue Jones illustrate, a productive difference in how philosophy is viewed can still result in the same (or similar) problems being addressed, with broadly similar conclusions reached. And, as a Wittgenstein scholar, I am honour-bound to disagree with *everyone* else's account of Wittgenstein: hence I differ from Sparshott concerning Wittgenstein's projects (as well as his methods) — and from Sue Jones (and from David Best) — and some of those disagreements are visible in my own offering.

As was also remarked by participants at the symposium, the contributions here differ in the degree to which they explicitly address the practicalities of dance. In part, this reflects personal knowledge, expertise and concern; in part, the issues the various chapters approach — and these two factors are, of course, not unrelated. Those whose practical concerns are with *dance* (especially dance performance) may find that the issues which beset them are different from those that vex people whose concern is (first and foremost) with concepts, with the abstract — though, again, this contrast is contentious. And some of the chapters here explicitly contend with it!

Nevertheless, dance is a central concern in all chapters: any apparent divergence is a matter of emphasis, or reflects a particular author's cast of mind.

The contents

A recent work (Sparshott, 1998), by one of the senior contributors to this volume, addresses the *future of* (philosophical) *aesthetics*, on the assumption that it has a future — or that it might have, if certain (basically political) conditions were fulfilled (Sparshott, 1998: p. 16). Believing in such a future, as it applies to the philosophical aesthetics of dance, requires at least three commitments:

- first, to artistic value, such that there are presently artworks to induce, and to provide substance to, philosophical puzzlements — and perhaps also *future* artworks to do this;

- second, to the idea "that depth in understanding comes from learning what the debatable issues are" (Sparshott, 1998: p. 100, note 2) rather than in finding resolutions to such issues (for, otherwise, it might seem that philosophy should have found the requisite resolutions ere this!);

- third, to the enduring vitality of debatable issues — for dance, this seems less contentious than it might be for other artforms, since key issues for dance studies are still being *discovered*. And this volume might be thought to contribute to that process.

In work of the quality and concern found here I find it easy to be optimistic about such a future.

Thus the chapters here represent a rich mix of differing, criss-crossing themes, opinions, conclusions, issues … — as one might expect. If I mention only some of them in this Introduction, it is not because these are the most important. Rather, they are among the features which I think might be lost to someone who dips into the volume, and which are worth reinforcing. Equally, I mention only some of the places each theme is developed. I will especially highlight three such themes: the nature of our knowledge of dance, the need for conceptual re-orientation once dance is recognised as a suitable topic for aesthetic consideration, and the interplay between understanding works and identifying them.

Our first theme, then, revolves around the nature of our knowledge of dance — something of an abiding issue. So that, in his rich, discursive contribution, Francis Sparshott (Chapter Five) explores what is involved in knowing what dance is — in recognising it, understanding it, commenting on it in an informed way (contrasting the perspective on these issues *assumed* to be that of the professional philosopher with a more realistic conception of, at least, his own perspective). In contrast, Sue Jones (Chapter Six) throws light on the nature of our knowledge of dance by considering what account might (consistently) be given of cases which — while not dance in the sense it has been discussed here — are nevertheless *called* "dance". Again, her discussion throws light on the normative intentionality of dances. There is a connection here, too, to Aaron Meskin's discussion (Chapter Four) of the various 'objects' — performances, performers' interpretations, abstract works, etc. — that constitute a typical dancework: and hence might be known about in knowing about the dance. In a related vein, David Carr (Chapter Eight) explores the knowledge that one has in understanding dance — although his central preoccupation is with the educational place of such understanding.

A second theme throughout this text is the need to re-orientate one's thinking once one takes dance seriously (as all the authors here do): that pre-theoretical analyses may not deal with the complexities of dance — and, perhaps, this implies some more general limitation! Thus David Best (Chapter Seven) argues for a recognition of the fundamental character, for dance, of human actions not themselves helpfully explored in terms of some prior motivation: *in the beginning was the deed*. As a result, the starting point might be a world of *agents*, capable of doing certain things, which are only *then* open to explanation or justification ('after the fact'). Such a conception would diverge radically from that adopted by some contemporary theorists of arts education, as Best demonstrates. Equally critical of some trends in contemporary educational theory, and drawing inspiration from Aristotle, David Carr (Chapter Eight) suggests a reconceptualisation of the knowledge which is embedded in the activities of dance practitioners: that when practical knowledge is treated differently from, say, propositional knowledge, the sense in which dance study might be educational is clarified. Similarly, Chris Challis (Chapter Nine), considering the importance (for our dance understanding) of the idea of a 'dancing body', urges that the specificity of such a body — rooted in the daily class of dance companies — means, first, that in the aesthetics of dance one disregards the 'dancing body' at one's peril; and, second, that there is then no reason to take the ballet class (and hence 'the' ballet body) as *obviously* preferably to others. A reconsideration of the role of 'bodily' learning here will make us re-think the parameters of our dance studies. In my own contribution (Chapter Ten), I urge that an adequate 'cognitive stock' for dance studies can, and perhaps must, involve *technical* expressions, including (especially) those from other parts of philosophy — and that this idea will be reinforced if philosophical enquiry is granted some central place within dance studies (as Challis too implies).

From such a context, questions of the specificity of our understanding of dance naturally arise. And this introduces our third theme. Given what dances are like, and granting their art-status, how should our understanding of them be characterised? To what degree is it perspectival (Aaron Meskin: Chapter Four) or historical (Bonnie Rowell: Chapter Three)? To what degree does it embed some 'narrative' of dance theory? The discussions in this volume suggest that this question can never be fully separated from questions about dance-identity: when do we have *the very same* dance for consideration? For that might depend on the precise features of particular dances. But what are these? And would our answers here be different if we focused on some of the more obviously dramatic issues, such as dance's representational or depictive possibility (Carroll and Banes: Chapter Two), rather than on others — for example, those of postmodern choreography (Rowell: Chapter Three)? Here, Noël Carroll and Sally Banes lay out one carefully presented answer in their scholarly reconsideration of the past of dance. From there, they offer a reconstruction of a taxonomy for representation which — faced with dances that *are* representational — suggests how representation in dance differs from that in other artforms and how this difference is grounded in the character of dance itself. And Aaron Meskin (Chapter Four) disputes the application — at least to dance — of an analysis of the appreciation of performances popularised for music in contemporary aesthetics. While Bonnie Rowell (Chapter Three) sketches how an alternative, offered quite generally across the arts, might be articulated and elaborated in the face of postmodern dance — and how it might contrast with other currently popular descriptions. Although each of these aspects of the more general issues might be raised for all (or most) artforms, the discussion here recognises and explores the specific 'twists' generated by attention to dance — a physical, performing art.

Also worth stressing here are some of the commonalities among authors. Of course, some of those result from our commitment to dance. As Roger Scruton (1998: p. 20) writes (of literary discussions, but the point holds):

> … in the nature of things, the arguments of a critic are addressed only to those who have sufficient reverence for literature; for only they will see the point of detailed study and moral investigation.

And this is true of the writing of the aesthetician too. But can we be more precise as to (some of) what that might amount to?

As noted initially, chapters here typically make two fundamental assumptions: first, that the primary concern is with the *artform* of dance, or with those dances (or danceworks) that are (also?) artworks; second, that dances so conceived are valuable — to put that another way, there is a commitment to the value of art, which *this* concern with dance inherits. Each of these assumptions could be the topic of extensive discussion. To take them in reverse order, it is the value of dance-as-art that somehow justifies its educational role; but how? Clearly such a value is *intrinsic* to the particular dancework at issue, rather than being conceived instrumentally. And only this sort of value (essentially non-monetary) could justify an educational role, whether in schools or in Higher Education. Yet how is this artistic value to be understood? No direct answer is given here, although elements of the chapters by Carr and myself bear directly on this issue.

Again, picking up the other assumption, the concern with *artworks* might simply indicate a preference for considering certain cases; equally, it might be thought to rest on — and to sustain — an *artistic/aesthetic* contrast (Best, 1992: pp. 166–

167 and this volume, Chapter Eight; McFee, 1992: pp. 42–44; and this volume, Chapter Ten), on which appreciation of artworks is radically different from the appreciation of other 'objects of aesthetic appreciation', even when similar *words* are used to evoke each. Thus — at its most extreme — one might urge that a term used in both artistic and aesthetic judgement (a term such as "gaudy", for instance) is systematically ambiguous in these two uses. And that ambiguity might be explained by the way that aesthetic concerns are different (in particular, differentially cognitive) from what I have been calling *artistic* concerns: that is, explained by noting how the very different issues approached in each type of case mean that the same term might *amount*, in each location, to something different (Travis, 1996; Travis, 1997). How we explain this contrast will, of course, have a bearing on precisely *what* contrast is being drawn; and it is far from clear that our authors would agree about that. These are not topics to pursue in an Introduction. My point is both to identify kinds of consensus among authors here, and to suggest that at least *some* such consensus might be more apparent than real.

My purpose in thus sketching some of the thematic features of this book is twofold: partly, of course, I am simply trying to offer a route-map through the text; but I am also trying to articulate features of the field of dance studies as I see it (and as it might be practiced via philosophy). For the issues and assumptions at work in this volume suggest some fruitful areas of enquiry. Of course, the reader must decide if I have correctly located these issues and assumptions — it goes without saying that the contributors might not all agree on that! So, to summarise, I have suggested:

- that dance studies must assume the value of dance, although it must aim to produce arguments in explication and justification of that assumption. (This process might be very important too for arts education.)

- that dance studies should adopt an artistic/aesthetic distinction (in some form, where the precise form is a matter for debate) — not least because the heart of dance aesthetics lies in the artform of dance.

- that one direction for dance studies might begin with epistemology: that a revealing question concerns the nature of our knowledge of dance — what do we know in knowing what are, and what are not, dance (as well as recognising the grey areas)?

- relatedly, that conceptual re-orientation may be needed once dance is recognised as a suitable topic for consideration in aesthetics, since the issues generated by the study of dance may 'put pressure' on the traditional views of other matters.

• that the interplay between understanding works and identifying them deserves sustained investigation: that dance studies are definitely not positioned where it would be appropriate for studies of dance evaluation to be omitted (contrast Wollheim, 1980: §65; and pp. 227-229).

Of course, these are no more than some 'flags' to some issues discussed here. They are part of my effort to think through dance studies, in two senses: both in using my concerns with dance to better understand philosophy (as well as value and education) and in following as concertedly as I could the topics about its understanding thrown up by the 'fact' of dance. If these help direct the aesthetics of dance into some profitable avenues, even if only avenues of dissent, they will have served their purpose.

Acknowledgments

I would like to express my thanks:

— to Myrene McFee, who (in addition to preparing the pages for publication) contributed to the intellectual development of both the project and its editor;

— to all the contributors to the symposium and, especially, to the volume: to say 'it would not have happened without you', while truistic, makes the point. I am honoured to be in this company, and glad to be editing a collection of high-quality work from dance scholars with a range of backgrounds, and at different places in their careers. (I should also thank them for their forbearance with my requests, delays, and so on);

— to those who, although unable to attend the symposium, were well-wishers;

— to the Chelsea School, University of Brighton, for support (especially financial support) for both symposium and volume: in particular, to Elizabeth Murdoch and Paul McNaught-Davis (Heads of School from the symposium to date) and to Alan Tomlinson (Research Division Co-ordinator).

Notes

1 Modestly precludes my mentioning how many of these are by me!
2 In correspondence, David Best suggested that his chapter here was likely be his last writing on dance. Perhaps he will turn out to be wrong about this (I said something similar myself in print; McFee, 1994: p. 199) — I know many people will *hope* that he continues to write on dance; and I will be chief among them. As my predecessor in Chelsea, his example has been constantly before my gaze for 25 years.
3 Although all papers were solicited, the invitation to the various scholars was simply to *submit* for consideration: all submissions were subsequently subjected to a thorough process of peer review.

References

Ayer, A. J. (1977) *Part of my life*. Oxford: Oxford University Press.

Best, D. (1992) *The rationality of feeling*. London: Falmer Press.

Carr, D. (1997) 'Meaning in dance', *British Journal of Aesthetics*, Vol. 37, No. 4 (October): pp. 349–366.

McFee, G. (1992) *Understanding dance*. London: Routledge.

——— (1994) *The concept of dance education*. London: Routledge.

——— (1997) 'Education, art and the physical: the case for the academic study of dance — present and future', in G. McFee and A. Tomlinson (eds) *Education, sport and leisure: connections and controversies*. Aachen: Meyer & Meyer, pp. 103–117.

Scruton, R. (1998) *An intelligent person's guide to modern culture*. London: Duckworth.

Sparshott, F. (1998) *The future of aesthetics*. Toronto: University of Toronto Press.

Travis, C. (1996) 'Meaning role in truth', *Mind* Vol. 104 (July): pp. 451-466.

——— (1997) 'Pragmatics', in C. Wright and B. Hale (eds) *A companion to the philosophy of language*. Oxford: Blackwell, pp. 87-107.

Wisdom, J. (1965) *Paradox and discovery*. Oxford: Blackwell.

DANCE, IMITATION AND REPRESENTATION

Noël Carroll and Sally Banes

Introduction

The relation of dance — theatrical dance — to representation has undergone a seismic shift in the course of the modern period. In the eighteenth century, in the founding texts of the modern philosophy of dance in the West, notably those of John Weaver and Jean-Georges Noverre, dance, properly so-called, was identified with representation, narrowly construed as the imitation of action. By the twentieth century, however, this theoretical assumption came under attack, perhaps nowhere more fiercely than in the writings of André Levinson. Indeed, by the late twentieth century, the notion that there is any deep ontological affinity between dance and representation of any sort appears obviously outmoded. And yet representation, and even imitation, is still a feature of *some* dances, even if it is not regarded as a necessary condition of *all* dances. Thus dance theory must still take account of the relation of dance to representation, even though it is no longer possible to suppose that representation is the essence of dance.

In this chapter, we want to take a look at the relation of dance to representation. The first part is diagnostic. In it, we will try to explain why early dance theorists attempted to identify the essence of dance with representation. In this respect, they were mistaken, but their mistakes were influential, so influential that much — perhaps most — of the dance canon traffics in representation. Even if most of the ambitious dance produced today is not primarily representational, much — perhaps most — theatrical dance, historically speaking, is. Consequently, it is still incumbent on dance theorists to provide a framework for discussing dance in relation to representation. Thus in the second part of this essay, we will develop a way of talking about dance and representation which,

13

among other things, suggests a clue for contrasting representation in dance with representation in other art forms.

Dance as imitation

Western dance in the modern period is linked explicitly with representation in the early theoretical writings of both John Weaver and Jean-Georges Noverre. According to both writer-choreographers, dance is essentially a representational art, where 'representation' is primarily understood as imitation — the endeavor to refer to actions, events, and people by simulating their appearances. Both Weaver and Noverre attempt to annex the Aristotelian theory of *mimesis* as a theory of dance.

In this, Weaver and Noverre stand in contrast to Adam Smith, for whom anything is dance so long as it involves movement structurally composed of cadenced steps functionally aimed at displaying grace and agility. For Smith, dance, whether of the eighteenth century or not, could either be imitative or not imitative. Smith notes that dance is not necessarily or essentially mimetic, citing what he calls 'common dances' (social dances) as exceptions to any presumption that dance is by its very nature imitative. Smith, of course, realises that some dance is mimetic but, because he regards this as an optional feature of dance and not its quiddity, imitation does not appear in his philosophical description of dance, in which he claims that:

> ...a certain measured, cadenced step, commonly called a dancing step, which keeps time with, and as it were beats the measure of, the Music which accompanies and directs it, is the essential characteristic which distinguishes a dance from every other sort of motion. (Smith, 1980: p. 207)

Given the sort of dancing available to eighteenth-century observers, Smith's characterization of dance seems eminently commonsensical. As a comprehensive, descriptive account of dance, it seems more accurate than theories of dance that aspire to assimilate dance solely to imitation.

Yet Weaver writes, "I shall endeavour to shew in what the Excellency of this *Art* [dance] does or ought to consist; the Beauty of *Imitation*", and "the chief Business then, and aim of these *Pantomimes*, was, (as I have said) the *Imitation* of Persons, or Manners and Passions" (Weaver, 1712: pp. 159, 140); while Noverre adds:

A well-composed ballet is a living picture of the passions, manners, ceremonies and customs of all nations of the globe...; like the art of painting, it exacts a perfection the more difficult to acquire in that it is *dependent* on the faithful imitation of nature. (Noverre, 1966: p. 16; emphasis added).

Thus, unlike Smith, Weaver and Noverre appear to regard imitation as an integral, if not essential, feature of dance.

But surely, like Smith, they knew that a great deal of dancing was not concerned with imitation. So what could dispose them to place such great emphasis on imitation? Of course, the first difference between them and Smith seems to be that their domains of discourse are not the same. Presumably, Smith intends to be talking about all dance, including folk jigs and elite social dancing, whereas Weaver and Noverre are talking only about theatrical dancing and of what it 'does or ought to consist'. That is, Weaver and Noverre are dealing with dance for the stage, specifically autonomous dance compositions (rather than dance as part of drama or opera), and their theories pertain to what that kind of dancing is or should be.

Moreover, it is instructive that Weaver waffles between speaking about what such dance 'does or ought to consist'. Both Weaver and Noverre slip between advancing descriptive accounts of dance and normative accounts (accounts of what theatrical dancing should be). Clearly, both know that not all theatrical dancing is — speaking pre-theoretically — imitative. It is fair to say this, because both rail against the non-imitative tendencies of theatrical dancing of their own day, decrying what they see as an excessive emphasis on *divertissements*. Thus, from what we might call the statistical-descriptive, ordinary-language point of view of their own day, both Weaver and Noverre can agree that what is called dance — even with reference to the stage — is not definable in terms of imitation.

But both also regard such divergences from imitation as a failure to realise the *true* nature of dance (or theatrical dancing), since, by their lights, dance essentially *is* imitative. The non-imitative jumping and scampering that people call (theatrical) dancing is not accurately categorised, according to these theorists. Thus, Noverre asserts:

I am of the opinion, then, that the name of ballet has been wrongly applied to such sumptuous entertainments, such splendid festivals which

combine magnificent scenery, wonderful machinery, rich and pompous
costumes, charming poetry, music and declamation, seductive voices,
brilliant artificial illumination, pleasing dances and *divertissements*,
thrilling and perilous jumps, and feats of strength. (Noverre, 1966: p. 52)

Weaver and Noverre bolster their conviction that theatrical dancing is
essentially imitative in a number of ways. Weaver, especially, talks at great length
about ancient Roman pantomime, assuming that this is the genuine template
from which dance has subsequently deviated. In this, he invokes the authority of
past practice to identify the essence of dance and is perhaps convinced of its
efficacy because of the great power to move audiences that classical authors
attribute to it. Both Weaver and Noverre speak of *restoring* dance to its proper
state, which essentially involves the imitation of action. Both have a sense of the
correct nature of dance that prompts them to regard mere divertissements and
graceful airs as categorically defective or not proper instances of the species,
even if a simple statistical-descriptive use of language might count them as such.

A second reason that both Weaver and Noverre connect dance to imitation
essentially is their reliance on Aristotle. Both cite Aristotle explicitly. Aristotle,
of course, linked drama with the imitation of action ('drama' is intimately related
to the Greek word for 'doing'), and, inasmuch as theatre is drama, one supposes
that Weaver and Noverre thought it natural to infer that theatrical dancing is a
subspecies of the imitation of action — since the representation of action is,
according to Aristotle, the essence of drama (theatre). And, as well, classical
authors like Plato and Aristotle counted dance as a part of theatre. Moreover,
since on Aristotle's view all the parts of theatre are supposed to be subservient
to the plot — to the representation of action — in an Aristotelian theory of the
dance, such as Weaver and Noverre were advancing, it seemed evident that
dance, if it was to realise the *telos* of theatre, would contribute to the imitation
of action.

It is undoubtedly the authority of Aristotle that inclines Weaver and Noverre
toward the conception of dance as imitation, a conception of dance that continues
to dominate nineteenth-century ballet. But the question unavoidably arises as to
why theorists like Weaver and Noverre would have invested Aristotle's theory
of mimesis with so much credibility, especially in the face of so much counter-
evidence — that is, so many divertissements of the sort that exercised their
disapproval.

Here it is important to recall that as eighteenth-century theorists, Weaver and Noverre were writing at a time when our modern system of the arts was only just being consolidated (see Kristeller, 1980). That is, it is only in the eighteenth century that consensus on exactly what counts as the Fine Arts begins to emerge decisively.

Nowadays, this system is generally taken to comprise at least painting, sculpture, music, and poetry, with drama and film often added. That these practices go together seems natural to us. Together they are what we mean by the 'fine arts'; these are the *Arts* with a capital 'A'. For us, this group seems composed of practices sharing deep affinities. We may even think that there is no other way of grouping these practices. But until the eighteenth century, there were different ways of sorting these practices. The Greeks, for example, sometimes grouped music with mathematics.

But in the eighteenth century, the fine arts enlisted its core membership. According to Paul Oskar Kristeller, Abbé Charles Batteux wrote the first well-defined, systematic treatment of the fine arts. The title of Batteux's 1747 treatise was *Les Beaux-Arts réduits à un même principe* (The Fine Arts Reduced to a Single Principle). And that principle was none other than the Platonic-Aristotelian principle of *mimesis*. Batteux wrote:

> We will define painting, sculpture, and dance as the imitation of beautiful nature conveyed through colors, through relief, and through attitudes. And music and poetry are the imitation of beautiful nature conveyed through sounds, or through measured discourse. (Batteux, 1989: p. 101)

For Batteux, membership in the system of the fine arts required that a practice meet certain necessary conditions; namely that it be an imitative, or more broadly, a representational practice. In this, Batteux articulated a presupposition widely upheld in the eighteenth century — that art is to be defined in terms of the Aristotelian notion of *mimesis*.

Weaver and Noverre obviously share in this emerging consensus about the fine arts. One way of reading their commitment to Aristotle is to reason that, insofar as they believed that dance is a fine art, then dance as art must meet the conditions necessary for anything to count as a fine art. On this view, mere virtuoso divertissements were not dance — dance art — properly so-called, despite how people might talk pre-theoretically.

Another way of interpreting the polemics of Weaver and Noverre is to remember that they were reformers. Part of their self-appointed mission was to get dance taken seriously. In the context of the eighteenth century, an obvious way in which to get dance taken seriously was to promote its recognition as a fine art which, in turn, required the assertion that its identity was essentially a matter of imitation. Poetry and painting were accepted as legitimate instances of fine art in virtue of their imitative powers. Drama was accorded the status of fine art, again because of its capacity to imitate action. Similarly, Noverre agitated for the *ballet d'action*, we hypothesise, because this was conceptually the most clearcut way for theatrical dance to acquire the coveted cultural status of art.

This is not to suggest that Weaver and Noverre endorsed the position that dance is imitation simply for opportunistic reasons — that, for example, they would have been equally hospitable to any other slogan that might have lent theatre dance cultural prestige. They believed that dance is a matter of imitation in their hearts as well as their minds. But their minds were deeply shaped by eighteenth-century presumptions about the relation of art and imitation.

Weaver and especially Noverre are interested in analogies between poetry and painting — the arts of imitation discussed at greatest length by Plato and Aristotle. Moreover, since poetry for Plato and Aristotle is primarily dramatic poetry, Weaver and Noverre often draw analogies with drama. Noverre calls for dance to look to the work of dramatists such as Racine, Corneille, Voltaire, and Crébillon for inspiration. In this, we conjecture, Noverre is asserting not only that theatre dance resembles drama in its essential nature, but that drama provides a model for dance — a direction that dance can follow in order to recover its genuine nature, too long forgotten in the flurry of 'meaningless' divertissements and graceful airs. The point of emphasizing the relation of dance to drama was, in other words, not only as a way of enfranchising dance as art, but also as a way of implementing a dynamic new style in dance, a style that for being more like drama would return dance to its original essence and power.

Drama is especially important for Noverre as a model because of its emphasis on plot, which, of course, for Aristotle was the representational core of theatre. Through plot, Noverre saw a way to unify dance spectacles. But at the same time, Noverre did not wish to blur the distinction between dance and drama altogether. He criticises the intrusion of words in dance, regarding wordlessness as the quintessence of dance. He complains about dances that use long recitatives and banners with words on them as antithetical to the dance. Though dance shares certain features with drama, according to Noverre words are not something dance should take from drama.

What dance shares with drama — the common resource that it should exploit — is plot or story. Words should be avoided. But how can words be avoided, if dances are to tell stories, to represent actions? Here Noverre recommends that choreographers tell well-known stories, with plots familiar enough to spectators that they can recognise and follow their enactments without the accompaniment of speech. In this way, Noverre was convinced that ballets imitating unified actions could have the power and impact of tragedy (though to what extent this is likely is an issue to which we will return at the end of this essay).

The writings of Weaver and Noverre in their theoretical assertion of the view of dance-as-representation (imitation) sounds ambiguous to us. We wonder, even if we restrict our attention to theatre dance, whether they mean that dance is representational or whether they mean it should be. Given the data available to them, it seems hard for us to see how they could have thought that, just speaking statistically, dance is essentially representational. So they must have meant that dance *should* be representational.

However, granting them the Aristotelian framework in which they were operating, it is likely that they probably did not draw the distinction between whether dance is or should be representational in the same way that we draw it. For them, the *telos* of dance is imitation, and this sort of essence is normative. Apparent counter-examples to the theory, no matter how numerous statistically, are not genuine instances of dance, no matter how people talk, since the nature of dance is imitation. And this conception of dance, partially as a result of the reforms and influence of people like Noverre and Weaver, could have even mustered impressive empirical support in the nineteenth century. For after all, the Romantic ballet was primarily a *ballet d'action*[1].

But, by the end of the twentieth century, the suggestion that dance is a representational art clearly commands no support. The reason for this is not simply that by now the number of counter-examples is overwhelming, but also because the underlying representational theory of art, derived from Aristotle and assumed by Batteux, Weaver, and Noverre, has been shown false for art in general and for every artform, including dance, in particular. Counter-examples cannot be waved aside by appealing to some representational essence. Dances like Merce Cunningham's Events can be enfranchised by theories of art demonstrably more powerful than the view that art is essentially representational.

For us, the suggestion that dance *is* representational can only be regarded as a covert way of saying that dance *should* or *ought* to be representational, where *should* and *ought* here cannot be glossed in the Aristotelian idiom of essential norms, but must be understood as expressing an evaluative preference. When Weaver and Noverre maintained that dance should be representational, we may now reinterpret them as saying that they wanted, perhaps for good reason, dance to become representational. They wanted it to become representational because they wanted it to be art. But since we now realise that representation is not a necessary condition for art, their theory of dance is no longer compelling to us.

However, this does not mean that the relation of dance and representation is no longer of interest for dance theory. For even though the theory that *all* dance is representational needs to be discarded, much dance has been representational and some even continues to be. Thus dance representation is a topic that still requires philosophical attention. And it is to this issue that we now turn.

Dance and representation

Though the contemporary dance theorist readily concedes that the identification of dance with representation is inadequate, that theorist must nevertheless say something about how representation operates in dance and, if possible, what is characteristic of it, at least in dance as we know it. For, as already noted, much modern theatre dance is representational. Before the twentieth century, there are no ballets without stories (and, therefore, representation), while throughout the twentieth century not only does much ballet continue to tell stories, but so does a great deal of modern dance and even some postmodern dance. How dance represents is therefore a nagging theoretical question, as is the question of whether there is something characteristic of dance representation in contrast to representation in the other arts.

In order to facilitate a discussion of dance and its representational powers, it is useful to begin by looking at a continuum of different ways in which artforms represent. By 'represent' here we mean that **x** represents **y** (where **y** ranges over a domain comprised of objects, persons, events, and actions) if and only if:

1. a sender intends **x** (for instance, a picture) to stand for **y** (for example, a person), and

2. an audience recognises that **x** is intended to stand for **y**.

This definition is broader than the standard notion of imitation, for reasons that will become evident as we proceed, though imitation, as that notion standardly figures in discussions of art, clearly falls under this concept of representation. Moreover, as the admission that imitation is but one sub-category of representation entails, there are more kinds of representation than one.

Four types of representation are especially useful for our purposes[2]. They sit as on a continuum of representational practices in terms of the different, though sometimes overlapping ways that audiences can come to comprehend or recognise that x stands for y. These four points on the continuum include:

1) *Unconditional representation.* This is the sort of representation that obtains by triggering the audience's innate recognitional capacities — the capacities that enable viewers to recognise that the referent of the *Mona Lisa* is a woman simply by looking at the picture. In cases of unconditional representation, we can recognise that x stands for y on the basis of the same recognitional powers that enable us to recognise ys in, so to speak, nature. If we can recognise women in the real world simply by looking, then we can recognise that the *Mona Lisa* pictures a woman by means of the same perceptual processes we use to recognise women.

This dimension of representation is closely associated with the notion of imitation — understood as the simulation of appearances. When an actor on stage or screen represents eating by imitating eating — by lifting a fork to her mouth and simulating chewing — the audience recognises her actions as a portrayal of eating without recourse to any specialised codes. Often the mechanism subtending such examples of direct recognition has been discussed in terms of similarity, though, more recently, the idea of natural generativity has gained popularity (see Schier, 1986). Whether similarity or natural generativity affords the superior explanation of the phenomenon is a question we may leave to psychologists to resolve. Our only point is that much representation — for example, in mass-market movies and TV — proceeds by triggering innate recognitional capacities and, in that sense, is immediate (that is, not mediated by the manipulation of an arbitrary or conventional code).

2) *Lexical representation.* If some representation is unmediated by arbitrarily established codes, other forms of representation are coded or lexicographic. In these cases, in order to realise that x stands for y, a spectator must know the relevant code. In dance, certain gestures and movements are correlated to certain meanings in a dictionary-like fashion. An averted glance and a forfending

backhand raised to the face stands for contempt in certain balletic practices. One cannot realise this by looking; one must also know the relevant lexicon. Of course, the boundary between unconditional representation and lexical representation often yields mixed cases, since what we sometimes recognise in an unmediated way is a socially (rather than an artistically) coded signal (for example, we unconditionally recognise the fire truck in part because it is red, but its being red is the result of an antecedent social code).

3) *Conditional specific representation.* Sometimes we recognise what is being represented only on condition that we already know what is being represented. One is unlikely to realise that *poison* is being put in the king's ear in the play within the play in *Hamlet* unless one already knows that this is what the play within the play is supposed to represent. Once we know that this is what is intended to be represented by the playlet, we easily pick up what the otherwise obscure gestures stand for. But most of us, in all probability, would be at sea without such antecedent knowledge.

This is not a case of unconditional representation, since we wouldn't have a clue as to what is going on without being told. Being told, here, is, in other words, a condition for understanding the representation. However, once told (that is, once the condition is met), we can use our native recognitional powers to decipher the otherwise elusive gestures.

Nor is this a case of lexical representation, since there is no pre-established code for ear poisonings in drama. The actor proceeds by imitation, not by strictly coded signaling. Lexicographical or semiotic representation is, of course, conditional, insofar as it depends upon the existence of a code, but not all conditional specific representation need be lexical, since in many cases it can operate by engaging natural recognitional capacities once those have been cued in terms of what to expect. Deciphering a case of conditional specific representation can involve a complex interplay of cognitive abilities requiring natural recognitional capacities working in concert with fragments of lexicographical knowledge (along with homologies and linguistic associations, including our sensitivity to synesthetic or cross-modal effects). However, this category still marks an important difference, since in order to mobilise these capacities and structures, we need the clue that something is being represented. Indeed, these category 3 representations require that we know that something specific — for example, an ear poisoning — is being represented. In that, it contrasts with our next category.

4) *Conditional generic representation.* Here the spectator is able to detect or to recognise that **x** stands for **y** on condition that she knows that something is being represented. For example, unless you know that I am trying to represent *something*, you might not take my rolling arm movements to stand for waves. But if you know that I intend to represent something, even if you do not know antecedently what I want to represent, you would be likely to see my arm movements as waves right off the bat. It would be one of your first hypotheses. Likewise, if we know that a piece of music is a tone poem, then we are likely to interpret certain 'rushing' or 'flowing' phrases as water. Simply knowing that an artistic signal is meant to be representational, even if we are not told exactly what it represents, leads us to mobilise our natural recognitional capacities, our linguistic associations, our capacities for following homologies, our sensitivity to synesthetic effects, and our knowledge of strict semiotic codes to determine appropriately what the representation is a representation of, without being told its specific, intended meaning.

The contrast between conditional specific representation and conditional generic representation can be illuminated instructively by contemplating the game of charades. Imagine two teams — A and B. Team A gives a player on Team B a saying which she must elicit from the other members of her team by means of gestural prompting. Suppose, as well, that she tries to do this by acting out the whole saying. Since the members of Team A know the saying — since they know what her gestures are intended to represent — they relate to her performance as an instance of conditional specific representation. They are able to follow and to appreciate her gesticulations, because they know exactly what she is trying to signal. Her fellow team members, however, know only that she intends to signal something. They do not know exactly what it is. They try to infer what it is, using a variety of cognitive skills that they put into gear simply because they know that she is playing charades. If they were not playing charades, they might not think that she was trying to signal anything at all. But knowing that she is playing charades, knowing that she intends to represent something, they try to determine what. And they are quite often successful at this.

For Team B, their teammate's gestures are regarded as conditional generic representations at the same time that for observers from Team A, they are conditional specific representations. That is, members of Team B disambiguate her gesturing on condition that it presumes that something is represented, though they know not what beforehand. For members of Team B, the charade is a matter of conditional generic representation and, alerted to this, they use this understanding as a framework for disambiguating the array, exploiting all kinds of clues to infer what is being represented. Team A, on the other hand, knows what is being represented ahead of time. For them, following the charade is a matter of matching gestures with the saying they are designed to recall. They know the solution to the problem that the player from Team B is trying to crack, and they use that knowledge to appreciate player B's ingenuity.

Clearly, the players on Team A and the players on Team B are engaged in different cognitive tasks, which we can characterise as responding to conditional specific representations, on the one hand, and responding to conditional generic representations, on the other. Moreover, this is not simply a matter of charades, since artworks can employ either sort of representation as well — *Pacific 231* and *Symphonie Fantastique* are examples of conditional specific representation, while the thunder in Beethoven's *Pastoral* is more of the nature of conditional generic representation (one wouldn't hear it as thunder unless one knew the piece was illustrative).

The resources available to us for identifying such representations in the case of conditional generic representation, like those of conditional specific representation, are varied. They may involve recognitional analogies, fragments of lexical knowledge, synesthetic effects, homologies and the existence of certain common descriptions for musical or movement motifs and certain objects (for instance, 'flowing music', 'flowing movements', and 'flowing water'). However, there is still a difference between these forms of representation since, with conditional specific representation, you know antecedently exactly what is being represented whereas, with conditional generic representation, you only know antecedently that something is being represented. Both forms of representation may involve the deployment of natural recognitional capacities as well as fragments of lexicographic knowledge. But in order to access such information you need to be alerted to the fact that either something or something specific is being represented[3].

Clearly each of these types of representation is found in dance. Examples of unconditional representation would include: fighting scenes in Beijing Opera where the simulation of fighting stands for fighting, or peasant dances in *Giselle* that stand for harvest celebrations, or regal entrances in *Raymonda* that stand for royal promenades, or the enactment of children's play in Donald McKayle's *Games*. We see an example of this type of representation in *Coppélia* when

Swanilda impersonates the automaton by moving in a jerky, abrupt, mechanical way. She is imitating a puppet, and we can recognise this by looking, just as we recognise that she is running away from Coppélius without referring to a code. This most elementary and direct form of representation can range from reproducing the simple act of ordinary walking in order to depict walking, to creating a stylised, rhythmic, but nevertheless still recognizable rendition of an action.

For instance, in 'Taxi', the final number of the musical *Bring in 'da Noise, Bring in 'da Funk,* a number of African-American men from different class backgrounds and walks of life try unsuccessfully to hail a taxi. The dancers enact first a street kid, then a college student, then a well-dressed professional man, and finally Colin Powell making the familiar pointing gesture with an outstretched arm, and, in frustration mounting to anger, watching the cab drive by. They do this rhythmically, to music, gradually adding in more and more tap footwork. We understand instantly what this narrative means. We see four men in a row fail to get a taxi to stop. This is the literal content of the representation, although thematically we also understand the political implication that no matter how famous or successful a black man becomes, he is still invisible and considered dangerous in American culture. Nevertheless, at the literal level, this is an example of unconditional representation inasmuch as we recognise the relevant simulated activity by looking, although it is not altogether an unmixed case, since the simulated activity involves imitating a social (rather than a dance) gestural code for hailing a cab.

In terms of our second category, there are many different gestural codes in dance — from the mudras of Indian dance to the Delsarte system of bodily movements popularised by Ted Shawn and others. And in the 1980s, a number of postmodern choreographers began using American Sign Language as a gestural code in their dances, often speaking and signing simultaneously. Such systems exemplify the use of lexical representation in dance, as does the circular hand movement around the face that symbolises 'beautiful woman' in nineteenth-century ballet.

By the late nineteenth century, European ballet choreographers had elaborated a conventional code of pantomime gesture, which educated audience members learned to decode. Derived from the traditions of the Italian *commedia dell'arte,* ballet pantomime emerged as early as the beginning of the eighteenth century, when ballet separated from opera and thus newly required non-verbal means to advance the dramatic narrative. John Weaver, for instance, describes his innovative experiments with restoring ancient pantomime gesture to convey specific emotions in *The Loves of Mars and Venus* (1717):

> *Admiration* is discover'd by the raising up of the right Hand, the Palm turn'd upwards, the Fingers clos'd; and in one Motion the Wrist turn'd round and Fingers spread; the Body reclining, and Eyes fix'd on the Object....The left Hand struck suddenly with the right; and sometimes against the Breast; denotes *Anger.* (quoted in Winter, 1974: pp. 58-59)

Cyril Beaumont explains the use of ballet pantomime, as it had crystallised in the late nineteenth-century Russian Imperial ballet, in several passages in the Petipa-Ivanov ballet *Swan Lake*, for instance:

> *The Princess-Mother shows her disapproval of Siegfried's boon companions.* To convey this, she mimes: I pray you — these companions — have not. That is, she places both finger-tips to her breast, clasps her hands in entreaty, points to Siegfried, extends her arms towards his companions, then, turning her hands palms downwards, crosses and uncrosses them in a horizontal plane. All negative actions are achieved by first presenting the required phrase of mime in *positive* form, then negativing it by the crossing and uncrossing of the extended hands....

In another passage, Beaumont explains:

> *Odette declares that she is doomed to die.* To convey this, she mimes: I — here — must die. That is, she places both finger-tips to her breast, points to the ground, then raises her arms above her head, clenching the fists, crosses her wrists, lowers her arms straight in front of her, then, just as the arms fall vertically downwards, she unclenches her hands and sharply separates them. Death is conveyed by a gesture of strength which is suddenly snapped in two. (Beaumont, 1982: pp. 78-79)

Conditional specific representation is indispensable to much dance, for without titles, program notes, and other descriptive texts a great deal of dance movement would be utterly indecipherable. Indeed, this is the most important category of dance representation. To know which fairy gifts the dancing represents in the Prologue of Petipa's Sleeping Beauty, one must know the specific details of the ballet's libretto, while in order to realise that the eponymous *Radha* turns back into a stone statue rather than simply entering a state of repose at the end of her dance of delirium requires an acquaintance with Ruth St. Denis's program notes.

Likewise, in Graham's *Night Journey*, one must know that the dance retells the story of Oedipus (as well as knowing that myth) in order to grasp that the man on the 'pogo stick' is Tiresias.

In Noverre's *Orphée et Euridice* and equally in George Balanchine's *Orpheus*, background knowledge of the Greek hero's tragic adventure in the underworld is essential, just as in Balanchine's *Apollo* we need to know that he is the god of the arts, that the women he dances with are the Muses, and indeed, which of the Muses they are. When a Yoruba dancer in Nigeria or Dahomey dances the image of the spirit Egungun with swirling red cloths that appear to carry humans away like a whirlwind, the dance will be meaningless to spectators who are unfamiliar with Yoruba cosmology (See Thompson, 1974). In fact, whenever one encounters mythological or historical backstories in dance, whether in the Western ballet tradition, the many dance-dramas in both East and West based on the Hindu epics *The Mahabharata* and *The Ramayana*, African ritual dances, or other dance cultures, one is likely to find conditional specific representation.

This is equally the case for the many dances, in various cultures, based on plays, poems, and other works of literature. For instance, José Limón's *Moor's Pavane* is a distillation of Shakespeare's *Othello*. Using the choreographic form of a Renaissance court dance for two couples — the key characters Othello, Desdemona, Iago, and Emilia — the dance itself almost seems to create with its intricate floor patterns a tangled web of psychological conflict. That the dance represents the fanning of Othello's murderous jealousy and its vicissitudes is a meaning irretrievable for the uninformed spectator. To anyone unfamiliar with Shakespeare's play, the meaning of the choreography along with the significance of the lace handkerchief the dancers drop or pass from one to another (as well as the sequence of its passing), of one male dancer's whispering constantly into another's ear, or of the angry or anguished glances the dancers cast, will be lost.

An example of conditional generic representation may be found in Kei Takei's *Light*. Realizing the overall representational intentions of the piece warrants our interpretation of much of the imagery as cosmic. In Part 10, 'The Stone Field,' Takei holds the center of the stage, jumping and turning as rocks are flung at her feet in a way that prompts us to regard her as a goddess amidst a meteor shower. In Simone Forti's *Planet*, the title alerts us that representation is afoot. Thus we are predisposed to see the dancers moving from crawling on all fours to walking to running as a representation of the process of evolution. But whereas in the example of the Egungun dancer, one has to know the specific attributes of the spirit to recognise the object of the representation, in *Planet* the title suffices to signal representational intent, without telling us what specific attribute of our planet is being represented. That remains for the spectator to conjecture.

Admittedly, the boundary between conditional specific representation and conditional generic representation can become quite slim. Near the border sits, for instance, Balanchine's *Jewels*, where without the titles we might not see the choreography in terms of the representation of gem-like features.

If, as this brief inventory indicates, dance representation can fall into any of these categories, one may wonder whether the taxonomy can tell us anything particularly informative about dance representation. The taxonomy, it might be said, would be informative, if it turned out that dance representation fell into only one of these categories. But how informative is it if dance can exemplify all of the categories? Indeed, the problem may seem even worse, since it is not only the case that dance can exemplify all of these categories, but so can all the other arts, including theatre, film, video, sculpture, painting, photography, literature and even music. So can we learn anything distinctive about choreographic representation by being shown that dance can fall into all the same categories that all the other arts do?

We think that there is a way to use the taxonomy informatively. It is true that dance representation can fall into all of our four categories and it is also true that representation in other artforms can instantiate each of these categories as well. And yet it does seem that dance does rely on some of these categories more than the other arts do — or at least more than the neighboring arts of dramatic enactment (such as realist theatre, movies, and TV).

What we have in mind is this. Contrasting dance with theatre, film, and TV, dance seems to rely more on categories 3 and 4 (above) than do theatre, film and TV. This is not to say that dance does not employ categories 1 and 2; perhaps dance even employs these categories as much as or more than it does categories 3 and 4. Nevertheless, theatrical dance as we know it does employ forms of conditional representation more than the dominant forms of theatre, film and TV do in Western culture. Indeed, these artforms rely more exclusively on category 1 than on the other categories of representation on our list. Call this difference in choice of representational strategies a *proportionate difference* in representational means between dance and its dramatic neighbors.

This is not to deny that theatre, film, and TV as typically practised may use category 2. And in certain avant-garde instantiations — like Brakhage's

Anticipation of the Night — they may even deploy forms of conditional representation. Nevertheless, in the main (the mainstream), theatre, film, and TV use categories 3 and 4 to a lesser extent than they use category 1; whereas, while dance uses category 1, it also relies very heavily on using category 2 and, especially, categories 3 and 4 for purposes of representation. This should be clear from the degree to which even mainstream dance representations depend on accompanying descriptive texts — such as program notes and titles — for intelligibility, whereas mainstream theatre, film and TV are generally accessible without such enabling texts.

Thus, there is a proportionate difference in the choice of representational means between dance, on the one hand, and theatre, film, and TV, on the other. Dance relies more on conditional representation than they do. But what of music? Doesn't it also rely heavily on conditional representation? Is there no difference between music and dance with respect to representational means? Certainly there is: dance uses unconditional representation more than music does. So where dance differs from theatre, film, and TV by its emphasis on forms of conditional representation, it differs from music in its far more frequent use of unconditional representation. Moreover, it differs from the remaining temporal art — literature — insofar as literature operates primarily via lexicographic representation, relying on that category of representation far more than dance does; or, for that matter, than theatre, film, TV, and music[4].

By marking off four types of representation in terms of the way in which viewers come to comprehend them, then, we can say something about the characteristic, though not the unique, use of representation in dance. We are not speaking about what is unique about dance representation because, as we've seen, dance employs the same types of representation that other art forms do. However, dance characteristically relies on these different types of representation with different emphases than the other arts do. It mobilises unconditional representation more than music does, lexicographic representation less than literature, and it depends more on both types of conditional representation far more than theatre, film, and TV do.

Our taxonomy of types of representation can say something informative about dance representation, especially in relation to its neighboring dramatic arts: dance representation is far more frequently a matter of conditional representation — especially conditional specific representation — than are typical theatrical, film, and TV presentations. That is, there is a proportionate difference in representational means between dance and its near neighbors — the other temporal arts and the other theatrical arts.

The differences between dance and the other theatre arts is particularly telling because it may help explain why dance often requires the acquisition and application of background knowledge in order to be comprehended, whereas the other forms of contemporary dramatic enactment ride more exclusively on the audience's natural recognitional powers. Theatre, film, and TV are more accessible than dance to the degree that they rely more exclusively on unconditional representation.

Moreover, if the preceding analysis is correct, it may have some interesting ontological implications concerning dance representation: namely, that insofar as certain descriptive texts (like program notes) — or, at least, their propositional contents — are indispensable for parsing certain dance representations, such descriptive texts should be regarded as part of the dancework proper, and not merely as accompanying paraphernalia. That is, in the relevant cases, not only the choreography but the underlying story, no matter how generic, is an ineliminable part of the dance representation.

Earlier we noted that it was Noverre's ambition to get the words out of dance. He aspired to make ballets with the power of Racinean tragedies, but through movement. Yet it has never been clear that movement alone can secure such sustained effects. The movement needs to be contextualised; it needs a back-story[5]. And that may be one of the reasons that conditional specific representation remains such an important channel of communication for dance.

In this section, we have examined four categories of representation in terms of how viewers comprehend instances of them. These categories can be implemented by all the arts, including dance. But different artforms rely differently on alternative representational categories. Dance places greater emphasis on forms of conditional representation than arts like theatre, film, and TV, which, in turn, rely more heavily on unconditional representation. This suggests not only a contrast between dance representation and representation in the other arts, but also explains why, in general, theatre, film, and TV often appear more conducive for popular consumption than dance. In addition, we have argued that the backstory and other referents in dances employing conditional specific representation are proper parts of the dance ontologically and that the heavy use of conditionally specific representation in dance is connected to the challenge of trying to make dance dramatically powerful at the same time it is wordless.

Notes

1 For a broader overview of the relation of dance and imitation, see Cohen, 1983.

2 This taxonomy has been drawn in terms of different ways that viewers come to realise what x represents. We do not deny that different taxonomies could be constructed. Nor do we deny that more distinctions could be made with respect to the viewer's comprehension of representations than the ones we emphasise. We merely maintain that the distinctions we mark are useful and based in the facts. We also understand that some of our categories tend to blend into others. That is why we speak above of a continuum of categories.

3 For similar ways of drawing these and related distinctions, see Sparshott, 1995: p. 71 and Kivy, 1984: pp. 28-60.

4 We are uncertain about the gross proportionate differentials between dance and the nontemporal arts of painting and sculpture, though of course the representations in the latter arts differ from those in dance in that they are static.

5 In his 1803 preface to *Letters on Dancing and Ballets* (first written in 1760), Noverre writes, "There are, undoubtedly, a great many things which pantomime[-ballet] can only indicate, but in regard to the passions there is a degree of expression to which words cannot attain or rather there are passions for which no words exist. Then dancing allied with action triumphs" (Noverre, 1966: p. 5). Despite his belief in the emotive power of wordless dancing and his railing in *Letters* against any "complicated and long-drawn-out ballet...the plot of which I cannot follow without constant reference to the programme" (Noverre, 1966: p. 19), in the preface to his ballet *Euthyme et Eucharis* (1775) he nevertheless acknowledges the need for program notes as well as a backstory : "I shall admit that the Programme tells the historical or mythological story and states clearly what the Dance can only vaguely hint, because our Dancers are not Greeks and Romans" (quoted in Winter, p. 121).

References

Batteux, C. (1989) *Les Beaux-Arts réduits à un même principe.* Ed. Jean-Rémy Mantion. Paris: Aux Amateurs de Livres.

Beaumont, C. W. (1982) *The ballet called Swan Lake.* New York: Dance Horizons. (reprint of 1952 edition).

Cohen, S. J. (1983) 'Dance as an art of imitation', in R. Copeland and M. Cohen (ed) *What is dance?*. Oxford: Oxford University Press, pp. 15-22.

Kivy, P. (1984) *Sound and semblance*. Princeton: Princeton University Press.

Kristeller, P. O. (1980) *Renaissance thought and the arts*. Princeton: Princeton University Press.

Levinson, A. (1925) 'The spirit of the classic dance', *Theatre Arts Monthly* Vol. 9 (March): pp. 165-177.

Noverre, J.-G. (1966) *Letters on dancing and ballets*. Trans. C. W. Beaumont. New York: Dance Horizons; reprint of 1930 ed.

Schier, F. (1986) *Deeper into pictures: an essay on pictorial representation.* Cambridge: Cambridge University Press.

Smith, A. (1980) *Essays on philosophical subjects*. Oxford: Oxford University Press.

Sparshott, F. (1995) *A measured pace*. Toronto: University of Toronto Press.

Thompson, R. (1974) *African art in motion: icon and act*. Berkeley: University of California Press.

Weaver, J. (1712) *An essay towards an history of dancing*. London: J. Tonson. Reprinted in facsimile in Richard Ralph, *The life and works of John Weaver*. London: Dance Books (1985).

Winter, M. H. (1974) *The pre-romantic ballet*. London: Pitman.

THE HISTORICAL CHARACTER OF DANCES

Bonnie Rowell

Introduction

Within the study of dance in higher education in the UK, there has been an increasing tendency in recent years, as there has been within other disciplines, to adopt a post-structuralist perspective, one that privileges the viewer in the construction of meaning. Whilst I would welcome the acknowledgement of the viewer's role within the process of interpretation and the concomitant liberation from any notion of one single definitive meaning, there are two unfortunate by-products of this tendency. Firstly it has led to a certain amount of distrust of more traditional methodologies, specifically an approach to dance based upon Western philosophy. Secondly, and perhaps as a result of the first, it has led in some quarters to a wholesale acceptance of a post-structuralist concept of meaning together with a certain disregard for the logical implications embedded within it.

Indeed there appears to be a general tendency to consign any notion of objectivity to the single banner of 'positivist philosophy' without further consideration and to conflate an objective perspective with 'scientism'. Thus, while methodologies drawn from literary criticism, from sociology and anthropology can co-exist quite happily, there is still a tension with, and a deep rooted suspicion of, a primarily philosophical approach which seeks to establish an ontological basis for the study of dance and which foregrounds the *concepts* of meaning and understanding in a different way.

This chapter, then, considers the two positions by drawing upon an account of meaning within artworks which is helpful, I think, in clarifying the current position and which highlights important implications certainly within the current conception of 'meaning' held by some teachers of dance. It is prompted by two further issues: the current 'revisiting' of dance classics by choreographers as diverse as Mark Morris, Mats Ek, Matthew Bourne, Lea Anderson and Maguy Marin together with the dance world's increasing and understandable concern with preserving the past, with reconstruction and notation and with the problems of authenticity and identity which these activities bring to the fore.

My argument draws upon a response (or a response to a response) to a perception of meaning in artworks which is commonly attributed to analytic aesthetics. This perception deems that meaning is located within the artwork in some way. The implications of this conception of meaning are that meaning is 'fixed' and it is this view that has given analytic aesthetics its bad press (certainly within the dance world) over the last few years and it is this view that is challenged by Graham McFee within his historicity thesis (McFee, 1980, 1992a, 1995). I begin by rehearsing McFee's critique in relation to the arts in general, continuing with my own response in relation to postmodern theories of meaning and lastly, in relation to the issues it raises for dance.

McFee's thesis concerns the historical character of artworks and may briefly be summarised as stating that meanings of artworks might change — that the work might come to have a meaning at a later date, due to later events, that it did not have at the time of its conception; from this it follows that the changes will — from the perspective of the later audience — seem to reflect meaning-features that the artwork always had, since it has them now. This implies a certain fluidity to the concept of meaning. What I find particularly interesting about this idea is that it might be seen in some ways to be akin to a post-structuralist account of meaning, but at the same time it usefully highlights problems within that account.

'Forward retroactivism'

I begin with a more detailed account of McFee's thesis which is a way of articulating the claim that artworks have a historical character. The argument proceeds in three stages.

First McFee argues that an understanding of artworks can only be achieved via a knowledge of their context, that it cannot be dependent upon their perceptible features in isolation, but to the *appropriate* interpretation or description of those features. (Appropriate, that is, in relation to the cultural conventions which govern them, to issues of genre and style and so on). If we mistake the categories appropriate to artistic interpretation, then we will misperceive the works.

The second stage introduces the *standard* notion of historicity or 'backwards retroactivism': that we must locate works within their history to understand the artistic concepts (issues of genre, style etc.) appropriate to our perception of them, and hence not to misperceive them, and this follows from the first stage. We may modify our view of works of art in light of knowledge of a previous work which, for example, might clarify the tradition of the current work and thus cause us to change our views of the later work. Much of the impact of Mats Ek's *Giselle*, for example, would be lost without a knowledge of the Coralli/Perrot/ 'original'. That understanding is achieved via a knowledge of context would seem to be widely accepted. A further implication, though, is that understanding is always *indefinite* because knowledge of context can only ever be partial and this presents a more contentious issue. It is a view that is contended by most analytic philosophers, but broadly in line with current European theorists. However, it is the nature and limits of this idea of 'indefiniteness' that presents the problems and clearly distinguishes between the two camps.

The third stage gets us to forwards retroactivism - that later events can alter how we think about earlier works, by altering the concepts *appropriate* to the perception of those works. McFee's preferred example serves to clarify the matter. He argues that Picasso's series based upon *Las Meniñas* shows us new things about the Velasquez original, such that we change our views about the earlier work. He gives another example of this process *in action*: Foucault, in his essay in *The Order of Things* (1989: pp. 3-16) discusses the Velasquez painting and he could only have arrived at the insights about the Velasquez, McFee argues (1992a: p. 308), via knowledge of Picasso's later works and the insights on the Velasquez inherent in them. This, for McFee constitutes a change in the meaning of the earlier work; and this is possible, he argues, because reasons for our judgements which were not available at the time of the work's inception, became available at a later date. Changes in the reasons we have for critical judgements imply changes in the meaning of those judgements and thus a change in the meaning of the artwork itself, given that both judgements are answerable to the perceptible features of the work. A crucial question here, then, is how do we identify and describe the perceptible features of the artwork and this question, of course, has particular resonance for danceworks whose identity is even more in dispute than some other artworks as dances have no persistent *physical* identity.

It would seem unproblematic to acknowledge that particularly insightful accounts or interpretations of an artwork, in the form of say verbal criticisms or in the form of other artworks like Picasso's *Las Meninas* or Mats Ek's *Giselle*, might make us see the original artwork in a new light. What is contentious is that this constitutes a change in the meaning of the earlier artwork, for it presupposes a certain fluidity to the notion of meaning and it implies a possibly indefinite evolution of artworks which some commentators would want, if not to make synonymous with, then at least to nod in the direction of, the seeming subjectivism of postmodern criticism. As McFee has made clear, both in this series of articles, and elsewhere[1] this is not so for him. (His reasons would take us too far afield.)

To summarise then, we have seen that knowledge acquired later than the composition of the work is relevant to its meaning-relations. We also have that the possibilities for meaning are indefinite, because new reasons might continue to become available, indefinitely. These things are widely accepted by European theorists but I think it is interesting that they have been argued through here from a Western philosophical perspective. This is an attempt to do away with the conception of *artistic value as timeless*, and, as McFee states, it is just such a conception that has been a source for criticism of the whole project of aesthetics in recent years. This is an account of the arts which is in favour of both acknowledging and accepting certain features of current critical debate, such as the indefiniteness of value and meaning, whilst at the same time making clear a distance from some other features, such as subjectivism. For McFee, there is a key limiting concept to the notion of 'indefiniteness': and it is Wittgenstein's 'principle of permanence'[2] (just as it is to instability of meaning in general). This principle of permanence is really a sort of principle of 'least effort', in which, though changes occur throughout human experience, there is a tendency to retain the overriding linguistic structures, and by extension, cultural structures. This model, then, while permitting the text and its perceptible features a certain fluidity, provides some restraints.

This account may be contrasted with a position on meaning which is inherent in a model for dance analysis used widely within dance teaching. Pauline Hodgens' chapter on interpretation in *Dance Analysis, Theory and Practice* (Adshead, 1988: pp. 60-89), for example, gives an account of the process of the interpretation of danceworks which, while acknowledging the relevance of the conditions of their production, makes a distinction between the dance and its context, such that you 'read' the dance-features *against* the background of their context and *informed by* concepts of genre and style and so on. The distinction is somewhat uneasy in that the role of the 'reader' within the process of interpretation is acknowledged but the dance 'text' remains intact as a readable and immutable object. It does not explore the logical parameters of 'text' and 'context'. This original model has been revised to a more radical account of the 'non-fixed text' and I take here as my example Janet Adshead-Lansdale's paper for *Dance Research* (Adshead-Lansdale, 1994: pp. 15-20) in which she repositions the relationship between text and interpretation:

> The process of interpretation has its own logic in so far that *different things* are perceived, upon which meaning is constructed, it is not necessarily that the *same things* are perceived differently. This view is more radical in being less reliant on the notion of a fixed text. (1994, p. 16)

So dance now has a text which has doubly disappeared: disappeared in the first instance in that it has no persistent physical identity, and in the second instance in terms of our perception of it, and I would want to get to grips with these ideas in a more substantial way. It is unclear to what extent Adshead-Lansdale holds that the text has disappeared in favour of "… a tissue of quotations drawn from innumerable centres of culture" (Barthes in Adshead-Lansdale, 1994: p. 18); and "innumerable" here does not mean indeterminate, but the centre of reference is most certainly slippery. However, her strategy is certainly to conclude in these terms: Michael Worton, co-author of *Intertextuality Theories and Practices*, is quoted:

> Intertextual analysis is possible only if the reader accepts that such an analysis must be founded on the speculative creativity of ambiguity. There is no *knowing*, but there are different modes of understanding, of responding, of reading. (Worton in Adshead-Lansdale, 1994: p. 18)

If, as Worton asserts there is no knowing (and I presume he is here referring to the notion that perception is interpretative), then still the implications for this assertion must be fully acknowledged, and examined. Perhaps the difficulties in applying theories of literary criticism to dance need first of all to be clarified. In terms of 'the creativity of ambiguity' as and when applied to dance *performance*, then two cases need to be acknowledged. Either *some* of the possibilities for interpretation are instantiated in a staging, in which case the dance is not ambiguous in those dimensions; or we consider *just* the possibilities for performance in which case we have underdetermination, rather than ambiguity.

If, instead, the idea of 'creativity of ambiguity' is to suggest that there are many possible *critical* interpretations of the dance, then this claim is true — but it is true of a fully determinate dance performance; in which case, if the dance were the 'text', the ambiguities would not concern it, but only emphasise the variety of critical interpretative possibilities suggested by it. In either case the possibilities are rich, but not unlimited — as the notion of 'speculative creativity' might seem to suggest.

To announce (as above) that "... analysis must be founded on the speculative creativity of ambiguity", without a consideration of what the boundaries to this creativity might be, is to overlook important consequences: and if the term "ambiguity" is not to suggest that any meaning can be imputed to anything, then what limits its possibilities? If the answer to this involves reference in some way to 'the text', and to its perceptible features, then we are back to where we started — with the text — and it does not tell us very much about the nature of interpretation or of its relationship to the artwork. These are things that McFee, whilst acknowledging the text's lack of fixity, is centrally concerned with, and I think we must be too.

I have mentioned earlier that this question of textual identity has particular resonance for dance due to its nature. Dance, as Marcia Siegel maintains, exists forever at "... the vanishing point" (Siegel, 1972) but the concept of a meaningful artwork is crucial to our understanding of later productions and versions, however undefined that concept may be, and particularly in light of the dance world's current, well founded concern to preserve its past and its present, if for no other reason than to understand its future. But we must be clear what it is we are preserving and, since there are of course no easy answers on that issue, debate and the attendant scholarship is crucial: here, the notion of a 'non-fixed text', left at that, does little to advance our understanding of the area. There are two problems we can at least avoid: firstly, the view of meaning as unitary and definitive; secondly, the view that anything has equal claim to be regarded as a meaning. Denying the first does not lead one into accepting the second.

Ek's *Giselle*

A specific dance example might serve to clarify some of the issues raised so far and to highlight their importance to dance. The revising of past dance narratives is rife amongst choreographers within all dance forms: it is prompted by a response, according to Sally Banes (1987: xiv), to the postmodern crisis in our approach to notions of originality and authenticity. This feature too informs my concern with understanding these dance works.

Mats Ek's *Giselle*[3] concerns itself with a reinterpretation of the original theme, in light of subsequent thinking, particularly in the realm of psychology and female sexuality: in this sense it is a discussion of the earlier dance. So it can be argued that Ek's dance draws our attention to a reappraisal of the Romantic impulse and might cause us to have new reasons for seeing an 'original' version in a different way, and this, according to McFee may lead to a change in the meanings of the 'original' *Giselle*. I am using the term "original" loosely and I want neither to rehearse the debate about dance-identity, nor to delve into the complex history of production of *Giselle*. However, there is generally acknowledged a concept of *Giselle*, such that we can point to versions and say that they are not it. What this concept is, is a complex matter involving historical scholarship and judgement: but the inter-relationship of scholarship with judgement is taken as read within other disciplines. Neither am I claiming that Ek's dance is a 'version' of Giselle, but it does stand in the same relation to the original as a particularly insightful discussion might: it tells us something new in ways that draw on the past of the artform of dance and that draws upon later events in ways that might make us 're-draw' the 'narrative' of that artform (as well, of course, as being an art work in its own right).

Ek's *Giselle* draws our attention to the Freudian concept of hysteria, locating the second act in an asylum for women with Myrtha as the matron, and the dance foregrounds the role of female reproduction in Giselle's madness. Giselle has a red rag doll which she produces from between her legs and uses both as comforter and substitute baby. It gets passed between the inmates during Act II as most desirable possession. During Act I the villagers roll on huge white eggs as part of their harvest celebrations — giving us more evidence of Ek's concern with fertility and female reproduction, this time by contrasting the individual's sexuality and obsession with reproduction with the corporate, socially acceptable norm in a quite sinister way. Gwen Bergner and Nicole Plett in their recent work on *Coppélia*, draw our attention to similar concerns within *that* ballet:

> Nestled within its comedic marriage plot lie a host of cultural anxieties — about ... the survival of community structure, ... and the threat posed by unregulated male desire. (Bergner and Plett, 1996: p. 159)

Now to what extent these cultural anxieties were evident to the nineteenth century audience and how sharply focused they were is uncertain.

Giselle herself possesses both childlike innocence and adult sexuality, without the social adroitness to be able to distinguish appropriately between the two, and is thus an outcast. Her dances in Act I display a child's exuberance as she approaches the newcomer Albrecht, but she lifts her skirt in an open display of attraction and invitation. Her madness then stems from the possession of a womb and her inability to subsume her sexual impulses in the socially acceptable roles of wife and mother. As such, this conforms to a post-Freudian 'reading' of the story of *Giselle* and gives us possible 'reasons' for the narrative, but it does much more than that.

Movement in Ek's dance does not derive from the 'original' but from European 'modern ballet' which fuses classical and modern values, though direct reference is made to certain motifs within the original: Myrtha's *pas courus*, for example, appear in Ek's version as gliding steps on a flat foot. Giselle's dances are aerial and fluid yet their emphasis is towards the ground and make reference to flexed hands and feet, both of which aspects give a childlike openness and intensity. Albrecht has a similar classical fluency which is however unbounded by any classical allusion to courtliness. Instead, his aristocracy is stated in a certain urbanity and suaveness, almost that of a ballroom dancer and he wears a white tailcoat. The backdrop is surrealist in style for both acts: for the first, a landscape which includes overtly breast-like hills; for the second, a skewed perspective room with disembodied anatomical parts as decoration. Historical period is thus ambiguous, but the production makes clear reference to post-Freudian psychology as well as to post-Freudian related artistic concerns. Thus in the treatment meted out to Giselle and her fellow inmates for their sexual transgressions, Ek appears to be offering a critique of Freud's version of female sexuality as well as a comment upon the narrative and the cultural anxieties of the time[4].

Ek says that he wanted to offer an alternative interpretation of Romantic themes in dance to the saccharine ones that they have become[5]. This implies that he believes Romantic dance always to have held the possibilities for such interpretations but that they have become bowdlerized in some way. But according to a 'realist' account of meaning, a post-Freudian interpretation of the 'original' *Giselle*, if we are to accept it as significant now, would always somehow have been a possibility, but of course, one which was never realised, and this seems to be an absurdity. Alternatively, if we discount the significance of post-Freudian ideas as anachronistic to an interpretation of the original, this would mean to say that Ek's interpretation can have no role in the meaning-relations of the original work. Now his interpretation stems from an appraisal of Romantic dance in relation to Romanticism in the other arts, and this would seem to be in accordance with the process by which any interpretation is effected, that is, in relation to its context. Ek's production offers an interpretation of the 'original' *Giselle* the reasons for which could not possibly have been available at the time of that ballet's inception. Merely to state that the *significance* of the work has changed because of our contemporary views will not do, for that implies that these interpretations were always available, just not disclosed to the nineteenth century viewer. It would seem more plausible to assert that the later interpretation offers us insights into the original such that its meaning has changed.

Turning now to an earlier pre-Ek version that *does* claim to bear a relationship to the original, I would like to examine the emphasis placed upon female sexuality in the 1979 Nureyev production[6] for Lynn Seymour, Monica Mason and dancers of the Bavarian State Opera. For my purposes, it is significant in two ways: firstly, for Lynn Seymour's mad scene and, secondly, for Monica Mason's chilling portrayal of Myrtha. As Giselle, Seymour's interpretation points us towards a psychology of female sexuality in terms of the abandonment of social constraint and the power which is thereby generated. It is unlikely that reasons for those interpretations would have been available to audiences at the time of the dance's original production. These interpretations are reinforced by the dramatic power and physical strength of Mason's Myrtha. She is both awesome controlling spirit and demonic nightmare, associated with the unknown both in nature and in the subconscious and as such embodies the powers of the sublime. Female sexuality is thus portrayed as something to be feared and something closely associated with the governing powers of nature. The evidence for this claim lies in the technical virtuosity, strength and control of the dancing in this particular production, qualities which are most certainly foregrounded, and yet it could be argued that the interplay between physical control and human limitation are qualities at the very heart of the Romantic revolution in dance, particularly female dancing and thus properties which were ever in the dance. Or it could be that knowledge acquired by watching Ek's version has informed my interpretation of this earlier version. It is possible that Mason's interpretation of the role of Myrtha would *not* be regarded as appropriate to that role by an audience that is used to a more traditional account, a more saccharine account in Ek's view of Act II *Giselle*, that the physical strength that Mason makes evident and does not seek to disguise would appear inconsistent with the illusion of weightlessness and effortlessness that many would deem the essence of Romantic ballet. Mason's interpretation is authoritative and self-aware — her focus does not extend beyond the boundaries of her body (or not far) and her performance seems significantly anti-illusionist. Ek's version draws our attention to the possible appropriateness of this interpretation in Nureyev's version.

My point is that Ek's version focuses our attention on the power of women *en masse*, and that this draws our attention to the power of Mason's dancing in the earlier version, a power that is wholly consistent with the role of Myrtha by Ek's account, and that means that we must possibly reappraise our concept of *sylph* and *wili*, to say nothing about the role of women in general, but that reasons for this reading of either version were unavailable to the nineteenth century audience, or, for that matter, available to inform nineteenth century performance.

Conclusions

Perhaps in some ways Ek does offer us a more authentic version, devoid of an over-emphasis on ethereality, or upon technical and production feats; and in doing so, offers us fresh possibilities for the dance narrative and for its performers' interpretations — and this would be to serve the purpose of keeping the concept "Giselle" alive. So perhaps, choreographers' current obsession with revisiting dance history at best produces dances that illuminate that history, that provide fresh possibilities for their meaning-relations and help keep the works alive. In this way, postmodern dance-makers are telling us something new and something important. The notion of the non-fixed text opens possibilities as to our imaginative engagement with artworks, but it does nothing to tackle the complex problems that arise as a consequence. I have found it valuable to have an account of meaning that does acknowledge the implications and that also tackles head on the complex relationship between text and context. I need that sort of systematised examination of the area that I find lacking in European theorists.

During a recent conference[7], theatre and opera director Tim Albery asserted that "... the text is a fluid and elusive thing that can change from moment to moment", but he drew these conclusions *after* a detailed examination of the complex inter-relationship of elements that constitute and inform a notion of the text, *and not* as a starting point from which all the audience's meanings can contribute to an artwork's overall meaning, and are given equal validity. 'Meaning' needs to be placed centre stage in just this way within the study of dance whereby the nature of dance works, the complex inter-relationship of their materials and how we understand them as artworks, rather than as social signifiers, is the central concern.

Notes

1   The position is clearly made for example throughout his *Understanding Dance* (1992). The details of his response to such criticisms can be sought there.

2   See McFee, 1980: p. 315.

3   *Giselle*, choreography by Mats Ek (1982), for the Cullberg Ballet. First screened on BBC2, as part of the *Dance International* series, September 30th, 1989.

4   Peggy Phelan's chapter on "Dance and the history of hysteria" in Susan Leigh Foster's *Corporealities* offers a fascinating account of Freud's notions of the relationship between the body and 'truth' that seems especially pertinent to Ek's dance here. Phelan draws upon Freud's *Studies in Hysteria* of 1895 and discusses the great faith he placed in the truth of bodily performance. In classical psychoanalysis, she argues, the trauma manifests itself *physically* in the paralysis of a body part for example, and the cure is effected *physically* — by the re-enactment of the trauma, or the touching of a relevant body part by the analyst to trigger memory. (This emphasis is later abandoned in favour of the 'talking cure'.) The choreographer might well have had this former aspect of Freud's work in mind.

5   Mats Ek in interview preceding the BBC2 screening of *Giselle*.

6   *Giselle*, after original choreography by Jules Perrot and Jean Coralli (1841), with Pas de Vendanges by Mary Skeaping, directed by Stanley Dorfman and Rudolf Nureyev in 1979 for Rudolf Nureyev, Lynn Seymour, Monica Mason, Youri Vamos and members of the Ballet of the Bavarian State Opera House.

7   "Preservation Politics: A conference on issues and methodologies in dance revived, reconstructed, remade" took place at Roehampton Institute London, November 8-9th 1997 and included a cross-arts panel discussion with Tim Albery, Phyllida LLoyd and Professor Ann Thompson debating the issue: "Interpreting or remaking the text?" Conference proceedings forthcoming.

References

Adshead, J. (ed) (1988) *Dance analysis: theory and practice*. London: Dance Books.

Adshead-Lansdale, J. (1994) 'Dance analysis in performance', *Dance Research* Vol. XII, No. 2, Autumn: pp. 15–20.

Banes, S. (1987) *Terpsichore in sneakers: post-modern dance*. Middletown, Connecticut: Wesleyan University Press.

Bergner, G. and N. Plett (1996) 'Uncanny women and anxious masters: reading *Coppélia* against Freud', in G. Morris (ed) *Moving words*. London: Routledge, pp. 159-79.

Foucault, M. (1989) *The order of things*. London: Routledge.

Hodgens, P. (1988) 'Interpreting the dance', in J. Adshead (ed) *Dance analysis: theory and practice*. London: Dance Books, pp. 60-89.

McFee, G. (1980) 'The historicity of art', *Journal of Aesthetics and Art Criticism* Vol. 38, No. 3: pp. 307-24.

McFee, G. (1992a) 'The historical character of art: a re-appraisal', *British Journal of Aesthetics* Vol. 32, No. 4, October: pp. 307-319.

———— (1992b) *Understanding dance*. London: Routledge.

———— (1995) 'Back to the future: a reply to Sharpe', *British Journal of Aesthetics* Vol. 35, No. 3, July: pp. 278-83.

Phelan, P. (1996) 'Dance and the history of hysteria', in S. L. Foster (ed) *Corporealities*. London: Routledge, pp. 90-105.

Siegel, M. (1972) *At the vanishing point*. New York: Saturday Review Press.

PRODUCTIONS, PERFORMANCES, AND THEIR EVALUATION

Aaron Meskin

Introduction

My focus in this chapter is not on dance works, but on productions and perform-ances. I contend that productions and performances have been unfairly slighted by philosophical theorizing about the arts. They have not been taken seriously as works of art in their own right. Nor has there been much in the way of theorizing about their evaluation. Jerrold Levinson, one of the few authors who has thought seriously about performances, has argued that their evaluation has a perspectival element that is not shared by full-fledged works of art (Levinson, 1987). In this chapter, I argue that Levinson is wrong about performance evaluation. In so doing, I seek to counter the slights that productions and performances have received at the hands of aestheticians.

In the first section of the chapter, I offer an outline of dance ontology and attempt to make clear what sorts of things productions and performances are. I also argue that indeterminacy with respect to the individuation of dance performances is not a serious worry. In the second section, I argue that per-formances and productions count as works of art in their own right. I also offer some criticisms of Paul Thom's claim that dance performances and productions are not works of art, and then deal with one other objection to the idea of performances and productions as works of art. In the third section, I argue that understanding performances and productions as works of art in their own right will keep one from accepting a perspectivalist view of dance performance and production evaluation. I also argue that dance performance and productions should be evaluated from the perspective of their audiences, and that these audiences are importantly different from musical audiences.

Dance ontology: work, production, interpretation, performance

Dance ontology is complex. There are dance works, dance productions, the performance interpretations of companies and individuals, and performances themselves. There may also be stagings of productions, distinct from the productions themselves, but they will not be discussed here.

Dance works (such as *Trio A*, *The Moor's Pavane*, or Frederick Ashton's *Cinderella*) are multiples. They are abstract entities called 'types' in the philosophical literature (Wollheim, 1980[1]). Dance performances (for example, the performance of *The Moor's Pavane* that I attended on October 25th, 1997) are concrete, spatially and temporally extended event-tokens. We can distinguish also between performances of entire companies and the performances of individuals in those companies. Both are objects of evaluation and critical attention, although performances of individual dancers are not artworks in their own right unless, of course, they are performances of solo works. The performance of an individual dancer in a dance performance with more than one performer is properly considered part of an artwork, not an artwork itself.

What about performance interpretations and productions? Performance interpretations are, as R.A. Sharpe and others have argued, also multiples: that is, they are also types (Sharpe, 1979, Levinson, 1987[2]). They are, more precisely, performance types. So, for example, when we speak of Carlos Orta's interpretation of The Moor's role in *The Moor's Pavane*, we are speaking neither of an individual performance nor of a critical understanding of the role, but of a performance type (which may or may not be underwritten by a critical understanding of the role). Just as individual performers produce performance interpretations, there are performance interpretations which are collectively produced by entire dance companies: the recent production of Mark Morris's *L'Allegro, il Penseroso e il Moderato* at ENO, and the production of Hanya Holm's *Homage to Mahler* performed in 1997 by the Dance Plus company of Rutgers University are two examples. These are also properly thought of as performance types. And these types, as I have already suggested, are commonly known as productions.

Dance works, productions, and performance interpretations are all multiples properly classified as the abstract objects known as types. Performances are concrete tokens. Productions are, in fact, sub-types of works and concrete performances are tokens of both those sub-types and the broader types of which those sub-types are interpretations.

It is not difficult to spell out the sub-type relation. For any two types A and B: A is a sub-type of B if and only if necessarily, all tokens of A are tokens of B, and it is possible for there to be tokens of B which are not tokens of A[3].

Individual performances are tokens of at least two types: the work, and an interpretation (that is, production) of the work. This is not problematic. To make an orthographic analogy: the letter "a" is a type, individual letters "a" are tokens of that type, italic "*a*" is a sub-type of the type "a", any token of the type italic "*a*" is a token of the type "a"[4].

But this is not to say very much. Can we say anything more?

I think we can. I follow Monroe Beardsley, David Carr, and Graham McFee in thinking of dance as human action rather than mere movement[5]. And, of course, dances are typically composed of sequences of actions. Dance works and dance productions are, then, roughly speaking action type sequences (like the British pub crawl), and dance performances are concrete temporally extended sequences of individual actions (like last night's pub crawl). But this is only roughly speaking. First of all, action type sequences are abstract and, hence, might be understood Platonically: that is, as transcendent entities subsisting outside the causal order. This would be a mistake, since dance works and dance productions are made, but Platonic entities are not. Dance works and dance productions are probably better thought of as *indicated action type sequences* (Levinson 1980). But this is still not quite right either, since auditory, costume, lighting, and setting elements may be (although they need not be) elements of a dance work and are almost always elements of a dance production. Dance works and dance productions then are indicated action-sound-lighting-costume-setting type sequences. Let us, for the sake of simplicity, ignore the added elements and just think of indicated action type sequences (e.g., the sequence: *ronde de jambe*, pull left ear, roll both shoulders forward — as indicated by the author). Dance performances are concrete action sequences which are intended to realise a work and a production type and, in virtue of this intention, largely succeed in doing so[6].

This account of dance performances entails some indeterminacy since "largely succeed in doing so" is an indeterminate characterization. McFee claims this is unacceptable:

> Is the ballet I see on Tuesday night the very same type, *Swan Lake*, as the ballet I see on Wednesday night?'.... The answers to such questions must

be determinate, at least in principle. For if it were in principle impossible
to answer these questions, whether or not two performances were of the
same dance would simply be a 'matter of opinion'. And that leads to an
unacceptable subjectivism. (McFee, 1992: p. 92)

But one is not forced to unacceptable subjectivism upon giving up determinacy.
Even if the criteria for being the same dance are vague and, hence, in some
borderline cases, there is no determinate answer to the above question, it does not
follow that there are not determinate answers in other cases. So, for example, the
answer to the question whether or not a particular man is bald may be in principle
impossible to answer, since "baldness" is a vague predicate. However, in many
other cases, for many other men, the answer is determinate. Even if indeterminacy
leads to subjectivism, then, it may not lead to an *unacceptable* subjectivism, since
this subjectivism may only be in the borderline cases.

Yet indeterminacy need not lead to subjectivism. If it is vague whether or not
a man is bald then it may be objectively vague. If the answer to whether two
performances are of the same dance is indeterminate, it may be objectively
indeterminate, not subjective, not a "matter of opinion".

Quite frequently, perhaps typically with modern and contemporary dance, the
choreographer of a dance work also functions as the artistic director of the only
company that ever performs the work. In these cases all actual tokens of the work
are tokens of the same production. But it is still possible and important to
distinguish the work and production in cases such as these. For it is clearly
possible, in these cases, that there could be other productions of the work.

Productions and performances as works of art

Productions and performances count as works of art in their own right. Both
productions of works and performances can possess aesthetic and artistic qualities
and values that works themselves do not. Performances are not simply means of
transparently presenting a pre-existing work (as film screenings are), but are
subject to evaluation of their own — "it was a lousy performance of a mediocre
production of a brilliant work of choreography". Furthermore, performing artists
are called "artists". If this appellation is correct, then it is plausible to think that
they are artists in virtue of making artworks.

A further reason to think productions and performances are works of art is that
performing artists may, in the making and execution of productions, interpretations, and performances, be creative. Productions and performances may be

new, valuable, and possess intentionally-produced valuable aesthetic and artistic features — features which are not determined by any pre-existing rules, plan or recipe. In those cases they count as creations and the performers who make them count as creative. Although creativity is neither necessary nor sufficient for art-making, it is certainly a frequent correlate of it and lends credence to the claim that performances and productions are works of art in their own right[7].

Paul Thom has argued that performances cannot be works of art because works of art are enduring things and performances are events:

> Performances are not works of art ... to perform is to engage in activity, and to that extent a performance is an event or process, whereas a work of art is a thing. (Thom, 1993: p. 3)

The argument seems to be that thinghood is a necessary condition for being an artwork. Performances are events. Events are not things. Hence performances cannot be artworks

But, as Peter Kivy has pointed out in reply to Thom's argument, events are things at least in some sense and, hence, performances cannot be excluded from the category of artworks merely on the basis of being events. (Kivy, 1995)

Thom also claims that artworks are (necessarily?, constituitively?) enduring and fully present at each instant of their existence, whereas performances are events which are not enduring and are not wholly present at any instant. But this bit of conceptual analysis is suspect. As Kivy points out, there is no good reason to think that all artworks are enduring: improvisations and 'happenings' seem obvious examples of non-enduring works of art. It also seems unlikely that the distinction between enduring things and un-enduring events would hold up to a four-dimensionalist conception of objects and events. Finally, Kivy also argues that some performances are enduring: "some of them ... have one characteristic of permanence: they are repeatable; they are types with tokens" (Kivy, 1995: p. 127). Here, however, I think we should be clear that Kivy has shifted from talking about performance tokens to performance types (That is, interpretations and productions) and that Thom was only clearly interested in excluding performance tokens from the category of artworks. After all, performance interpretations are not events, they are event types and, insofar as they are event types, they are abstract objects which do endure (or, perhaps more accurately, subsist).

In any case, Kivy is right: Thom's argument that performance tokens cannot be works of art rests on suspect premises. And he has no argument against considering productions to be works of art[8].

One additional objection to the view that performances and productions count as works of art is that this view seems to imply that when we go to an evening-length dance performance, we typically encounter not one work of art but three (choreographic-work, production-work, and performance-work)[9]. But this seems intuitively odd — attendance at a standard dance performance seems as though it should allow you to experience one work of art, or at most a series of works of art, not three at once.

The choreographic work is the intuitively obvious candidate to be the work of art that you see when you attend a performance. The performance gives you access to that work of art; it allows you to experience the choreographic work. But if this is true, and there is only room for one work of art in our experience, then productions and performances cannot themselves be works of art which are experienced.

One possible response would be to deny that one actually experiences the choreographic work at all — all one actually experiences when one goes to a performance is that performance. On this view, the performance is a work of art, and it is the only work of art experienced. The choreographic work and the production work are, after all, abstract objects, and hence out of the realm of our possible experience. They might be works of art. But they are not experienced in the performance.

I believe both of these views are mistaken. When we attend a dance perform-ance, we do experience three works of art. And this is not, after all, that counter-intuitive. Consider, for example, the fact that we typically experience multiple actions by experiencing a single event (for example, I see the arm movement *and* I see the baseball pitch, both by experiencing the same event). And if I should happen to meet Bill Clinton, I would see both Bill and the current holder of the US presidency (at the time of writing). So I think we should simply accept the fact that attending dance performances gives us experiential access to multiple works of art — the performance, the production, and the choreographic work.

Perspectives on dance performances

I turn now to an argument that Jerrold Levinson has made about the evaluation of musical performances and interpretations. If this argument is correct, then it has important ramifications for dance performance and production evaluation. I will argue that Levinson's argument fails, at least in part, because he does not take productions and performances seriously as works of art in their own right. Levinson argues for a thesis he calls PREP which is as follows:

> performances of music are *legitimately* evaluated from a number of different perspectives, and thus, as a result, there is little use for the notion of a good performance simpliciter of a given piece of music. (Levinson, 1990: p. 376)

Note that Levinson means "performances" to refer to either individual performances, or to performance types (that is, interpretations or productions).

One can construct a similar thesis about dance — call it DPREP: performances and productions of dance are *legitimately* evaluated from a number of different perspectives, and thus, there is little use for notions of a good performance (or production) simpliciter of a given piece of dance.

If DPREP were true, then questions such as "Was Carlos Orta's performance of the Moor's role last night a very good one?" or "Is the Royal Ballet's current production of *Cinderella* an excellent one?" would not, strictly speaking, count as having a single correct answer, but instead a variety of answers relativised to various perspectives. On the perspectival view "The performance is good" is not strictly speaking well-formed, true or false. Instead, if we want to say anything true we would have to say something like: "The performance is good-for-an-audience-A".

Note also that the view has the unfortunate result, typical of relativised views of a domain of discourse, that much apparent disagreement about the value of performances will turn out to be pseudo-disagreement (that is, not really disagreement at all). On Levinson's view, one-time listeners of a performance of John Adams' *American Elegies* who appear at first blush to be disagreeing with experienced listeners about the evaluation of that performance may not, in fact, be disagreeing at all. If DPREP were true, the same would go for apparent disagreements about dance performances.

The perspectives of various roles

I turn first to a consideration of Levinson's claim that the perspective of the audience is not the only legitimate one from which to evaluate performances. Consider, for example, performers. Levinson writes: "Music is not exclusively something affording aesthetic experience through pure audition, but is also a vehicle for aesthetic involvement via the production and shaping of sound events"

(Levinson, 1990: p. 381). Dance, too, affords aesthetic and artistic experiences for dancers.

Certainly what is good for an audience may not be good for performers (and vice versa). A dance performance that is suitable for an audience (because it makes clear the basic structure of the dance being performed) may be an absolute bore for the performers. An interpretation which allows the performers to explore their technical mastery or to lose themselves in the immediacy of the movement may well be valuable for them but not as valuable for an audience. Levinson claims, then, that the perspective of the performers, as performers, is a legitimate one to evaluate performances against. "Music," he says, "is for listeners ... but it is also for performers" (Levinson, 1990: p. 382). Isn't dance for performers as well as viewers?

Dance *is*, at least in part, for performers. Executing steps gracefully and skillfully, or even as clumsily as this author does, can be a quite valuable experience. Improvising can combine the value of dancing with the value of composition.

But the issue at question is the evaluation of performances. Dance and musical performances and productions are largely intentional action sequences which are intended to be perceived by audiences. Part of what makes something a performance is this directedness towards an audience. Performances may be evaluated from a variety of perspectives. Anything can be evaluated from a variety of perspectives. But what we are primarily interested in with respect to performances is evaluating them *as* performances. If we are concerned to evaluate a performance as a performance then we ought to evaluate it from the perspective of the audience.

As an analogy, consider teaching. We can evaluate an example of teaching (for example, a lecture on metaphysics) from a variety of perspectives. A lecture might be of value to a group of students in that it clearly presented some material which they found interesting, or needed to pass an exam. From the student's perspective, it is a good lecture. But it might be dull for the teacher who has given it eighteen times before. On the other hand, a lecture in which the teacher was able to work through a problem that had been puzzling her might be a good one from her perspective but a lousy one from the perspective of her students.

Nevertheless, I think we do not want to rest content with the claim that a class lecture is legitimately evaluated as teaching from a variety of perspectives ("The lecture is bad for the students"; "The lecture is good for the teacher"). Teaching is directed at students. In fact, the function, or *telos*, of teaching is the education of students. The perspective of the students is, therefore, the right one for evaluating class lectures as teaching. If we are to evaluate the lecture as teaching then we ought to evaluate it from the perspective of the students and their education.

Performances are directed at audiences. Their function, or *telos*, is to make dances available to audiences and, in so doing, provide them with valuable experiences of dance. It follows that we should evaluate them with respect to this function (that is, from the perspective of the audience). We can evaluate performances of dances or musical pieces from the perspective of their performers. But if we do so, we are not evaluating them as performances, we are evaluating them as mere dancings or playings of the work in question[10]. The same argument can be made against Levinson's suggestion that performance evaluation can also be legitimately made from the perspectives of the composer (Levinson, 1990: p. 382). And, insofar as one can make sense of evaluating a performance from the perspective of the work, the argument would apply in that case as well.

Of course performers and composers may be audience members. In fact it is not incoherent to think that performances may be self-directed; that is, that one can perform for one's self or one's co-performers. These are not the cases that Levinson is discussing.

The perspectives of various audiences

I have argued that performance evaluation is essentially concerned with evaluation from the point of view of the audience and not the performer. I have not shown that performance evaluation should not be relativised to any points of view, for there is still Levinson's argument that there are a variety of different, yet legitimate, audience points of view from which to evaluate. I do not believe that this is right. And even if it is right for music, I do not think it is right for modern and contemporary dance.

There are a variety of different sorts of listeners for a musical performance: first time listeners, one-time listeners, jaded listeners. Levinson points out that different interpretations of the same musical work may be suitable for these different listener types. An interpretation which makes the basic structure of a piece clear (through choice of tempo perhaps) will be suitable for first-time listeners (that is, it will provide them with valuable experiences), but may not be as suitable for jaded listeners if it does not provide a novel way of hearing the piece. The same seems to be true for dance.

Levinson argues that, although we may evaluate musical performances from the perspective of a one-time listener, it just isn't typically the case that listeners have access to only one performance of a work. Musical listeners are not typically one-time listeners. With respect to music, Levinson points out that "we have available, for numerous works, an amazing multiplicity of live and recorded performances, to which one can return on many occasions" (Levinson, 1990: p. 387).

It is true that musical audiences have access to, and typically take in, multiple performances and productions of the same work and, even, multiple listenings of the same performance. Nevertheless, although ballet audiences often have available multiple performances and productions, this is not nearly as true for modern and contemporary dance audiences. There is *some* modern and contemporary repertory. Fans of Ailey, Graham and Limón certainly have the chance to see multiple performances and productions of the same work. And even post-modern choreography (for instance, Mark Morris, Trisha Brown) can now be seen in repertory. Nevertheless, it is still the case that a huge portion of the dance audience sees the vast majority of contemporary and modern choreography only one time. We do not have an 'amazing multiplicity' of live performances of contemporary dance to which we can return on multiple occasions. This, of course, is a contingent fact about the institutions of modern and contemporary dance. Perhaps in this regard it is not much different from the institution of contemporary classical music.

A deeper difference emerges when we consider recorded performances. We have access to musical performances through recordings in a way that we do not have access to dance performances through video or film recordings. Recordings of musical performances allow us to hear past and distant performance. And they allow us to hear the same performance over and over again. Sound recording is a transparent medium insofar as it allows us to hear what is recorded and not merely hear representations of what is recorded. Of course it is true that there are aspects of musical performances that audiences do not have access to by means of sound recordings. Much rock music performance, for example, is importantly visual. So sound recording does not grant access to all aspects of musical performance. But it does allow audiences to hear the music and, in virtue of this, to have access to the performance.

Video and film recordings of dance performances, however, do not allow us access to those dance performances. We do not see dance performances when we look at video or film; we see representations of them. The video and film media are not transparent since they do not present us with the first-person spatial information that is essential to vision[11]. With dance this means that important spatial information, and spatial experience (for example, the experience of having the dancers move towards you), is unavailable from recordings.

Therefore, even those viewers who do see video or film recordings of dance performances do not see dance performances; they see representations of them. In contrast to the musical case, much of the audience for modern and contemporary dance works does consist of one-time viewers.

Thus, I hold that Levinson is right in claiming that it is artificial and unrealistic to evaluate a musical performance as if they were the sole representative of a work since, in the standard situation, many different performances of the work will be available to a listener. With modern and contemporary dance, this is simply not the case. Only infrequently do we have the opportunity to see multiple productions of a modern or contemporary dance work. Our access to multiple performances of the same production is also rather limited. And we simply cannot have multiple viewings of the same performance.

An alternative to perspectivalism

Let us return to Levinson's claim that the various audience perspectives are all legitimate ones from which to evaluate musical performances and, by extension, dance performances. I think we can accommodate some of Levinson's insights in a theory of performance evaluation by recognizing that the value of performances and productions may stem from a variety of different sources. There may be many reasons why we count a performance or production as valuable. This realization does not force us to a perspectivalist approach to performance evaluation. I suggest we replace Levinson's formulation: "The performance of work W is good-for-audience-A" with the alternative: "X has value as a performance of W because it has the capacity to satisfy audience type A".

If we take performances and productions seriously as works of art in their own right, then it will be odd to give a perspectival account of the evaluation of performances and productions while refraining from that view with respect to the evaluation of musical works, dance works, and other works of art. Works of art are valuable largely, although not solely, in virtue of their capacity to provide valuable types of experiences. Artworks are not valuable simply because they offer a single valuable type of experience. Instead, valuable works of art offer a variety of experience types for a variety of different audiences. This is, in part, the reason why great artworks pass the test of time.

For example, a great painting, such as Vermeer's *Girl with a Pearl Earring*, has the capacity to provide valuable experiences for first-time viewers, one-time viewers, experienced viewers, sophisticated viewers, late capitalist viewers, etc. The painting's capacity to provide valuable experiences for first time viewers is one good-making feature of the work. Its capacity to provide valuable experiences for experienced viewers is another good-making feature. The work is great because it has the capacity to provide many different types of valuable experiences.

Valuable works of dance, because of their capacity to underwrite multiple productions and performances, have the capacity to provide many different sorts of valuable experiences for many audiences. What of productions and performances? Since they are works of art in their own right, their value should also be understood as primarily stemming from their capacity to provide a variety of valuable experience types. Furthermore, understanding the value of all artworks as dependent on a capacity to provide a variety of valuable types of experience helps us to see why works are typically considered more valuable than productions and performances. A dance work may have the capacity, by means of underwriting a variety of productions and performances, to provide many different valuable experiences for many different sorts of audiences. Productions, being more determinate, have a more limited capacity. Individual performances, because of temporal and physical limitations, have an even more diminished capacity to provide a variety of valuable experiences.

Nevertheless, productions and performances can provide different valuable experiences for different types of viewers. A production or a particular performance of a dance might bring out the basic structure of its choreography (and, in this way, satisfy first time, unsophisticated viewers) *and* present a novel way of bringing out the dance-historical features of the work (and, in so doing, manage to satisfy sophisticated viewers). A dance production or performance which fulfills only one or the other of these functions possesses some value, but if it does not have the capacity to provide valuable experiences for different sorts of audiences we will be hesitant to evaluate it highly[12].

I have claimed that dance performances and productions are, like other artworks, valuable *largely* in virtue of their capacity to provide valuable experiences for a variety of types of viewers. This should not lead us to relativizing performance and production evaluation to types of viewers. In the vast majority of cases a valuable production or performance is one that has the capacity to satisfy a wide variety of different sorts of audience types.

Perspectives stemming from various performance objectives

I now turn to Levinson's argument that there is a relativity in performance evaluation that stems from "variation in endorsable performance objectives" (Levinson, 1990: p. 385). For example, Levinson suggests that a performance which would be judged as highly valuable on its own, because of the interesting interpretation of a work that it offers, might be thought of much less highly in a context where it is part of a series of connected works. We must, he argues, relativise the evaluation of performances to performance objectives. The idiosyncratic performance might be good with respect to one objective, bad with respect to another objective.

In the first place, a perspectivalism of this sort exists in the non-performing arts just as much as in the performing arts. Consider, for example, museum curating. Our assessment of the display of a painting will differ depending on the context and objective of the exhibit in which it is in. If a museum has put up a retrospective show of the work of Vermeer, intending to show the course of his artistic development, then we will be tolerant of, perhaps even pleased at, the inclusion of his early works as they may aid in making clear the underlying moral and religious unity of his *oeuvre*. But the inclusion of these not entirely successful early works in an exhibit meant, for example, to highlight the connections between Vermeer's achievements in painting and the technological developments that lead to the invention of the camera, would be inappropriate and worthy of critical disapprobation. Just as performance is a "practical, socially embedded, variably purposed activity" (Levinson, 1990: p. 381), to use Levinson's phrase, so too the displaying of paintings is tailored to situations and tied to concrete uses.

Note, however, that even though a painting may be hung in exhibits with different purposes this fact does not effect the evaluation of those paintings as artworks. Our evaluation of *Christ in the House of Mary and Martha* (an early Vermeer painted in 1655) is not dependent on the exhibit in which it is shown. Instead, what is relativised is our evaluation of the inclusion (hanging, incorporation) of the painting in an exhibit. The *inclusion* of *Christ in the House of Mary and Martha* is valuable in a retrospective show. The *inclusion* of this early painting in a show about Vermeer and optical technology might not be nearly as valuable.

Levinson gives the example of a hypothetical cycle of "[p]erformances of the sixteen Beethoven quartets that were odd and unusual, *each in a different way*" (Levinson, 1990: p. 386). If we negatively evaluate this hypothetical cycle, we are not negatively evaluating the individual performances, we are instead negatively evaluating the choice to include performances of those types (that is, those interpretations) in a complete cycle. If they are good performances we may recognise that fact but still register our negative evaluation of their inclusion in that particular context.

Therefore, it is not performance evaluation which is perspectival, but the evaluation of the use, choice, or inclusion of performances which has a perspectival element. An inept radio programmer may play a wonderful performance of a Mozart piano concerto in an entirely inappropriate context. A dance company may brilliantly dance two works of choreography which have been foolishly and disastrously put together on an evening's program. Our evaluation of the programming is negative. The evaluation of the wonderful performances need not be.

Conclusion

Dance productions are collective interpretations (that is, performance types) of dance works. Performances are concrete sequences of actions which are intended to realise these interpertations. Both productions and performances may count as creations. Furthermore, both productions and performances are works of art in their own right. Since productions and performances are works of art, their evaluation does not involve any special perspectivalism or relativization. Their value stems primarily from their capacity to provide a variety of different valuable experience types for audiences. Although the *inclusion* of a performance in a programme is appropriately evaluated with respect to the purpose of that programme, the performance itself is not[13].

Notes

[1]   See also Chapter Ten of this volume, where McFee offers an fuller account of the type/token relationship. (However, I shall be criticising some of the conclusions for dance that McFee draws from this distinction.)

[2]   I disagree with Sharpe about the status of works. He does not think they are types. On my view both works and interpretations are types.

[3]   It follows from my definition of the sub-type relation that types are not sub-types of themselves.

[4]   Dance performances are tokens of two types—work and production—both of which are distinct artworks.

[5]   There may be some mere movement involved in some dance (for example, in contact improvisation).

[6]   I claim that both dance works and dance productions are, roughly speaking, indicated action sequence types. In what ways then do they differ? A dance works and a production of that work typically, although not always, have different creators. In the paradigmatic case the dance work is created by a choreographer while the creation of a dance production involves an artistic director and company working together. Of course one individual may play multiple roles. Another significant difference between works and productions is that productions are typically more specified than works—that is, productions place stricter conditions on what count as performance of them.

[7]   My account of creation and creativity is indebted to Jack Glickman's essay 'Creativity and the arts' (Glickman, 1976).

[8]   Graham McFee disagrees, he writes "[to say that] the elaborations of performer's interpretations are creative activities in the sense in which choreography ... or composition ... are creative ... is plain crazy" (McFee, 1992: p. 104).

[9]   It is important to note that I am not arguing for an additional category of secondary artworks. Instead, I am arguing that performances and productions should be included in the general category of artworks.

[10] The issue concerns danceworks: of course, this continues to put aside the sense in which one experiences a work of musical art.

[11] Mere dancings and playings are not audience-directed. Note here that I hold that one can dance a dance (and play a piece of music) without performing.

[12] I have been influenced in my views by Gregory Currie and Noël Carroll who have both provided powerful arguments against the transparency of film and video (Currie, 1995; Carroll, 1996) Although I do think their arguments are successful, they do not transfer to the case of sound recording. The core idea is that the difference between sound recordings and visual recordings rests on differences in the primary functions of the two sensory modalities. Spatial localization is a primary function of vision, not of hearing.

[13] Note that this would not preclude a performance from having high artistic value. I did not claim that the artistic value of a work of art is determined *solely* by the value of the experiences that it provides. I claimed only that a work has value *largely* in virtue of the valuable experiences it provides. There are other sources of artistic value.

[14] Previous versions of this paper were presented at the Rutgers University Graduate Philosophy Colloquium; the Dance and Philosophy Symposium at University of Brighton; the University of Maryland College Park Graduate Philosophy Colloquium; and the American Society for Aesthetics Eastern Regional Meeting. My thanks to Tobyn DeMarco, Graham McFee, Catherine McKeen, and Saam Trivedi for helpful comments.

References

Beardsley, M. (1982) 'What is going on in a dance?', *Dance Research Journal* Vol. 15, No.1: pp. 31–36.

Carr, D. (1997) 'Meaning in dance', *British Journal of Aesthetics* Vol. 37, No.4: pp. 349–366.

Carroll, N. (1996) *Theorizing the moving image*. Cambridge: Cambridge University Press.

Currie, G. (1995) *Image and mind: film, philosophy and cognitive science*. Cambridge: Cambridge University Press.

Glickman, J. (1976) 'Creativity in the arts', in Lars Aagaard-Mogensen (ed) *Culture and Art*. Atlantic Highlands, NJ: Humanities Press, pp. 130-146.

Kivy, P. (1995) *Authenticities: philosophical reflections on musical performances*. Ithaca: Cornell University Press.

Levinson, J. (1990) *Music, art, and metaphysics*. Ithaca: Cornell University Press.

———— (1987) 'Evaluating musical performance', *Journal of Aesthetic Education* Vol. 21: pp. 75-88.

———— (1980) 'What a musical work is', *Journal of Philosophy* Vol. 77, No. 1: pp.5-28.

McFee, G. (1992) *Understanding dance*. London: Routledge.

Sharpe, R.A. (1979) 'Type, token, interpretation and performance', *Mind* Vol. 88, No. 351: pp. 437-440.

Thom, P. (1993) *For an audience: a philosophy of the performing arts*. Philadelphia: Temple University Press

Wollheim, R. (1971) *Art and its objects: an introduction to aesthetics*. New York: Harper & Row.

ON KNOWING WHAT DANCING IS

Francis Sparshott

Introduction[1]

The concerns discussed in this chapter were raised sharply by events at a conference on Indian dance held at the University of Toronto in April 1985. Somewhat to the surprise of the organisers, the conference was attended by distinguished scholars from the Indian sub-continent. The conference was conducted throughout in English. But the emphasis of much of the conference was on "classical" Indian dance, the kind of dance discussed in Sanskrit texts, and in those texts it seems that there is no word that corresponds closely to the English word "dance". The key concept is that of a complex form of musical dance-drama; there is a word for what an English-speaking theorist might call the dance component of this form, but that word does not pick out any actual artistic dance practice. This situation, emphasised in every introductory work on Indian dance, would seem to make the very project of a conference on Indian dance culturally problematic; but in fact it caused no difficulty. No participant even referred to it as a possible problem. Much of the conference was indeed devoted to dance outside the classical tradition, or not centrally related to it — to folk dance, or adaptations of Indian forms to Western theatrical contexts, or choreographical syntheses of elements and genres of varying cultural provenance; but no one seemed to consider that this introduced any radical incoherence or heterogeneity into the proceedings, much less that it represented an imperialistic or colonising imposition of European concepts and practices on indigenous materials and conceptualisations. How was it possible that this should not be felt as a problem?[2] But it was so far from being one that, when I raised this concern at a round-table discussion with which the conference ended, I was interpreted

63

as ethnocentrically maintaining that only European concepts were valid. And this, of course, was the opposite of what I intended.

It was clear that the participants in the conference unproblematically shared a flexible conceptualising skill of which they may not even have been aware, a sense of the subject under discussion that seemed conceptually inexplicable. In what may be a similar way, recent years have seen the formation of a "World Dance Alliance", a global union within which regional centres are being formed to facilitate communication and co-operation among practitioners, administrators and scholars of dance world-wide[3] . I have not taken any part in this organisation beyond paying my membership dues and reading brochures I am sent, but the very concept of such an alliance must seem to a philosopher to be fraught with problems. What could it be an alliance of?

Three possibilities suggest themselves *a priori*. First, technologies of communication are world-wide and rapidly assimilated into their own cultural patterns by people of the most diverse cultural formations. Videotapes are made and exchanged world-wide, and dances are cross-culturally notated. A world alliance could be generated simply as the field within such communicational practices arise, and for its purposes "dance" would be identified as that which is felt to be properly subjected to them. This could be an entirely pragmatic matter, engaged in without any self-consciousness or conceptual reflection, and would be compatible with any degree of inner reservation as to the cultural centrality or spiritual significance of what was thus communicated. A second possibility would be generated by the bureaucratic operations of UNESCO or comparable international agencies. In much the same way as a national Arts Council can influence, or even impose, the category of Art on some practices and deny it to others, giving edge to its judgements by its decisions as to what is and what is not eligible for funding, an official international bureaucracy could give a definite content to "world" practice by its recognitions and decisions. And such a bureaucracy would have to use some international *lingua franca* or other (no doubt with provisions for translation and translatability), a language whose conceptualisations would necessarily acquire a *de facto* privilege. A third possibility would be the privileging of certain forms and procedures at inter-national festivals and ceremonies. An example that comes forcibly to the mind at the time of writing, during the Winter Olympic Games at Nagano in Japan, is the spectacular ceremonies and displays with which the Games open. The Games are in a sense fully international, but the events in which the athletes compete fall under a single set of rules and understandings which are defined as international by their acceptance rather than their origin; and something of the same sort applies to the festivities, which include drills, dances, musical performances, firework displays and what not, in which the culture of the host country is cunningly perfused with what is now accepted as "world-wide". The 1998 opening ceremonies began with the lighting of the Olympic flame by the Japanese figure-skater Midori Ito to the accompaniment of an orchestral rendering of *"Un bel dì"* from Verdi's *Madame Butterfly*, and ended with a mass singing (or at least an opening and shutting of mouths) of Schiller's "Ode to Joy" in Beethoven's setting, led by the Japanese conductor Seiji Ozawa (former conductor of the Toronto Symphony Orchestra). What is one to make of a world in which such things can not only be done but accepted as normal and even in some sense exemplary?[4]

In all three kinds of international unification, what makes the goings on organisationally possible is what makes them somehow workable: contemporary methods of transportation and communication which mean that even in the most isolated enclaves there are aspects of immediate or accessible experience that relate one to a multi-cultural world whose dimensions are within one's grasp. From that point of view, the idea of a fully ecumenical World Dance Alliance is viable. But what would it be an alliance of? In what language could it communicate, and whose language would that be? No doubt most peoples have practices that Anglophone anthropologists or tourists of one or another stamp might call "dance", but in the languages of many of those peoples there may be no word that comes even close in coverage and purport to the English word "dance", and one might then be at a loss to see what it could mean for them (or at least, for those of them who had not studied abroad or in educational institutions set up by imperial or cosmopolitan powers) to think of these practices as akin to other practices elsewhere that English-speakers from this or that dominant community might equally call "dance". In fact, English itself embodies traces of a linguistic fission — as so often, French-type and German-type locutions coexist in idiosyncratic ways. "Dance" and "ball" (with "ballet") have different heritages, Germanic *Tanz* and Gallic *bal*; and Germanic "danse" has penetrated French as well. The further we look and the deeper we delve, the more varied and specialised the practices and ceremonies we would call "dance" appear, and the more strikingly and subtly varied the vocabulary applied to them. And yet, the *concept* of a World Dance Alliance has not seemed bizarre or even problematic.

Understanding and the 'danceworld'

How is a World Dance Alliance possible? A clue may be found in the "Institutional Theory of Art"[5] . On this theory, roughly (for the theory took many forms and underwent many developments), the concept of an "artwork" was to be understood through that of the "artworld": the loose, interactive institution within which art was produced, criticised, marketed, displayed, and stored, together with the teaching institutions that reinforced it. Different people would have different access to this institution, different understanding of it, and different operations within it, but everyone concerned had some idea of what it was, what was within its domain and what was not. An "artwork" was what was understood to be operationally within the domain; and whatever status one might assign to artists, critics, museum directors, or others, what defined art was relationship to the institution and hence, ultimately, the functioning existence of the institution itself. Nothing more, and nothing less.

One can adopt a sort of minimalist version of the institutional theory and say that the meanings of terms like "artwork" are indeterminate, but that, in so far as one is talking about "art", what is crucial is always the relation of the phenomenon under discussion to the artworld — a relationship that might not be anything so simple as inclusion or exclusion — and that the "artworld" itself might be broadly or narrowly construed according to the context of discourse; this variability itself being something of which different discussants and participants might from time to time show themselves variously aware and variously tolerant.

One can then envisage a sort of shadow of the institutional theory of art: an institutional theory of dance, invoking the danceworld. In much the same way as such formal organisations as galleries, museums and art schools constitute a visible skeleton for the "artworld," and are actually identified with the "artworld" in many minds, so the sorts of formalised international and cosmopolitan dance organisation I mentioned above form a sort of core for what could be called a "danceworld", to which a World Dance Alliance could relate. Actual procedures, customs, performances, and institutions of any sort whatever could then be conceptualised as "dance" or "dancelike" or "dance-related" according to how they related to this core. There would be no need for any consensus about such relationships, because there is no need for any consensus among any community as to what is and is not "dance" regardless of context. It is enough that, in any conversation or discourse, it would be possible for enough participants to follow enough of each others' arguments and examples.

It has been a common practice among philosophers in the latter half of this century to discuss these phenomena of conceptual adjustment and orientation by invoking Ludwig Wittgenstein's metaphor of "family resemblance": just as members of a family can share a perceptible family resemblance although there is no one specific set of resembling features all of which they all share, so phenomena to which a concept is actually applied need not share any set of necessary and sufficient criteria; it is enough that a phenomenon should be perceived as in some way sufficiently like some phenomena to which the application of the concept is uncontroversially apt. But this "family resemblance" analogy is not what I have in mind. Wittgenstein is talking about the structure of concepts as they enter as terms into logical arguments, which themselves can be thought of as conducted according to variable successions of "language games". What I wish to draw attention to is rather the dynamics of mutual understanding among participants in communication. Wittgenstein, always essentially a logician, is drawing attention to the fine detail of logical structures and their use; what I have in mind is rather the way logical structures are used[6].

The flexibility and mutual adjustment of understanding among participants in international and multi-cultural exchanges surely reflects a corresponding flexibility of understanding that is necessary to any linguistic exchange among individuals. Philosophers, at least since the time of Socrates, have sought to eliminate or mitigate this flexibility, ideally substituting the requirements of logic and formal grammar for the velleities and evasions of conversation and persuasion. Only this substitution would make honesty, criticism and science possible. One way of thinking about the necessary transition from private worlds of thought to the real world of science was to think of the private "conceptions" of a matter that individuals have as united by their relation to the common "concept" of that matter, in terms of which public and constructive thinking was carried on. One sees the point; but this way of thinking suggests that the variability of conceptions can be eliminated, and ignores what must surely prevail, the necessary dynamic of understanding among people with different conceptions using language to communicate with each other. Again, some people draw attention to the way children learn languages, picking up the complex grammar of a language from the fragmentary and debased samples with which they are confronted. Here too the model (a very powerful one, which underlies some of the most influential advances in linguistic theory in our time) suggests an ideal of stable and correct language-use that makes determinate intelligibility possible[7]. The model has a double appeal. It provides an explanation of grammatical order, enabling us to think in a tidy way about a mass of seemingly miscellaneous linguistic data. At the same time, it links language use with the orderly world of modern science, sorting out and promoting the explicable while discounting the aberrant. But it does not correspond in every respect to the ways in which children are exposed to language, acquire it, and use it when acquired. On the contrary, it appears to endorse the older contrast between *langue*, the linguistic system, and *parole*, the context-bound communications in which language-users engage, excluding the latter from systematic consideration. But what are language-learning children exposed to, what do they learn, and how? The topic requires (and has received) empirical investigation, but one can be sure of at least the following. An infant is addressed directly, in modes varying from non-linguistic emotive vocalising, through "baby-talk" merging linguistic aspects in non-linguistic vocalising, through simplified and modified modes of linguistic address, all the way to normal adult language-use, all being embodied in behaviour directed towards the child and embracing it. At the same time, the infant is surrounded by a world of older children and adults engaged in talk among themselves, some of which at any given time will be more intelligible to the infant than others, and some of which will be less recognisable than the rest as linguistic at all, or as belonging to the same linguistic system to which the infant is being introduced; and all of this linguistic environment is continuous with the language and language-like behaviour that involves the child directly. What the infant acquires is obviously not only the ability to recognise and use grammatical speech within the prevailing language system, but the skills to recognise and operate the whole mass of language and language-related behaviour in which it finds itself immersed. The basic skill with which it operates is that of functioning in a world of intergrading and interlocking societies that communicate linguistically. The human brain is an enormous ramshackle mass of neurons flexibly interconnected, and what distinguishes it from the computers we find it easiest to devise is its limitless adjustability to variation and variability. And a large proportion of this mass seems to be devoted to language use. The innate linguistic/grammatical competence identified by Noam Chomsky is an essential and central part of this necessary ability to use language in communication, but cannot be the whole of it, because it would be useless without the ability to deal with other possessors and users of that and other competences. The function of language is to enable people with different experiences and conceptualising methods to communicate and co-operate with each other, not merely to interact with other individuals identically prepared.

'How do you know?'

Now, how can I know what dance is? What is the form, what is the basis, of my understanding of what dancing is? The possibility of a World Dance Alliance must in the last resort depend on the sort of forms this knowledge takes in individual users of language, including words like "dance", and their understanding of the phenomena to which such words relate. What, in general, is there to say about that? Where should one begin? And how should one go on?

Logically, I think, one should start by considering the basis of one's own understanding. This basis must be the ground of one's own underlying ability to use and understand the words we use when talking and thinking about dance (including, of course, the word "dance" itself and its congeners) — and, if one is in any degree a dancer or an observer of dance, to dance intelligently and to appraise dancing. And this ground can only be the experiential basis of one's learning to speak and respond to speech about these matters, and to engage in them. To each of us, the initial question is: how can I have learned what I know?

This last question is one that most people find it very difficult to ask. Perhaps only philosophers, or people who are on the way to becoming philosophers, can ask it. The difficulty is vividly portrayed in Plato's "Socratic" dialogues: it was Socrates's singular talent to get people to question their own self-understanding in this way, by devising ways of getting them to realise that they did not know what they had always thought they knew — by reducing them to *aporia*, to intellectual helplessness. And even Socrates's success may be largely owing to the fact that he was a fictional character in a dialogue.

I am no Socrates, and when I once confronted a class of students of dance theory with the question how they knew what dancing was, I got nowhere. They were baffled. Philosophical reflection was alien to them, and they had no antecedent expectations as to what I as a teacher of philosophy might be getting at. More importantly, they, like most people I have encountered, were utterly incapable in a classroom setting of reflecting on and drawing on their own life-experience, as opposed to what they had read or been taught in school[8] . Almost the least rewarding from my point of view was the most academically competent among them, a doctoral student, who very articulately produced one familiar definition after another. To her, in effect, dance had become transformed from an activity to an intellectual construct, grounded not in her experience as dancer and dance critic but in her experience as seminar-goer and thesis-writer. I was left to surmise that the other students, less articulate, were transforming the task of self-knowledge from that of plumbing the dancing self to that of exploiting the resources of the seminar-attending self. For the question "How do I know what dancing is?" they substituted the question "How would a good student answer the professorial question, 'How do you know what dancing is?'?" — and, of course, since they had no relevant academic experience to draw on, they had no idea what a "good" student would say and were left without resource.

The background to understanding

The fiasco with the dance theory class was entirely my fault, and should have shown me that my proposed question was a spurious one. How do *I* know what dancing is? I actually have no idea. What I really wanted was for the students to make up a story for me, a story like the one I myself would make up. And they had no way of guessing what the story was. What the story would be has been suggested by the earlier part of this paper. Here it is[9] .

For me personally, the question "How can I know what dancing is?" has a special bite. I have written a pair of large books on the philosophy of dance without any special training or professional standing in dance[10] . True, I had read and was reading a great deal of theorising about dance, and had extensive knowledge of the philosophising that had been done about the fine arts generally, but one might still wonder how, without specially deep and wide knowledge of dance itself, I could evaluate the quality and relevance of such material. People who learned I was engaged in this project raised that question in different ways. Some of them thought I must be travelling all over the world to observe all the different sorts of dances there are. Some of them thought I must spend a lot of time going to dance performances, especially in New York. Some of them thought I must have been a dancer, or had dance training. In a way, they were right. If I had never done any dancing at all or had any dance lessons, if I had never seen a dance performance, if I had never witnessed a variety of dance from exotic traditions, I would certainly have felt disqualified. As it is, my total lack of practical experience in choreography and in public dance criticism, and my profound amateurishness and ineptitude as a dancer, make me uneasy. But these sceptics were not entirely right, and this for two reasons.

In the first place, it is not clear what use such experience would have been. If I had been to see exotic dance practices all over the world, how could I have know that what I witnessed was dance, unless I already knew what dance was? Or, if I was assured on the best authority that what I saw was really dance, how could I be sure that they really were the best authorities, and that what they were the best authorities on was really what dancing was? Or, if I did somehow know that, how could I have known just what part or aspect of what I was seeing was dancing, rather than something else that happened to be going on at the same place at the same time? And how could I know any of that, unless I already knew what dancing was? Again, if I had kept making pilgrimages to New York to find out what was new in the dance scene, how could I have known how much in what I saw was showing me what dance was, and how much was some local variant on dance, the singularities in which might distort and corrupt the idea of dance formed in my mind and realised in my experience? And yet again, if I had made myself a trained dancer, how could I know that what I had learned to do was dance, and not the specifics of some dance-practice that differed radically from other dance-practices of equally validity and authority, with the possible result that, the more I knew about how to dance in the way I had learned, the less I knew about dancing in general?

The second thing wrong with what the sceptics were implying is that they seemed not to have asked themselves how much knowledge was *enough*. Enough for what? Well, enough to write the book I was writing. In the event, critics have found lots of mistakes and omissions and misunderstandings in what I wrote, but few have suggested that these lapses and lacunae amounted to a disqualifying ignorance overall. And the truth is that in this world pretty well everyone knows as much as everyone else. We just know different things. Even in the world of books and scholarship, there are only so many hours in a day, and only so much capacity in a brain. The time I had spent learning about the specifics of dance and dances would have been time taken away from learning about something else; the time and energy my critics had spent learning the things I did not know had left them with no time to learn the things that I did know and they did not. As Plato suggests in that very subtle dialogue *Meno*, all knowledge is interconnected, one can get from any place in one's head to any other place, it is just a matter of discovering the right pathways. Everyone, in fact, knows something about dance, starting perhaps from the ways their ignorance and lack of interest in what they take dancing to be fits into the very specific forms of their life-style and self-understanding. Everyone, in fact, can write a book about dance, some book or other — provided, of course, that they can write a book at all. It is simply a matter of working out the strategies. But then, working out such strategies is not at all a simple matter.

Everyone can write a book about what dancing is, conveying true knowledge of how whatever they know and surmise about dance fits into a very real pattern of understanding, the pattern they live by. On any subject, every person has a unique perspective and a unique collection of relevant data, interconnected by a unique set of perceived and conjectured relationships, on the basis of which a distinctive contribution can be made. It is a matter of estimating one's own knowledge and one's own ignorance — no matter that these estimates themselves may not be shared by anyone else.

It thus appears that no specific amount of knowledge is in general "enough" to constitute an understanding of what dancing is. There are innumerable understandings, corresponding (in each case) to how a given direct knowledge of and about dance fits into knowledge and experience of other things. But though, in that sense, anyone *could* write a book about dance, not everyone does, or is going to; and not for everyone would it be a sensible, or even a thinkable, undertaking. There is equally a sense in which not everyone does know "enough"; not everyone has the equipment that makes it a practical proposition. But is there anything that one can say in general terms about what that equipment would be? Perhaps not. One obvious possibility would be the possession of exceptionally abundant or various experience and information about (some sort of) dance itself, together perhaps with an exceptional ability or willingness to reflect on that. Another possibility would be a smaller amount of such experience and information, together with some kind of general hermeneutical skill at divining the meanings of practices, or a comprehension of the scope of arts and practices in general, or a developed ability to empathise imaginatively, or an attentive regard for the active human body as a centre of experience. But it might be merely a talent for devising theses and narratives that will sound plausible and attractive to the devotees of whatever practice one is discussing. In this last case, what passes for a sufficient understanding of what dancing is may be no more than a linguistic facility for the continuation of any discussion in which one may immerse oneself, without any real understanding of what it is that makes people talk and write as they do.

Whether or not there is anything concrete to be said about how much and what sort of knowledge of what dancing is would be "enough," it remains true that, on any subject, every person has a unique body of data and a unique perspective sufficient to make a distinctive contribution to discussion. What is not yet obvious is whether and how such necessarily unique personal contributions can fit together to make some sort of unified discourse.

Thought and talk

That individual perspectives on dancing can be fitted together is shown by the fact that histories and anthropologies of dance can be written and understood. People can write coherent stories and descriptions of how dance has changed through time and how it varies across the globe. No doubt many different stories and descriptions can be written, and no doubt all are challengeable and incomplete; but coherence is possible and can be judged — can be recognised as satisfactorily present or absent. There has to be some way in which dance everywhere forms a single practice: if we say that dance differs widely from place to place and from time to time, what we say is intelligible only if there can be seen to be something that differs. What each of us knows as dance from our individual perspectives will fit in a determinate way into this mass of possible stories and descriptions. What we know is what we have learned, and what we have learned must have been available for us to learn. When each of us learns to dance, or learns about dancing as a practice of our own culture, what we learn can only be what in some way passes current at the place and time at which we are. But the "place" and "time" at which we locate ourselves are indeterminate: through reminiscence, anecdote and expectation, the stretches of space and time we think of as "here and now" will vary according to the context of our talking and thinking. This variability for each of us is a function of our being in a unique social and physical setting *in the world*; that is, our being situated in the one world in which everyone lives, but which is encountered by each of us in a different way. Histories and anthropologies of dance are possible because each of us learns what dancing is, not as a precise mode of behaviour nor as a systematically scannable range of possibilities, but as a body of practice intimately known, but known dynamically in its changes through place and time in our immediate neighbourhood, and hence inevitably as susceptible to more and more change the further we get from where we are. Part of this knowledge is our learning that on every issue the way things seem to us is never quite the way they seem to other people. To learn what dancing is is to learn something of the ways in which dancing as we encounter it modulates into dancing as we have not encountered it. If I am to live in the world, my special understanding of what dancing is, grounded in the unique intimacies of my personal life, has to co-exist in my mind with a general understanding of how the comparably special understandings of others correspond to the unique intimacies of the lives they live in the same world. Some people are sharply aware of this necessary flexibility in their own understandings, some deny it, some are conscious of it only fitfully when some social or intellectual accommodation makes it unavoidable; but necessary it is.

The variabilities in our perspectives on what we recognise as our common practice of "dance," or as versions of that practice, are negotiated by subtleties in our use of language. Words like "dance" and "dancing" can be straightforwardly used to classify things we apply them to, or to characterise them in specific respects. But even in this straightforwardness there is variation. Sometimes a word is the most appropriate name for the thing we are applying it to, sometimes it is only one among many things it might be called, sometimes it is not meant to be literally correct but to be recognisable as a metaphor. Sometimes it is simply the wrong word, a malapropism or a word we would not have used if we had mastered the set of distinctions accepted as appropriate by the people with whom we are trying to communicate. Use of a word may be stigmatised as pedantic, or vague, or philistine, or affected, which are ways of saying that the word is used in a way unsuitable to the context — and one can hardly say such a thing without recognising that on another occasion it might be our own usage that was out of line. In short, our knowledge of what dancing is incorporates an immense amount of understanding of the ways in which people think of dancing and of the mental attitudes they take to aspects of what they and other people think of, on various occasions and for various purposes, as dancing. Besides, more generally, in speaking of dance (as of anything else), we have to be perpetually aware of the fact that no two people use any word in precisely the same way, or have quite the same style of talking. We are all always at least subliminally on guard against misunderstandings. To learn to talk is to learn to cope with this individual variability. It is not a defect in language that such adjustments are necessary and possible; it is the way language works from the beginning, and no doubt the only way it could work.

Learning what dancing is involves learning how to answer such a question as "What is dancing?" whenever it might be asked, and that is part of learning a language, and that in turn is part of learning language, which involves learning how to talk with language-users other than oneself, which is a large part of what it is to take one's own place among other people.

Learning to understand by learning to do

Learning what dancing is is not just learning to talk about it, it is learning to do it. How do people learn to dance, and how does this involve learning what dancing is? Clearly, one might learn all sorts of different things, which would interact in different ways, and the practical sharing of these different learnings and knowings would amount to a mass of knowledge variously distributed within a community. One might, for instance, start as a novice by being given specific instructions: "Stand like this", "Put this foot there", "Do it this way and not that way". But however specific this sounds, the beginner has to gather what "this" refers to, so that the lesson can be applied next time, and must also understand what a "dancing lesson" is so as to know what counts as "next time" for applying the lesson. Since a similar pattern applies to all learning, all humans must possess and develop immense and subtle skills in these sorts of generalisation. As such a learner, I build up a stock of recognisable "thises" and "thuses", in relation to each other, forming an individual repertory of interrelated skills, assimilated into my own more general skills and tendencies of deportment according to my personal pattern of assimilation, in relation to the individual patterns of teaching my instructors are using. Since there will most likely be other learners in my class, and we may have other teachers, and we will sooner or later be dancing together with other people, all these individual patterns of learning and teaching must in the long run be practically reconcilable. All these patterns of reconciliation and variation together constitute what is learned as a single practice of dancing, one domain of potentially co-operative action among indefinitely many others in each of which we learn to engage through a comparable process. And an important part of what we learn is how to allow for the different ways our fellow dancers, with their different backgrounds and behaviour patterns and histories of learning, do and understand the things we share in.

In extensive and complex societies, what we learn and do as dancers is not likely to coincide with what we speak of and hear spoken of as dancing. This involves our understanding of what dancing is in a double complexity. What we do and find others doing as we dance is unlikely to be the same as what we allow dance to be when talking with people who belong to our social circles but are not (or not necessarily) dancers. And the dancing we have learned to do will not coincide with dancing we know of only by hearsay, and potentially recognise as dancing only by a sort of imaginative projection. A working knowledge of this sort of double complexity, whether or not it is explicit or reflective, is an integral part of knowing what dancing is.

In sufficiently large and loose societies, the complexities mentioned in the preceding paragraph are matters of degree. We are likely to learn about and actually encounter people who belong to groups whose interactive ways of dancing and understanding dancing correspond to a web of samenesses and differences different from our own, arising from a different set of accommodations and inclusions. As representatives of our own community, we can accommodate our understandings to theirs in just the same sort of way as we already adjust our individual doings and understandings to those of other individuals in our own group. But, as soon as we say that, we have to recognise that the "groups" in question may overlap, or shade into one another, in all sorts of ways. The identity of a "group" is simply a matter of the amount and manner of interaction among individuals, and of the ways in which and purposes for which people adopt and assign membership in groups.

Within a sufficiently large society, there may well be enclaves in which people work together and talk together almost exclusively, as in a close-knit school or company or any other effectively closed community. But, just because it is in some sense (by stipulation) *within* a society, such a group cannot cut itself off completely. Its members must at least be aware that there are things that others are doing, and that they are not doing themselves. Within such a closed group, some may contrast their own speech and practice with those of other groups, others may just (affect to) ignore them. Among the former, some may regard what "the others" do as simply different, others as inferior or plain wrong. Some may restrict the scope of what they find acceptable to what is current within their own group, or even to the narrowest understanding (compatible with co-operation) of the practice and speech current within the group itself. Such exclusions, however, become self-defeating to the extent that they are emphatic. What one repudiates as *essentially not* dance is ipso facto being rejected as *essentially dance-related*. In short, to have only one way of doing things can itself take place in different ways, and is in any case impossible without some understanding of what the (same) "things" are that are being done differently.

Our understanding of what dancing is, then, has to be a function of the totality of our own systems of speech and practice, of the systems that we recognise as alternatives to our own, of the facilitations and constraints of these recognitions, and, beyond that, of our sense of how all the likenesses and differences that confront us must ramify into likenesses and differences that we have yet to encounter or may never encounter. That is, dancing as we understand it is neither an essence nor a dialectic, but a perpetually re-adjusting set of accommodations, rooted in what is basic in our own speech and practice, but incorporating some degree of recognition that other people with whom we do or may co-operate and converse will root their own accommodations in personal bases different from our own. This being so, we cannot say what anyone knows when they know what dancing is, we can only say how that knowledge is built up. This has to be so because, in the end, the knowledge remains that of an animal whose brain is very unlike a computer, but is designed to cope with a perpetually changing world that is (and is known to be) partly familiar and partly novel.

Theorists of deconstruction have enabled us to see more clearly than before how knowledge dissolves into chains and nets of difference. But they have tempted some of us to forget that organised life must go on with a certain stability. What anyone will call "dance" on any given occasion, and what will be meant by calling it "dance", will depend on the nature and context of the communication, and communications take place within a partly shared sense of the prevailing variability; but, if that were all, nothing would ever get done. What makes practical life possible is that contexts have a certain stability and predictability, often enshrined in formal institutions. To engage in an organised practice is to restrict oneself to a certain range of possibilities, however much we know about other possibilities, and however conscious we remain of the implicit restrictions we are placing on the scope and stringency of this self-restriction.

Complexes and complexities

This paper has hitherto envisaged a linguistic/cultural complex with a single history and an unbroken network of intercommunication, however complex and tenuous these may be, within which "dancing" is practised and located. But it is possible that more than one such complex should develop on the same planet without mutual acquaintance, and then become aware of each other. What then? One possibility is that our original complex should decide that the other is irrelevant, that whatever these people do it is not what we are doing; so that if we are dancing, they are not. (When I say that the complex decides this, I mean that some people decide this and their decisions have authority, however that may happen.) Another possibility is that it should be decided that, although what the alien culture does is not really dance but something different, fruitful interaction is possible: that study of what they do may help us to new ways of dancing, or that some of what they do will actually be dancing once we assimilate it to our own dance traditions. A third possibility is that the conceptualisation of one culture should expand to embrace the practice of the other, deciding that the aliens have "a different way of dancing". And all such decisions may change, for instance if individuals find ways of incorporating alien practices into their own and these discoveries become influential, or if a borrowed practice comes to be rejected when it is felt to be after all incompatible with what dance has always meant and will continue to mean for "us". But what is most likely is that some groups and individuals will reject what others will welcome, that some will steal or adapt what they discover and others will seek to adopt the whole point of view of the alien culture.

The preceding paragraph considered the case of a culture with the concept of "dance" (that is, within which "knowing what dancing is" is a possibility) when it encounters a culture that lacks that concept. But one must not forget that the situation is symmetrical. The culture that lacks the concept of dance will have its own concepts, its own ways of doing things and thinking about them, structured in the sorts of ways I have described, and the question for them will initially be how to deal with the practices that the other culture calls "dance", but which for them are nameless and may well be unidentifiable and incomprehensible.

Our actual situation in the world today is for the most part neither one of unlimited intergrading nor one of unmediated encounter between incomprehensions. Perhaps since the start of the Bronze Age, human communities have largely operated in the domain of what I call "empires". I use this word to mean the sorts of grouping of societies and their cultures in which a common administrative and educational system imposes its own methods of practical and conceptual organisation on a heterogeneous domain. Within an empire, if the official cultural system has at its disposal a concept such as "dance", and recognises and supports a way of dancing and thinking about dance that is enshrined in the official language and practice of the dominant group, whatever is reasonably dancelike in the practices of all the subordinate cultures within the imperial domain will be done *under the concept of* dance, the word "dance" now being abstracted from the sort of dense vernacular I have described into the official jargon of a bureaucracy. Whatever was done and thought before may continue to be done and thought in much the same way but, to the extent that the official leadership looks towards the central authority, everything will be subjected to redefinition in terms of a hierarchy. Dances other than those enshrined in the official educational system will be redefined, for themselves as well as for officialdom, as "folk dance" or "ethnic dance", as provincial or social or in some other downgrading terms masquerading as classifications. Even in the groups furthest from the centre, someone (and someone, necessarily, who is close to the sources of official power) will be aware of the structure of this hierarchy, or of some of its manifestations, if only as a conceptual possibility. The "concept of dance" under which everything dancelike is done is that of the hierarchy as orientated towards the educational system of the central group[11] . The people within the ambit of the imperial system will accordingly tend to think of dance ambiguously, both in terms of what they know from experience that dancing (or whatever they call it) is, and also in terms of what the metropolis or the palace stipulate that it must be aspiring or failing to be.

An empire, by the impetus of its own nature, is ready to digest anything. Its organising concepts, concepts like "education" and "science" and "philosophy" and "religion" and "art", will have been re-tooled to accommodate any remotely comparable phenomenon as variant or as deviation. That means that when two mutually independent cultures encounter each other, as in the case we were puzzling about before, and have to decide whether what the other people are doing is another way of doing the same sort of thing or something entirely different, and if so how, an imperial education comes prepared with a prearranged set of strategies of accommodation — and, presumably, for asserting and justifying its own cultural hegemony.

If an empire spreads wide enough and lasts long enough, like the Chinese and Roman empires, it may seem to itself to be universal in scope, to represent the level of organisation, integration and sophistication that humanity must eventually reach as local practices and perspectives in all their immense variety become mutually illuminating and supportive. In our own day of air travel and electronic communication, in which oblivion and obscurity no longer cushion the shock of alien cultures, the dream of a universal empire and a hierarchy of hierarchies seems to be reborn. UNESCO seems to portend a sort of ghost of empire, a universal clearing house in which all languages are translatable into all other languages[12] . The over-riding concepts of our post-imperial age will eventually be the concepts of whatever UNESCO can most successfully mount an international congress of. People learn surprisingly quickly who should go to such a congress, and what they should do when they get there — perhaps a more powerful solvent than a proselytising religion is a world-wide practice of exchanging videotapes. It is in the world of UNESCO that a World Dance Alliance is not only thinkable but feasible.

The universality of dance

People often say that human beings everywhere dance, that there are few if any societies without some institutionalised practice easily recognisable as dance. What can they mean? In terms of our earlier discussion, they could be referring to a loose web of practices converging under the imperatives of coercion and co-operation, with the possibility of a history and anthropology of dance meaning no more than that one can move outward and backward from wherever one happens to be. On this understanding, the web would be self-sustaining, and the study of its existence a form of epidemiology[13] . But we can hardly rest there. Some constancies in human culture seem explicably ubiquitous, even essential. Every society has a language, a kinship system, a system of deviance control, a system of food practices. All humans have bodies and brains and developmental patterns that impose a common pattern of constraints and facilitations. We never encounter these in an unmediated form — "there is no human nature, there is culture", as anthropologists used to say — but they do mean that humanity does not simply invent itself as it goes along. If there is something in observable reality that makes us want to say that dancing is something people everywhere do, can we say anything about what that something is? If so, that would help to explain how we can "know what dancing is", how there can be something to know over and above what we learn as part of our discovery of social and conceptual actuality. Many attempts have been made to specify what this might be, even though in the end we have to say that they are merely alternative attempts to provide a "best available explanation" of something that may not need explaining. What should such an explanation look like?

Perhaps we should look beyond the constancies of human anatomy and the human condition to the constancy of human culture itself. Human cultures vary, but there are no humans without culture; the fact of culture is centrally the fact of necessary freedom. Humans must be such that they can and do learn the ways of life into which they grow, whatever those ways may be. That calls for a practical freedom of autonomous movement, the possibility of which must be maintained from generation to generation. But cultural forms within a society must at some level be stable — that is what culture is. So some freedom of movement beyond what the cultural forms prescribe must itself be sustained by the culture. In our own society, this corresponds roughly to what we think of as the fine arts; in other societies, it would take other forms, but we would expect to be able to recognise these if we got to know the society well enough. And the constancies of the human anatomy and condition would be expected always to give rise to recognisable sorts of occasion for such freedom: poetry, music, sculpture, dance. If these considerations are in place, and it is hard to see how they could not be, it is not at all a contingent fact that dance seems to be ubiquitous. It is incomprehensible that it should be otherwise. Dance could be excluded only by suppression; and, in order to be suppressed, it would have to be present and recognisable. This does not mean, of course, that one's own practice and reflection thereon afford a basis for any other society's practice; but the strategies of sympathy and integration that people must already have in place if they are to take their part in a world of free individual agents will take them as far as they care to go.

In addition to the forms of necessary freedom, we are tempted to surmise that any society will need to single out some occasions as special. One thinks of weddings, coronations, funerals, harvest festivals, comings-of-age. Surely any society will need to mark *some* such occasions. If so, how are they to be singled out? Presumably as ritual or ceremony; or, to speak more generally, by providing special circumstances or by doing special things. But how many possible ways are there of doing special things? Not all that many, one would think. Special clothing, special food, special words, special music — and special forms of body movement. And what would we call those special forms of body movement, if not dance? If that is right, one would expect something recognisable as dance to become established in many human societies, if not in most.

In conclusion

The sort of reasoning I have been using in the last few paragraphs seems compelling to some minds, attractive to others, tedious or even repugnant to others again. Even without it, the earlier part of the paper was meant to show that every participant in a culture where the word "dance" or a synonym is current, or in which dances are danced, is in a position to know what dancing is, and must indeed have such knowledge at some level of awareness. This knowledge need not be reflective or articulate, but shows itself in the ability to co-operate and communicate within the society. And there is no such thing as a *complete* knowledge of what dancing is, because it rests on the exercise of a generalised skill of integration and differentiation operating on an indeterminate mass of practice to which each of us has a distinctive access and within which each of us has a personal strategy. These accesses and strategies, if pursued with conscious energy, could take us as far as we wished to go. We can all know what dancing is, and we all do know it. We could even write a book about it, if we could write a book about anything. No two of us know quite the same thing, and it is always good to learn what somebody else knows.

Notes

1 All the sub-headings in this chapter are the editor's.

2 One gathers that the officially accepted line about "classical" Indian dance and the status of the Sanskrit documentation is heavily political and politically contested, and the conference was attended by at least one scholar with powerful political connections. It may be that the apparent lack of conceptual uneasiness among the participants arose partly from an unwillingness to talk Indian politics in Canada. Like all such post-colonial controversies, this one is really inaccessible to outsiders

3 According to a recent *International Calendar* (Winter/Spring 1998), there are at present three: centres: Americas, Asia Pacific, and Europe. The secretariat is in Tokyo.

4 A fourth possibility is that what purports to be world-wide is really confined to America and the Americanised, a relic of the centuries when the overweening power of Western civilisation led it to claim universal status (compare Huntington, 1996, especially Part III). If that is the case, all such institutions can be expected to disappear or to undergo radical trans-formation within a few decades. It is, of course possible that the World dance Alliance is an illusion, dreamed up by North Americans and endorsed only by those who have been sucked into the orbit of the American Empire, so that any centres established outside America will in the long run consist only of persons deeply alienated from their native cultures; but it may turn out not to be that way at all.

5 The most striking and influential presentation is that of Dickie, 1974. [Editor's note: The account offered represents a traditional reading of Dickie 1974. Dickie has since modified his theory, however (Dickie, 1984), and argued in various papers (Dickie, 1993a; 1993b; 1998) that his earlier views had been misunderstood.]

6 Followers of Wittgenstein used to exhort each other, "Don't ask for the meaning — ask for the use". But, of course, such a request could have no

finite answer. Wittgenstein knew this, which is one of the reasons he had no patience with Wittgensteinians.

7   Post-structuralist theories of language have developed an alternative view, according to which discourse reduces to an interplay of signifiers in which the signified plays no part. Here, too, one sees the point, but hardly knows what is to be done with it. Critics usually point out that if you invite the proponent of such a theory to give a lecture he or she will expect the fee and airfare to be paid with actual currency, to be met at the physical airport by a solid person, to be lodged in a hotel with palpable bed and bath, and so forth.

8   Karl Jaspers once said, "There is no communication of *Existenz* in the classroom". This is sometimes forgotten by teachers to whom the classroom has become almost a native environment, and one in which they feel safe.

9   The following material is adapted from my article Sparshott, 1993. Differences from what I wrote there are not necessarily to be attributed to changes of opinion, rather than to the decision to say different things on a different occasion.

10 Sparshott, 1988 and Sparshott, 1995. These were planned as a single book, but grew to a length so impractical that it was decided to turn them into two volumes.

11 The "central group" and its educational system are functionally defined. One tends to identify them as the ethnic group that has succeeded in oppressing all others, but this is not necessary, especially in stable and long-established empires. The ruling class tends to become a mandarinate, recruited by co-option, with its own quasi-culture distinct from that of any ethnic group whose conquest or guile may initially have won power. For more remarks on empire, see Sparshott, 1998, chapters 4 and 5.

12 The argument here supposes UNESCO to be the cultural arm of a truly international organisation. Since international organisations are the creatures of nations, and wealthy and powerful nations are likely to support only such international organisations as they can subvert into instruments of their own domination, it has to be admitted that this supposition has a certain absurdity.

13 I owe the concept of philosophical epidemiology to a colloquium present-ation by Professor Lynd Forguson.

References

Dickie, G. (1974) *Art and the aesthetic: An institutional analysis*. Ithaca: Cornell University Press.

——— (1984) *The art circle*. New York: Haven Publications.

——— (1993a) 'An artistic misunderstanding', *Journal of Aesthetics and Art Criticism* Vol. 51 (Winter): pp. 69–78.

——— (1993b) 'A tale of two artworlds' in M. Rollins (ed) *Danto and his critics*. Oxford: Blackwell, pp. 73–78.

——— (1998) 'Wollheim's dilemma', *British Journal of Aesthetics* Vol. 38 (April): pp. 127–135.

Huntington, S. P. (1996) *The clash of civilizations and the remaking of world order*. New York: Simon and Schuster.

Sparshott, F. (1988) *Off the ground: First steps to a philosophical consideration of the dance*. Princeton: Princeton University Press.

——— (1993) 'How can I know what dancing is? in Jolanty Brach-Czainy (ed.) *Primum Philosophari*. Warsaw: Oficyna Naukowa, pp. 148–161.

——— (1995) *A measured pace: Toward a philosophical understanding of the arts of dance*. Toronto: University of Toronto Press.

——— (1998) *The future of aesthetics*. Toronto: Toronto University Press.

DO RABBITS DANCE?
A PROBLEM CONCERNING
THE IDENTIFICATION OF DANCE

Sue Jones

Introduction

The question 'do rabbits dance?', when asked by a three year old, proved very difficult to answer. We sometimes describe the movements of rabbits, flowers and clouds as dance but should we do so? Judith Hanna advocates that:

> ... dance is human thought and behavior (sic) performed by the human body for human purposes. (Hanna, 1979: p. 5)

This view is even more persuasive when we consider an argument, in brief, which suggests that dance, properly understood, is behaviour that is only available to human beings. This argument revolves around the idea that dance is an intentional activity governed by rules. These rules act as guides for any behaviour that can be appropriately termed "dance". Since following a rule must involve intention (we are not forced to follow these kinds of rules and they are not causal), we cannot perform dance without our knowledge nor by mistake. However, in order to prove we know that something is dance (and no mistake has been made), a justification must be available that can make our actions accountable and make possible agreement (as to whether something is a dance). Such a view seems to disallow the use of the term "dance" with reference to the movements of, for example, clouds, plants and animals. The notion of being guided by rules cannot apply to these phenomena because clouds, flowers and animals cannot justify their dance-like behaviour in ways that show they intend to perform actions known as dance. However, we do use the word "dance" in relation to the movements of swans, bees, butterflies and flowers, so something seems to be awry.

Suppose we assume that, as Wittgenstein reminds us,

Philosophy may in no way interfere with the actual use of language; it can in the end only describe it. (Wittgenstein, 1953: 124)[1]

Then Hanna must be mistaken when she claims that dance is exclusively human behaviour; and so will be Graham McFee (1992: pp. 293-294), who also eshews dance as an activity available to plants and animals. Given McFee's explicit allegiance to the philosophy of Wittgenstein, it would appear that he ought to endorse the idea that plants and animals are capable of dance, for he is unlikely to disagree with Wittgenstein's view (quoted above) of the scope of philosophy.

My aim here is to attempt to reconcile 'actual use' of the term "dance" with the objections, concerning rules, which *prima facie* seem to "… interfere with the actual use of language". It may appear, on first sight, I am arguing that some of the movements of animals, plants, etc. *are* dance. However, it is my intention to show that the actions of rabbits, bees and flowers are *not* dance but can be seen (and are seen) as dance; and to explore how this is possible — or what it might show us.

In order to address the issue in hand, it would seem apposite to clarify what would be needed to explore to resolve, or at least shed some light upon, what is happening when we identify something as dance. Firstly, if we are looking at the identification of something we need to know what we are looking for and that would, in this case, initially seem to require an answer to the very slippery question '*what is dance*?' Secondly, as we shall see it is not sufficient, for the task characterised above, just to find (or suggest) the answer to the question 'what is dance?' by, for example, providing a list of essential qualities found within the activity: that is, providing a traditional definition of the word "dance" in terms of conditions (individually) necessary and (jointly) sufficient. Indeed the usefulness of definition like this for *dance* is questionable because the form of such definition cannot allow for degrees of understanding. However, the word "dance" can be used from perspectives that encompass varying degrees of understanding of this concept and this in turn can affect how the word is used. When we explore ways in which we acquire a concept, such as dance, we are able to see how different levels of understanding are possible. Exploration of these issues will also enable us to expose the relationship of things that are unquestionably dance to those that could be *called* dance. It then becomes possible to unravel the difficulties inherent in my claim that something is *not* but can be *seen* to be dance because this sounds very like a mirage!

I make no apologies for drawing very heavily in this chapter upon the work of David Best and Graham Mcfee, since they have trodden many of the paths we shall have to travel in our explorations. Their work has been used here rather like a map because they have indicated the tracks for me to follow — I am stopping on the way to scrutinise a feature of the area that has particularly attracted my attention. For many of the issues about to be addressed, I shall present a précis of aspects of their work, since there is no room here to explore these concerns in more depth. (I am aware of the difficulties of exegesis of these authors, especially when their work focuses mainly on dance as art and I am not concerned with such an exclusive use of the word.) To continue with the map analogy, many of the issues raised here only serve as rough, hand drawn sketches pinpointing the features salient for getting to the place I have identified. The works of McFee and Best, however, are more akin to a series of 'Ordnance Survey' maps that contain much in-depth information about the surrounding area[2].

What kinds of things do we call dance?

When we begin addressing the first part of our quest, which requires us to examine the question 'what is dance?', it might seem appropriate, on first sight, to look for a definition offering necessary and sufficient conditions. But, as above, Best (1974: pp. 22-32) and McFee (1992: pp. 15-21) have both shown that it is a futile occupation pursuing a 'traditional' definition for a word such as "dance". Rather than repeat arguments well rehearsed and eloquently presented elsewhere, I shall take a short cut by quoting Best (1978: p. 35) who says that,

> ...it may not be possible to produce a *definition* of the meaning of the term ... which is of interest to us ... After all, it is impossible to produce a verbal definition of the names of primary colours, yet that does not prevent our knowing what 'red' means, and being able to apply it correctly.

Acknowledging this point removes the problem of having to specify a definition of dance (in the 'traditional' sense) because we can argue that we know something is dance if we are able to apply the term "dance" correctly. An objection emerges here because to say that we apply a term correctly implies that we need a measure against which we can assess the correctness of our application. This leads, on first sight, back to the need to specify what dance is, by identifying essential qualities in actions known as *dance*. These essential qualities seem to be required as a template against which we could measure actions in order to check whether they could be rightly called "dance". Yet it seems impossible to find such qualities; and, more importantly, it is not the way we go about applying terms like "dance" — that is, we do not *wait* for such a list of qualities.

To explain this point further, imagine a group of Martians (who understand English!) asking the question 'what is dance?'. In reply one would probably choose to show them examples of dance rather than try to list essential qualities by, for example, giving them a dictionary-type definition of the term. Indeed, having given them a dictionary-type definition, it would still be doubtful whether they would ever be in a position to recognise dance for themselves! However, by showing them samples of the kinds of actions we call "dance", it would be possible for them to begin to understand what is meant by the term, because this is precisely how we come to learn the meaning of words such as "dance".

This example also shows that a new solution to the 'traditional' definition problem emerges if we change the question from 'what is dance?' to 'what kinds of things do we call dance?' Rephrasing the question in this way puts a different gloss upon the problem. The focus becomes directed towards the things we might call *dance* and, more importantly, can lead to other ways of providing justifications for our use of the term "dance". For, if we identify something as dance in a way that does not refer to essential qualities found in *all* dances, we must still be able to provide an adequate explanation for our use of the term "dance". Otherwise there can be no common understanding of the meaning of that term and as a result it can have no common use in practice:

> Speakers agree in the use of a word, share a common concept, if they accept the same explanations and if they use the word in the same way (in what is called 'a correct use') in accord with those explanations (Baker and Hacker, 1985: p. 51)

It would be nonsense for anyone to claim they had a concept of dance if their explanations (justifications) could not make sense of their use of the word.

How can we justify that an activity is dance?

Something now needs to be said about what counts as a justification or explanation for the use of a term and about how rules feature in those justifications. In examining this issue, we can also begin to articulate how justifications will make direct reference to examples of the 'kinds of things we call dance'.

Justifications only need to be sufficient to show that, when a word like "dance" is used, it is used correctly. These justifications will appear as rational statements that appeal to the rules which guide behaviour and enable the hearer to confirm the appropriateness of that use of the word. Reference to rules in justifications is important because implicit in the concept of a rule is the notion of standards of correctness. However, it must be noted that rules rely on correct *use*, not mere statistical predictability, otherwise they would be based upon what was done by most people in society[3]. This is exemplified when we consider the rules for mathematics because the rules for some calculations, if based upon statistical predictability, would then rely upon the activities of children, who are the ones who most regularly do, for instance, long division; and they, in practice, tend to get their sums wrong (see Baker and Hacker, 1984a: p. 72). The rules for mathematics can only been seen through *correct* use or we could never agree upon what counts as a correct calculation.

So far, we have proposed that the identification of something, such as dance, will rely upon reference to the rules within this activity and this will make it possible (at least in principle) to provide justifications for the correct use of the term. However, a new problem emerges because, before we can claim to be able to recognise dance, it appears that we would need to know *all* the rules. For otherwise a rule we did not know might be what justifies such-and-such as dance. This in turn also seems to imply that, since some rules may only apply to one dance (as in the case of art works which are unique — for further explanation, see McFee, 1992: p. 118: McFee, 1994: p. 22), we would need to see *all* dances before we truly have a concept of dance! Clearly this is nonsense: it would render such learning impossible. And it is not how understanding of concepts, such as dance, is achieved in practice.

This is made perspicuous if we look, by way of comparison, at how colours are learned. When we learn the correct use of the word "red", it is not necessary to have seen all reds in order to recognise that something is that colour. Indeed there are some reds within the spectrum of colours that we may argue could be seen as purple and it is very difficult to say when the colour black becomes dark grey, but generally we can agree upon whether something is red or black. Agreement is possible not because we have acquired a totality of rules but because we commit to a particular use of the word "red" or the word "black". The rules for use are not something separate from the word "red" or the word "black" for they can only be identified through the correct application of these words. We therefore only need to see enough reds to establish an ability to use the term. If we refer back to the example of the Martians we see that this method was suggested as an appropriate way of teaching Martians (or anyone else) to correctly recognise dance. Correct application of words such as "red" or "dance" can be agreed by justifications that convince us of appropriate use of the word. These justifications will make reference to the rules implicit in the use of these terms. However, we do not have to refer to every single rule (even if all the rules were available to us) in order to come to an agreement about whether a word has been used correctly. There comes a point where agreement can be reached and further explanations are not required because we are convinced that the word has been used appropriately.

Are dances rule-formulations?

It should now be clear that the proper use of words such as "dance" relies upon reference to the rules connected to and within the activity. But this could lead to the belief that all such rules can be made explicit in a kind of list or 'rule book' of the sort we would expect to see for a game. However, there are many different kinds of rules: for example, formal rules such as laws; conventions that involve informal, unspoken rules perhaps for a specific social group; recipes that provide guidelines; and instructions issued by an authority for others to follow (see Baker and Hacker, 1984b: p. 250). In the case of dance, the rules we would appeal to, as justification for calling such-and-such *dance*, occur in paradigms or examples of the activity. The rules are evident in samples of this activity because the dances will formulate them. In other words, samples of dance serve as rule-formulations.

Before proceeding further, clarification of some of the issues concerning rule-formulations is required. Firstly, rule-formulations do not always appear in sentence form. They can, for example, occur as blueprints, recipes and charts. To develop this point, let us look at how a chart may be used. All the rules for the safe navigation of a particular area can be found on the appropriate chart (to try to translate these rules into sentence form would not prove very helpful). Secondly, the same rules will not occur in charts for different areas of sea because each chart will necessarily be unique (we are referring to a *type* rather than a *token* here: McFee, 1992: pp. 90-97; McFee, 1994: p. 20). Now if we were to try to apply the rules encompassed in a chart showing a particular section of the sea, near Orkney, to a completely different area, near Portsmouth, we would find problems with navigation because all the rules shown on the chart for Orkney would not apply to the Portsmouth area. The land masses and the depths of the sea, for instance, would not fit with where we were sailing. As we might say, the *content* of each rule shown on each of the charts is different. But, there would still be some rules that would apply to both charts, such as how to use them. One might think of such rules as (roughly) procedural: they form a background to my use of the chart — indeed, to my taking it to be a *chart* at all. Knowing these rules would enable me to navigate any area of sea successfully (if I could apply the rules and was in possession of a chart appropriate for that area). This analogy is useful when applied to dance both because dances (like charts) can serve as rule-formulations and because, when we see a dance, there will be certain rules that may only apply to that dance (as many dances are unique). However, there are also more general rules (akin to the rules we might use when reading charts) which relate to the traditions and the background of other dances; and these will help us successfully to identify and understand something as a dance.

Another consideration is appropriate here. We may appeal to rules but this does not necessarily mean that they have been followed. In the case of dance, many choreographers have broken apparently established rules in order to produce something original and different. However, we must still appeal to those established rules if we are to understand the work, because we need to identify the rules they have broken in order to understand the dance. In the case of some of the experimental work of the Judson Dance Theatre, if we did not appeal to the rules, seen in the traditions of dances that have gone before, the works might not appear to be dance at all. For example, at first the work *Carnation* (1964) by Lucinda Childs — with its use of props purchased in Woolworths and limited pedestrian movements — could appear to bear little resemblance to dance. However, when we examine the aesthetic of the Judson Dance Theatre which opposes some of the more opulent and technical dance forms, it is possible to see how the movements and props can be viewed within a perspective that would include *Carnation* as a dance. Therefore, in order to understand *Carnation* as a dance, we must make reference to these other dance forms. This case confirms that, in order to identify and understand something is dance, we need to appeal to other dances because they embody the rules that we must refer to in our justifications and explanations.

Several issues concerning rules and rule-formulations have been considered, emphasising their similarities; but clarification of the differences between them is also required, because we must not consider them to be equivalent. Rules are not rule-formulations because the rule will always remain the same but rule-formulations can be altered; for example, we may apply colour to the countries on a map or create a globe from a map of the world. A dancer could wear a slightly different costume and the music could be taped or live during different perform-ances but it could still be the same dance[4].

Why can't rabbits dance?

One more point needs to be made about rule-formulations that has particular significance to the problem involving the identification of the activities of plants, animals and natural phenomena as dance. Even though rule-formulations *need* not take sentence form, it is true to say that the rules they formulate are language-dependent. This is made clear when we consider that although an animal can appear to *follow* rules, such as when a sheepdog is working with a shepherd, it is in essence only *acting in accord* with the rules the shepherd has set because:

> ... it cannot *justify* its behaviour by reference to a rule, cannot *consult* a rule in guiding its behaviour in doubtful cases, cannot *correct* its behaviour by *referring* to the rule and cannot *criticise* its own or other's behaviour by alluding to the rule (Baker and Hacker, 1984: p. 255)

These capacities are language-dependent; and lack of access to language means that clouds, plants and animals cannot explain their actions. Therefore, being unable in these ways to account for their behaviour, they cannot follow or be guided by rules. This provides a very convincing case for us to say that it is not possible for animals, plants or natural phenomena to dance: if this is granted, it would be inappropriate to say that rabbits *do* dance. The points raised concerning rules, justifications and the necessity for language mastery (the foundations of the argument) disallow animals (etc.) from rule-following. However, in raising these considerations, we have laid the foundations for showing how rabbits might be *seen* to dance — the task in hand — because those ideas which relate to rules and how we know when something is dance will actually prove to be just what is needed here.

It is helpful at this point to summarise what has been argued so far. We have said that it is possible to agree upon what can count as dance because we are able to show we understand the term "dance" by providing explanations and justifications that appeal to rules seen within dance activity. Justifications that enable agreement are possible because the rules we appeal to serve as standards of correctness. The rules of dance, to which we appeal, are only found by reference to examples of this activity because they formulate the rules. It has also been said that language is necessary to justify/explain the use of a rule. Without language it is not possible to explain why we call certain actions *dance* because public debate enables the possibility of confirmation, evaluation and justification and, inevitably, this will involve language as well as samples of dance[5]. These arguments have helped to show that identifying dance is not a problem if we refer to examples of this activity. The arguments also make clear that, in using justifications that make explicit how we have been guided by the rules seen within dance actions, we show understanding of what dance is.

Can dance be different things to different people?

Now that a way of recognising dance has been established, we can proceed to address the issues surrounding the acquisition of knowledge about the rules that enable us to understand the concept of dance. It has already been stated that we do not need to know *all* the rules in order to apply a concept (Indeed a totality of rules is not possible — a new dance may change or establish new rules). We can also say that some people will inevitably know more rules than others.

To explain this further, consider an example from botany. A young person may be able to identify some tall plants with trunks and branches as trees, another person may have sufficient knowledge to call them oak and ash trees and a serious botanist may name them *quercus robur* and *sorbus aucuparia*. A personal example in dance reiterates this point. At a recent performance, I witnessed a piece by two dancers using very different South East Asian dance styles: one performed in the Bharata Natyam style, whilst the other performed Kathak. Having previously seen other dances in each of these two styles, I was able to see the conflation of these very different dance forms juxtaposed within one dance. On speaking to another spectator after the performance, I found that she was not aware of the presence of two styles within the piece, although she was aware the dance had South East Asian origins. So she had a different perspective; and I am sure that a person with a South East Asian cultural background would have been privy to aspects of the dance that were not available to either of us. (It must be pointed out here that I am not talking about *appreciating* the dance but about what features were *identified* and how this was affected by the rules that were available to each person. Best (1978: p. 115) has succinctly shown the difficulties of claiming to appreciate the_meanings in dances from a different culture).

We can now see that our perceptions of a dance will be affected by what we know. To elaborate upon this issue consider an analogy concerning the development of the concept of *person*. A child just learning language may initially call all people "man". This may just be sufficient to enable him/her to distinguish between persons and tables or lamps, for example, where "table", "lamp" could be other words within his/her vocabulary, concepts within his/her grasp. Only once words like "woman", "boy" and "girl" are used correctly can the child can be seen to have developed a concept of gender, and s/he has acquired a concept of age when words like "child" and "adult" are accurately put into use. But all of these are (arguably) aspects of the concept *man*. So only after the child has mastered at least a good proportion of such distinctions has he/she grasped that concept — despite using the word earlier.

In the case of dance, it would be possible for someone to identify an activity as dance in a way that is merely distinguishing it from other activities such as eating, sleeping or writing. This is not to say that *anything* could count as dance if it was not eating, sleeping or writing! For, as we have already seen, a justification for the use of the word "dance" must be available: and a 'justification' which failed to draw contrasts key for the situation at issue would be disallowed. Any such justification needs to refer to rules but because the number of rules available to an individual varies according to knowledge and experience, different levels of justification will result. However, if the rules applied in the justification are appropriately and correctly applied, then agreement is possible.

In the example cited above, the concept of dance will be applied in a very inchoate form but it can still have the potential to provide an adequate explanation of its application. As more knowledge and understanding are acquired about a concept such as dance, more complex justifications are possible because more rules can be applied. In the analogy relating to persons, it was shown that concepts, such as gender and age, are layered upon the initial concept of *man*. This point is also applicable to dance because as knowledge and understanding are increased more aspects of dance become available, such as the recognition of different genres like ballet, tap and Graham-based work. Therefore, with this additional knowledge/understanding, justifications for the use of the word "dance" can become more elaborate and complicated because reference to more rules is made possible.

Who says it's a dance?

The focus of the discussion above has emphasised the importance of rules in the development of a concept of dance. It has also been suggested that various levels of knowledge and understanding are possible but this has addressed only part of the problem. We also need to look towards the *perspective* of whoever is applying these rules if we are to overcome the difficulties, initially identified, surrounding what can and cannot count as dance.

There are two (main) perspectives from which dance can be identified and these are from the viewpoint of the performer or the spectator. It is usual for the performance of a dance action to be considered as dance by both the performer and the spectator; however, there may be occasions when an action is regarded as dance from one perspective but not from the other. In other words, it is possible for someone to *see* (in the role of spectator) an action as dance that is not intended to be considered as such by the performer and visa versa. Hanna (1979: p. 18) admits that she would include in her definition of dance that which:

> … has the appearance of what is generally considered dance, even though, for the participants concerned, it is not dance, because they have no such concept.

She seems to be talking about a similar situation to the examples cited of rabbits or flowers dancing. The rabbits and flowers have no concept of dance but their actions may, on occasions, have the "… appearance of what is generally considered dance". What is going on here, we might say, is the application of the rules implicit in behaviour known as dance within what Wittgenstein describes as one "form of life" (human) to another "form of life" (rabbits) who do not apply or even recognise these rules. The performer (rabbit) is not guided by the rules of dance; at best, he merely accords with them. However, there is a sense in which the person watching the rabbit is *guided* by the rules.

If we refer back to our previous discussion about rules, in relation to the use of words such as "dance", we see that the correct use of this word relies upon the possibility of a justified, intentional application of it. However, the use of the word "dance" is not necessarily restricted to ways that mean that a performer of dance must acknowledge his/her actions as dance before observers can apply the word to what they see. Rabbits and fireflies do (cannot) not intend to perform a dance, but can still be said to be acting in accord with the rules for dance. But persons, seeing these actions as dance, can be guided by the rules because they apply the word "dance" with intention, and this action can be understood by, and justified to, others. Such a spectator is applying the rules of one normativity to another, in a way that implicitly acknowledges that the movements of the rabbit or firefly can be structurally the same as actions intended to be dance in another normativity. It is possible for activities to be witnessed in nature that conform to rules usually only applied to dance as normative human behaviour. In other words, we know what someone means when he or she says that the fireflies are dancing in the air. There is no linguistic mistake here; the words have been used correctly. A justification for why we perceive the fireflies to be dancing is available and agreement is possible. To refer back to the quote from Wittgenstein in the introduction to this chapter, we are able to describe how language is being used here in a way that does not interfere with its actual use.

Now, using the term "dance" in this context would not have the same implications as when we use it in relation to a dance, such as *Les Sylphides*, performed by the Royal Ballet, because the contrasts drawn would be very different. In reality, it would be inappropriate (as well as very offensive to the dancers) to make a comparison between the dance of the fireflies and the Royal Ballet. What is being argued here only concerns the identification of dance in a very broad sense. In addition, even though we can apply the rules connected to dance to the behaviour of fireflies, we are not using the term "dance" to show that we understand the *meaning* of the fireflies' dance. Indeed, the said 'dance' would *have* no meaning for us as human beings[7]. We are not concerned with the fireflies' dance in the same way as when we are appreciating the meanings in a performance such as *Swan Lake*. The concern in this chapter has been with the identification of activities that may be considered dance and it has not been our remit to consider what it is to appreciate the meanings in a dance. (Although appreciation will inevitably be touched upon because reference to rules will also provide justifications for the appreciation of a dance.)

Conclusion

The argument is now complete: we have shown how a spectator can provide good reasons for believing that actions not occurring within the realm of normative human dance activities can be considered as dance. This is not to say that we can use the term "dance" for anything that approximates the activity but that *appropriate* use of the term is *possible* within contexts other than human behaviour. And what makes it appropriate here concerns the understanding (of dance) of the spectator.

However, there are three other related issues that are also well worth touching upon because they provide insight into how we acquire a concept of dance and will affect what we regard as dance. Firstly, a person with a good understanding of what dance looks like would, quite rightly, consider that cases concerning the dances of rabbits and fireflies are examples of anthropomorphism. Indeed, the kinds of dance actions (of rabbits, fireflies, flowers etc. not the Royal Ballet!) to which I have been making reference are generally anthropomorphic, or make use of analogy or metaphor. However, in order to understand metaphors, analogies and anthropomorphic statements, we need to know how they work; in other words, to understand the rules for metaphor, analogy and anthropomorphism — which means that unless someone understands the way that, for example, anthropomorphism works, then the point being made would be missed (if the intention of the speaker was purely anthropomorphic).

Secondly, it is possible for a speaker to use language in a way that can provide many layers of meaning, as in the case of 'double entendre' in pantomimes. This enables the provision of different levels of entertainment, applicable to both children and adults, within the same audience. In a similar way, it is possible for one person to see a dance as anthropomorphic and another to just recognise it as dance and both can be correct. This will depend upon the level of understanding of the spectator; for example, a child may just see the movement of the rabbits as dance, whilst a critic might also acknowledge that human attributes are being bestowed upon the rabbits; in the same way these attributes are applied in a dance such as *Still Life at the Penguin Cafe* (choreographed by David Bintley in 1988).

Finally, by giving examples of dance from a variety of sources, including samples that involve anthropomorphism, metaphor and analogy (I have used analogy extensively in my argument here!), we can have different ways of accessing the kinds of rules and their application that will enable us to identify dance. They provide us with a variety of ways of explaining what we mean by *dance* and we can choose to use them in explanations to aid and develop understanding of the term "dance".

The language we choose in explanations will always be dependent upon the level of understanding of the person we are addressing. There are times when we have to simplify our explanations sometimes to the point that some details, in the eyes of an expert, are controversial and inaccurate; for instance, when we try to explain complex scientific theories to children. However, deeper understanding becomes possible when we build upon initial explanations and develop more concepts, as shown in the example concerning the acquisition of the concept *man* (5 above), which made clear that as more dimensions within the concept are encountered new levels of understanding are possible. As Stanley Cavell (1969: p. 42) notes, in our explanations:

> … the meaning of words *will*, of course, stretch and shrink, and they will be stretched and be shrunk.

The way we use and explain the word "dance" needs to have some flexibility (to stretch and shrink) depending upon whom we are addressing. We also need to recognise that there are ways in which we learn to identify dance that need not necessarily entail reference to activities that are 'in themselves' performed as dance. They serve as paradigms which show us 'what kinds of things we might call dance'. Perhaps, on occasions they could also serve as paradigms for what we would not want to call dance. (For there will be times when we would want to deny that the actions of rabbits are dance, such as in discussions about dance as art!)

It can be seen that, rather than hindering our understanding of the concept *dance*, anthropomorphism, metaphor and analogy can provide valuable ways of achieving understanding of what might be meant by this term "dance" — into its variety, so to speak. So, when asked the question 'do rabbits dance?', we could answer 'yes' because sometimes rabbits may be *seen* (by spectators knowledgeable about dance) to be performing actions we intentionally *choose* to call dance.

Notes

1   It is important to locate this remark within the key themes of meaning and understanding found in this section of Wittgenstein's *Philosophical Investigations*. The meaning of a word is found in its use and the possibility of understanding a word is rooted in how we *explain* the word and its uses. Wittgenstein stresses that this will not limit concepts to particular or confined meanings and therefore does not restrict the contrasts or comparisons that we may draw

2   I have also referred extensively to the work of Baker and Hacker who have studied, in depth, the writings of Wittgenstein. Reference below to their interpretation of Wittgenstein's notion of rules has alleviated my responsi-

bility for exegesis of the original texts.

3   The notions of rules and rule following are very complex and they are merely being sketched here:

> The concept of following a rule is complex and many-faceted. This is hardly surprising in a concept so central to so many distinctly human activities (Baker and Hacker, 1985: p. 180).

It should also be noted that in the case in hand we are talking about the use of rules in the application of terms, not about the kinds of rules of choreography that we may employ in the construction of dances. However, these rules will be related because the rules for choreography could well be cited as part of a justification for the use of the term "dance". Also, since the rules for choreography are not fixed they will contribute towards the dynamic nature of terms such as dance.

4   There are other difficulties within this issue, which make it more complex in relation to works of art, that will not be addressed here. See McFee, 1994: pp. 19-20; McFee 1992 pp. 88-94 on different versions of *Swan Lake*.

5   Public debate only needs to be possible, its occurrence is not a necessary condition. I can recognise something as dance without having to confirm this with another person although I could if I chose to do so.

6   See Baker and Hacker, 1985: pp. 238-243 for some discussion of *forms of life*.

7   It might, of course, be a symptom of some condition in the fireflies or an indicator of summer, say: so we might understand something from the fact that the fireflies behaved in this way.

References

Baker, G. P. and Hacker, P. M. S. (1980) *Wittgenstein: Understanding and meaning.* Oxford: Basil Blackwell.

────── (1984a) *Scepticism, rules and language.* Oxford: Basil Blackwell.

────── (1984b) *Language, sense and nonsense.* Oxford: Basil Blackwell.

────── (1985) *Wittgenstein: rules, grammar and necessity.* Oxford: Basil Blackwell.

Best, D. (1974) *Expression in movement and the arts.* London: Lepus.

────── (1978) *Philosophy and human movement.* London: Allen and Unwin.

Cavell, S. (1979) *Must we mean what we say?.* Cambridge: Cambridge University Press.

Hanna, J. L. (1979) *To dance is human*. Austin and London: University of Texas.

McFee, G. (1992) *Understanding dance*. London and New York: Routledge

——— (1994) *The concept of dance education*. London and New York: Routledge.

Wittgenstein, L. (1953/1976) *Philosophical investigations* (Translated by G. E. M. Anscombe). Oxford: Basil Blackwell.

DANCE BEFORE YOU THINK

David Best

Prelude

In an early publication (Best, 1978: Chapter 2) I criticised extravagant and fanciful claims made by pioneer devotees for the values, especially the educational values, of Movement and Dance. These claims were made in the heady days when Movement Education had reached the status of unquestionable doctrine — I once referred to its disciples as followers of the Gospel of St. Laban. It is sadly characteristic of educators' tendency to hasten to be seen to be adhering to the latest trend, that any teacher of a relevant activity who did not extol and practise the tenets of the Movement Movement was regarded with pity or disdain as deplorably passé, and even guilty of perpetuating quasi-militaristic drill. Terms such as "vault", "somersault", and "cartwheel" became heretical: student teachers were reprimanded for using them. Times have changed, and with them, inevitably, the trends: the pendulum has swung back from the extreme licence or freedom of, for instance, Modern Educational Dance, and Gymnastics, towards a more discipline-based approach.

Nevertheless the Movement Movement made an important contribution in its reaction against the prescriptive rigidity of what preceded it. The excesses were probably necessary in order to achieve a radical change of attitude and policy: such changes usually have to pass through a period of excess before a more balanced position can be reached. It is worth remembering what is owed by current practitioners to those pioneers: they may have been too fervently starry-eyed and doctrinaire, but their insights still inform good practice.

Thus, before I begin on my main thesis, I wish to record my tribute to the work and vision of such pioneers as Joan Russell, Vi Bruce, Marion North, and others,

101

and especially Laban himself. That I have criticised some of them for lack of philosophical care in their sometimes wild metaphysical flights of fancy does not in the least imply a lack of considerable respect for what they achieved. Moreover often, although exaggerated, their imaginative idealism opened valuable, fresh horizons of understanding and approach.

Thematic dance

In a chapter entitled "The Slipperiness of 'Movement'" (Best, 1978: ch. 2), I pointed out that one of the most obvious fallacies in these arguments for the values of movement was their dependence on an elision of very different senses of the term "movement". Thus, for example, it is obviously invalid to cite the movement of the earth and stars, and of oceans, heartbeats etc. in support of the importance of dance in the curriculum. (For examples, see Best, 1978: Chapter 2.)

However, I want to reconsider one kind of argument or claim which was frequently adduced, and which provided support for dance and movement on the supposition that they are "basic", "fundamental" and "primary". To quote (Best, 1978: p. 34):

> For example, Russell (1969) writes of movement as one of the first and a primary means of expression, and a basis of other forms of expression. From this sort of consideration she and others take it that dance is the basic, fundamental, primary art form.

It is clear from the context that Russell is partly importing into her case the illegitimate senses of "movement" and "dance" to which I have briefly referred, and there are other questionable assumptions implicit in her conclusions. Yet, as the central thesis of this paper, I want tentatively to propose a line of argument which might resurrect in somewhat similar terms support for dance and movement.

Subjectivism: the fundamental fallacy

In order to illuminate the conception of dance and movement for which I shall argue, it is necessary to outline, by contrast, the very common, and deeply ingrained misconception which it replaces. I shall broadly refer to this prevalent misconception as subjectivism: it is the assumption that dance, movement, or action is the external symbol or expression of an internal mental event. Subjectivism, or body/mind dualism, has been extensively discussed in a considerable body of literature, including some of my own work (see Best, 1974; Best, 1978; Best, 1985; Best, 1993) and it would be far too great a diversion to attempt to consider that complex issue in this paper. Hence, what is offered here is a condensed and simplified outline of a complex question: inevitably it omits qualifications which are necessary for an adequate account. Nevertheless, I hope that the incoherence of subjectivism will be made clear if I focus on its main tenets.

Subjectivism, or dualism, is of very wide scope: it is assumed to explain not only the relation of mind to body, but also that of meaning to language. That is, just as, for example, fear-behaviour is supposed to be an external manifestation of the "inner" mental/emotional feeling of fear, so language is supposed to be an external symbol of the "inner" mental thoughts, ideas, conceptions which give linguistic terms their meaning. Gilbert Ryle famously referred to such subjectivism or dualism as "The Ghost in the Machine" (1949) (Figure 1).

Figure 1   "The Ghost in the Machine"

It is crucial to my thesis to notice that the "ghost" is ultimate: it is he/she who sets off the "machine", and we, the external observers, are interested in the "machine" primarily in order to get at the individual meaning being expressed by the "ghost". This notion has been a deeply ingrained, virtually unquestionable assumption, for centuries. It underlies the general disregard, distaste, or rejection of the body, for instance in religious beliefs such as fundamentalist conceptions of Christianity: it explains the difficulty which some of us have experienced in trying to popularise dance in societies which are still influenced by residual fundamentalist religious beliefs. For, in these cases, it is the soul which is the "ghost", and which is of paramount importance: bodily functions are regarded as at best a temporary and unfortunate necessity, to be disregarded as much as possible, and at worst sinful. Dance is evil in that it involves and incites temptations of the flesh. I shall return to this question, but it is worth mentioning it already, since it is an important thread in my thesis.

Despite its widespread, unquestioned acceptance for centuries, the conception of the individual as a ghost in a machine can readily be seen to make no sense, since, according to the thesis itself, one can never get to the ghost: indeed, there is no way of knowing whether, in the case of others, such an entity exists, One can see the "machine" i.e. the bodily movements (although, in this sense, even this notion will subsequently be shown to be invalid) but one can never be entitled to infer to a meaning or mental event in a supposed "inner ghost". It would, of course, be illegitimate to try to generalise from one's own case, i.e. the supposed relation of my bodily behaviour to my mental events, since no valid inference can be drawn from only one case — my own.

In order to bring out the absurdity of the subjectivist doctrine of privacy, Rush Rhees once brought in to a philosophy seminar a picture of a swollen, bandaged face, in obvious agony of toothache, under which was the caption, "You can never really know what anyone else is feeling". The same point is made in the illustration opposite (Figure 2).

In order to bring out as clearly as possible this inherent, fundamental unintelligibility in subjectivism, let me illustrate by reference to meaning in language. I shall give an example from the well-known art-educator Elliott Eisner. (I apologise to those who know my work if this should be familiar: I use it because it is the clearest example I know.) Eisner's fundamental philosophical rationale for art in education is evident throughout his work, but the clearest brief statement of it is as follows. (I offer this example not to be negatively critical, but to bring

Figure 2   You can never know what anyone else is feeling

out my own positive thesis by contrast, and to give an example of an influential figure who is unaware that his commonly accepted theory of mind and art is self-defeatingly confused by subjectivism.) It cannot be over-emphasised that this is still a widely accepted assumption, and, until one thinks about it, it is quite plausible. In the abstract to his paper, Eisner writes:

Humans not only have the capacity to form different kinds of concepts, they also, *because of their social nature*, have the need to externalize and share what has been conceptualized. To achieve such an end, human beings have *invented ... forms of representation* [which] are the means by which privately held conceptions are transferred into *public images* so that the meaning they embody can be shared. (my emphasis)

This is a clear example of subjectivism, in that the "concept" is explicitly said to exist "in the mind" independently of and prior to any medium of possible expression: on this view, meaning is, at base, purely individual. How, then, do we understand and communicate with other people? Eisner illustrates his theory by reference to language, and says that human beings invented language in order to externalise and share private ideas, or thoughts, just as they invented the arts in order to express purely private, subjective feelings and ideas.

Let me explicate this schematically. In the illustration below, **A** represents one human being, and **B** represents another:

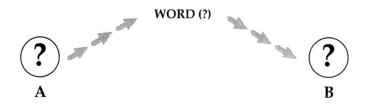

According to the subjectivist account (exemplified by Eisner), the mental experiences of A, her thoughts and feelings, are completely private, inaccessible to anyone else. But she wants to communicate them to B. So, as a start, she is supposed to invent a word to communicate one of her thoughts. B hears the word and is supposed to understand it. But how can he understand it? How can he possibly know what it means, since, in terms of the *subjectivist theory itself*, the thought which A expressed by the word is entirely private and unknowable? Indeed, it makes no sense to attribute to A or to B *any* mental experiences at all — hence my question marks, since we have no idea what, if anything, exists in this purely private world. Perhaps less obviously, it makes no sense to suggest that, in order to communicate her thought, A utters a *word*, for a *word* is already part of a *public, shared language*. Yet, according to the subjectivist account itself there is no such language, but only a group of bizarre creatures each of which is locked inaccessibly in its own private realm. Thus, it makes no sense to call it a *word*: it could only be at most a *meaningless noise*.

Imagine the situation in this supposed subjectivist world, where each person is what Kerr (1986, passim) aptly characterises as a "mentalist-individualist", i.e. a totally isolated thinking self, in a group of similarly isolated selves. Yet, according to the theory, each self wants to communicate with others, so language is invented in order to do so. How could this be achieved? Perhaps these beings set up a committee in order to create a language? It would be a rather odd committee, since no one could communicate with anyone else. For it must be remembered that not only do they have no verbal language, they have no communication with or understanding of the others *at all*. Not even signs, gestures or behaviour could be understood, since one could never know which meaning or mental attribute it expressed or symbolised. The only way to find out would be somehow to gain access to the private individual mental realm of the other to discover what correlation there was, *if any*, between what he did and what he was thinking or feeling. But such access is *impossible*, according to the theory *itself*.

To put the point in a paradoxical way, the only way in which language could be invented is if there should already be a language with which to invent it.

Of course, this is a brief outline of a complex argument, but it offers at least an indication of a conclusive refutation of the subjectivist, or dualist, conception. It should be said that the subjectivist would deny that this is an inevitable consequence of his theory, and he would claim that even on this theory meanings can be shared and communicated. But ultimately, in my view, subjectivism cannot avoid the consequence of unintelligibility which I have outlined.

Eisner, it may be remembered, states that it is because of their social nature that humans wish to share or communicate their "conceptions" with others. This is a highly misleading way of putting the matter; indeed it may be seen as back-to-front. For it is not that humans *began* with a social nature, which caused them to invent forms of communication and sharing, it is rather that their forms of communication and sharing ARE their social nature. It is not a causal but a logical relation: the forms of sharing, understanding, communication are what the character of their social nature consists in.

Even brief reflection reveals as absurd the contention that human beings could have invented language. It may take a little more reflection to recognise that it is questionable whether it makes sense even to suppose that these mentalist-individualist collections of creatures without language or any other form of communication, or sharing of common understandings, *could even count as human beings.*

The conversation which we are

By contrast with the fairly obvious (when one's attention is drawn to it) incoherence of subjectivism, or dualism, or the mentalist-individualist conception of human beings, it has to be recognised that the main root of meaning, understanding, and personal identity consists in the common, primitive reactions, in a social context, of human beings. That is, contrary to what is still widely assumed, it is not the isolated, individual thinking self which is basic, but what Kerr (1986: p. 115) aptly calls "the *conversation* which *we* are". This does not, as is sometimes thought, negate the importance of individual identity, but, on the contrary, it is what makes *sense* of individual identity. No sense can be made of such identity on a subjectivist basis, since, as we have briefly seen, there could be no justification for supposing even the existence of the ghost in the machine, still less its character. D. Z. Phillips (1970: p. 6) puts the point very clearly:

> The problem is not one of how to bridge an unbridgeable gulf between a number of logically private selves, contingently thrown together. On the contrary, unless there were a common life which people share, which they were taught and came to learn, there could be no notion of a person... Our common ways of doing things are not generalisations from individual performances, but the preconditions of individuality. The public is the precondition of the private, not a construct of it. This being so, what it means to be a person cannot be divorced or abstracted from these common features of human life.

It is difficult to grasp the implications of this conception, because we have all been brought up on the mentalist-individualist conception, and it is generally so deeply ingrained that it may be misleading even to call it an assumption, since it is such an unquestionable part of the way we think about ourselves and others. (Although I shall continue to use the term "assumption" and its cognates, this caveat should be remembered.) Yet, as we have seen, there are sound reasons, which are central to my thesis, for the rejection of the fundamental "I", in favour of the fundamental "we".

However, to repeat, this does not in the least belittle the importance of individuality: on the contrary, it gives sense to human individuality.

The two major issues for which I have been arguing can be brought together in the following assertion, which, to many, appears to be startling because of the dominance of entrenched subjectivist attitudes: Normally the use of language is not, as is generally believed, a symbolic expression of a thinking process going on in the hidden recesses of a mind: on the contrary, normally the use of language IS the thinking. Of course, that is not to deny that one can think and feel without *expressing* one's thoughts and feelings. But that ability is a secondary acquisition, as becomes clear when we recognise that in such cases the thoughts and feelings are *formulated in*, and *identified by*, the media of language and the other media of potential expression. For example, the feeling of remorse is possible only for a language-user, since it can be identified only by its formulation in language. It would make no sense to attribute to a dog a feeling of remorse for biting the postman last week. Moreover, think of how children learn to speak: they just react, respond, express themselves *immediately*, verbally.

To put a major point with oversimple brevity: Eisner states that human beings created language and social practices in order to express independently existing feelings and concepts. What I am saying, by contrast, is that *language and social practices create human beings*. That is, the thoughts and feelings characteristic of human beings, and thus the parameters and nature of personal identity, are created, at least to a very large extent, by language and social practices.

The two major issues to which I referred above, outlines of which I hope to have provided, are:

1) It makes no sense to regard language and behaviour as external symbols or expressions of private mental events: the use of language is the thinking.

2) Language is a *social* activity: it makes no sense to regard it as consisting in generalisations from individual "concepts". On the contrary, inextricably interwoven with other shared public practices, it is a *precondition* of individuality.

Roots

I considered the subjectivist theory of Eisner in order to illuminate my main thesis. We saw that it makes no sense to suggest that language could have been invented.

The question then arises: How did humans acquire verbal language? The answer is the central theme of my argument, which is that language evolved from common primitive gestures, responses and ways of life, without which language could not have arisen. As Wittgenstein has put it, at the basic level verbal expressions replace the natural, primitive, non-verbal expressions. For example, instead of simply removing my hand quickly from a hot plate, I might exclaim "Ouch! It's hot." (More likely, I shall do both, of course.) In such cases, what counts ultimately is what is *done*, rather than what is said. To give another example, the man who says he is not afraid, but cowers away and manifests other actions, gestures and facial expressions characteristic of fear in relevant circumstances, reveals unmistakably that he is afraid. Of course, this is a general point: clearly in certain circumstances it is perfectly possible to cower away etc. without being afraid, for instance if one were pretending or acting. In general, the meaning of a verbal expression such as "I am afraid" is inseparable from, underlain by, certain ways of behaving. The point is well made in the saying that the primitive sign of wanting is trying to get.

This aspect of my thesis reveals that it is misleading to suppose a sharp distinction between, on one hand, language and, on the other, natural responses and forms of behaviour. In direct contradiction of the radically confused conception of language as consisting in a mere system of symbols, or a code, or form of representation, it has to be recognised that language is an *activity* among other social activities.

Although it is not directly relevant to my main thesis, I should emphasise that from these primitive beginnings language has evolved in enormously varied ways, often far from its roots in natural reactions. That extensive and varied evolution has given commensurately extensive and varied possibilities of thinking, feeling and being. (I have considered this issue more fully elsewhere [Best, 1993]). Thus the rich use of language of Shakespeare has immeasurably extended our possibilities of experience.

Nevertheless, as I hope my brief examples reveal, primitive actions and responses are the roots without which linguistic and artistic refinements could not have developed. I use the word "roots" because it emphasises that such meanings are still fed, and given their life and possibility of further development, by these basic sources in natural response. The meaning of "wanting" and its cognates is rooted in the primitive action of trying to get.

Movement

I referred earlier to the ghost in the machine, and we have seen that that conception makes no sense. Behaviourists recognised the incoherence of an unattainable ghost, yet retained the machine. That is, having rejected as senseless the notion of a metaphysical ghost, they regarded the human being as a purely physical, mechanical entity. In various places (e.g. Best, 1978: pp. 78-83; Best, 1974: pp. 55-74) I distinguished between (intentional) action, and physical movement partly in order to show that the conception of the human being for which I argue is not that of the behaviourist. It is not possible here to offer an extended discussion of the issue, but let me make it clear that for the purposes of my argument and following the clear conceptions of the Movement and Dance pioneers to whom I referred earlier, I am not equating "movement" and its cognates with the mechanistic meaning of the behaviourist. Of course the movements of a human being can legitimately be considered from a purely physical, mechanistic point of view, for instance by a doctor, or in bio-mechanics. But that is not the normal way in which we see the movements of others.

This is an important question, which I cannot consider here. However, it is worth mentioning it because some approaches to the arts and other aspects of human life reveal deep misconceptions as a consequence of holding too mechanistic a view of human beings. For example, the currently fashionable and influential Howard Gardner contends that cognition and knowledge are based in the human nervous system, and he refers to the normal infant as "a well-programmed organism" (1991: p. 44). He frequently refers to mental processes as "mechanisms". (e.g. 1973: pp. 45 and 133). This is not the place for a considered criticism of Gardner[1], but, because of his prominence, it is worth drawing attention to one of the most fundamental sources of his confusions, which is that of taking too mechanistic a view of human beings. In education we are concerned not with mechanisms, or programmed organisms, but with human beings. That sounds blatantly obvious, but it needs to be emphasised. Purely physical things like nervous systems and mechanisms cannot develop understanding, cannot have emotions, cannot have artistic experience. Of course, Gardner is by no means alone in being immersed in this deep misconception: it is a great temptation for empirical psychologists to see human beings in terms which are conducive to empirical methodology. Gardner, for instance, writes (1973: pp. 37-38) of "electrophysiological measures" of feelings, including emotions, which he does not distinguish from sensations. For Gardner, all feeling is the same: it is neurological.

Yet at times he blatantly resorts to the inner ghost, since a mechanism needs something to operate it. His inherent dualism is also clearly revealed in his frequent assumption that language is a symbolic code, and he even likens language and the arts to the symbolic codes of traffic signals and the signs on supermarket shelves (1991: p. 59). Worse, he asserts that the arts communicate information about feelings (1973: p. 97 and passim). Most blatantly, he writes of "a mind struggling to get out and express itself" (1991: p. 5).

Gardner thinks he can measure feelings, because he regards human beings as machines. Perhaps he subscribes to the currently fashionable "Cognitive Science", with, as Kerr (1986: p. 186) puts it "artificial intelligence", as the model of human thinking. This is the modern version of dualism. Kerr continues (1986: p. 185):

> Roughly the internal states of information-processing machines have become the paradigm for the psychological states of creatures of our kind. If our mental processes once seemed a deficient form of angelic intuition, they have now become an inefficient kind of mechanical calculation. *The ghost in the machine has given way to the clockwork in the animal. ...* the age-old dream is repeating itself: thinking is something better done independently of bodiliness... (my emphasis)

This model of thinking, though now the trend, is radically misconceived. Thinking is done neither by a ghost nor by a clockwork mechanism, but by a human being.

Gardner conceives of thinking and feeling in terms of mechanisms, programmed organisms, electrophysiological tests. If we were concerned with that sort of entity then empirical psychology could, in principle, tell us all that we want to know about human thinking and feeling: but the enterprise is confused from the start, because human beings are not mechanisms. For example, it would make no sense to suppose that the expressiveness of facial gestures could be captured by geometrical measurements. As Wittgenstein trenchantly expresses the point (1953: p. 232):

> In psychology there are experimental methods and conceptual confusion... The existence of the experimental method makes us think we have the means of solving problems which trouble us: though problem and method pass one another by.

Dance in the roots[2]

"... savage religion is not so much thought out as danced out."

This incisive remark by the Oxford anthropologist R. R. Marett (1914: p. xxxi) captures the crux of my thesis. It indicates why I suggest that the claim made by Joan Russell for the "basic" importance of dance may be resurrected if the argument for it be reformulated.

I have tried to show that primitive reactions are the roots of concept-formation. (For a detailed exposition, see D. Z. Phillips, 1983.) For example, the concept of causation, which is of an importance to the empirical sciences which is difficult to over-estimate, is rooted in certain immediate, instinctive responses to situations. Wittgenstein (1976: p. 410) writes:

> *We react to the cause.* Calling something 'the cause' is like pointing and saying: 'He's to blame.' We instinctively get rid of the cause if we don't want the effect. We instinctively look from what has been hit to what has hit it.

One of the greatest difficulties in recognising the strength and validity of the kind of conception for which I am arguing is to grasp that there is a whole repertoire of movements, actions, gestures in which the meaning or significance is intrinsic. We have been for so long and so deeply immersed in the conviction that meaning or significance must somehow be behind the movement or linguistic expression that it is hard to grasp that, on the contrary, the meaning is on the surface. The point was made earlier that normally the use of language is the thinking or meaning: it makes no sense to postulate a ghostly mental process, of which the linguistic expression is a symbol. Similarly, the meaning or significance is the movement, in a particular context. Our actions, and gestures, are not expressions of supposed "inner" mental states: on the contrary, such behaviour is one's meaning or feeling.

This reveals even more clearly the fundamental but common confusion of theorists such as Howard Gardner who, as we have seen, regards language, the arts, and other social practices as symbols of mental or neurological states.

It is so difficult to recognise the obvious. For it is obvious that it makes no sense to try to locate meaning by occult delving into mysterious subjective states, or in mystical metaphysical universals. The solution to the problem of meaning is, in a sense, much simpler than that — so simple that it is difficult to see. For the meaning is right there in front of you; it can be found only in the movement or word itself. To repeat, because of the importance of the point, the meaning is to be found only in the movement or word.

Of course, in another sense this is not in the least to say that such meaning is simple: on the contrary, it may be immensely complex. But in such a case it is *possible*, if necessary, in principle, to work towards an understanding of it by reflection, discussion, or induction into that kind of activity, or that language, in its context of a *way of life* comprising a web of interconnected social practices. This is in complete contrast to the subjectivist, dualist conception which locates meaning in a realm which is inaccessible even in principle.

Wittgenstein (1967: §159) illuminates the point in this way:

> If a theme, or phrase, suddenly means something to you, you don't have to be able to explain it. *Just this* gesture has been made accessible to you.

Often, there is a great deal which can be done to bring someone, or ourselves, to understand meaning. Verbal reasons may illuminate the significance of certain features. Sometimes non-verbal reasons can be given — for instance parts of the music may be played with particular emphases. There is a wide and varied possibility of bringing meaning to light.

But sometimes it may be impossible to say or do anything to explain meaning. There is a great temptation to assume that meaning must always be explicable in terms *other than* the word, movement, gesture, work of art, or ritual. Yet that assumption is not only incoherent, it gravely reduces our possible perception of the indescribably rich panoply of uniquely discriminated meanings available to us, if we are sensitively, openly receptive. Martha Nussbaum (1985: p. 516) writes: "Our highest and hardest task is to make ourselves creatures on whom *nothing is lost*". Fergus Kerr (1986: p. 166):

> We simply give ourselves up to the features before us: people's faces do not normally mask their thoughts and feelings. Our language is not just a tolerable *façon de parler*, as if *faute de mieux*. It is not a failure on our part that we cannot say what the music expresses. We do better to *awaken to the possibility that our way of life is the incomparable thing that it is*, without compulsively contrasting it all the time with alien alternatives. The metaphysical picture of what we are, so far from securing our uniqueness, only obscures it. (My emphasis)

Particularity

Hence my emphasis on the *particularity* of artistic and emotional feeling (Best: 1993, Chapter 11). Often, in effect anyway, one can say no more than that a piece of music expresses itself. Yet this is difficult to grasp, because of the grip of the assumption that meaning is somehow lying behind, symbolised or represented by, the facial expression, the gesture, the movement, the word, the work of art. In many cases, it makes no sense to assume that something else must be the meaning. Wittgenstein: "if only you do not try to utter what is unutterable then nothing gets lost" (quoted in Kerr, 1986: p.166).

Confusion is also compounded by the use of general characterisations. Thus one sometimes encounters difficulty in arguing for the uniqueness of a personal relationship, such as love or friendship. While, of course, the use of such a generalised term may be legitimate, such use may also obscure the *particularity* of a relationship, say the love between John and Rosie, which could not occur except between those two people. This is not to say that John could not love someone else, say Jane. But there is an important sense in which his love for Jane could not be said to be the same feeling. (I discuss this question in Best, 1993, ch. 11.)

Of Orwell's description of the traumatic experience of a Belgian journalist, in the First World War, my late and much lamented friend R. W. Beardsmore (1973: p. 352) writes:

> … there could be no answer to the question: "And what was it like, then?" What death was like, was something which came out in the pathetic scene to which he has been a witness.

Moving to a conclusion

The conclusion to which I have been moving is, perhaps, most clearly revealed with respect to religious meaning. Religious rituals and practices are not expressions of "inner" spiritual states, nor are they normally, at root anyway, thought out in advance. On the contrary, the social activity, the ritual, the dance, is the meaning, and, if anything, it precedes and forms the root of religious thinking. This point is difficult to formulate accurately, because I do not wish to give the impression that these root-actions and rituals are thought*less*. That deep and persistent misconception that action or movement is distinct from or opposed to thinking is the source of considerable confusion, and highly damaging assumptions, reflected, for instance, in much educational theory. One seminal expression of it is the ingrained but disastrously misconceived supposition of the opposition between theory, or philosophy, and practice. It is rather that the thinking and rationality are implicit in, inseparable from, and spring from, the activity. When I said above that such activity precedes and forms the root of religious thinking, I was referring to what might be called "conscious" thinking, for example, that which can occur apart from the activity. Earlier I emphasised the importance of the conversation which we are: now I wish to emphasise that, at root, such a conversation is pre-linguistic; it is the vital root of conceptualisation. At this level it is the *dance* that *we* are.

In the beginning is the *deed*

It is interesting to notice how close we may be to the roots of concepts — roots of which we are often unaware. My colleague H. O. Mounce (1980: p. 192) makes a parallel perceptive point that an unsophisticate who sobs at sentimental Hollywood kitsch is closer to the spirit of art than an intellectual who regards his intellectualism as placing him in a position superior to emotional response:

> The unsophisticate responds to very bad art. But the response is at least genuine. The intellectual is deficient not perhaps in what he *thinks* good but in how he responds to it — he no longer feels its magic.

Similarly, one finds it almost impossible to keep still when listening to some forms of music, such as, in my case, some jazz; much folk music (especially Irish and Hungarian); South American (especially Brasilian) and African rhythms; Indian classical ragas; and much of the music of J. S. Bach. This compulsion to rhythmic movement springs from the roots.

A recent radio programme deplored the almost total destruction of the rich legacy of Scottish hymns and carols because of the dominating influence of strict Presbyterian religious codes, which banished any such supposed licence or frivolity. The condemnation was reinforced by the fact that it had been customary to dance to them. Even in relatively recent times, a visiting Englishman happened to enter a room in a Scottish village where windows and doors were covered in blankets, and there was dancing to quiet music. He asked what was going on, and was told that the dancers were muffling the sound and hiding the dancing for fear that the Pastor would hear of it. Yet, they said, it was so *natural* to express one's religious belief in dance.

In the tiny communities of some remote Scottish islands, until very recently (and the tradition may even persist, perhaps) a long tradition at Christmas was for neighbours to gather in a cottage where a baby would be cradled in the arms of one, and passed round, as they danced slowly in a semi-circle round the fire. If there were no baby in the community, a doll would be provided.

Joan Russell (1969) writes of children "dancing with joy and rage", and refers to pictures of the captain of the England football team, on winning the World Cup, leaping and dancing in an expression of delight. This is a natural, primitive reaction, close to the roots of what it is to be human.

An extraordinary example from my own experience occurred during a visit to Salvador Bahia, in Brasil, where I was privileged to be invited to attend a spiritual gathering of Candomblé. This is a dynamic spiritual ritual which was brought especially to the North East of Brasil, from Africa, with the slave trade. Roman Catholic images were superficially grafted on to the African ritual, originally to comply with the religious practices of the slave owners. Over a period of three or four hours, accompanied by continuous hypnotic drum rhythms, women danced round in a ring in the middle of the assembled gathering, the great majority of whom were black. The dancers worked themselves into a trance, possessed by their goddesses. The ethos permeated the participating congregation. One felt compulsively drawn into the intensely vibrant atmosphere of this powerful ritual. Occasionally a dancer, deep in trance, approached, and exchanged a ritual communication with, a member of the congregation, who touched the ground, then his or her forehead, chest, and then they lightly embraced each other on each cheek. I was included. Sometimes a dancer became so deeply absorbed in her trance that she "fainted" and was carried out.[3]

There was, for me anyway, no question of conscious understanding, yet there was a powerful feeling of connection with shared roots. It was profoundly disturbing, but not in a negative sense. Again, this is difficult to explain in our terms. In the far South of Brasil I had been warned by many people to be careful to avoid the "voodoo" of Salvador-Bahia. To some extent I could understand that now, although I would not have missed it, and I wished I had had time to attend again. I shall certainly never forget that night: the experience periodically haunts me. It was fascinating, in the original sense of irresistible attraction to something deeply frightening, if one were open-minded, sensitively receptive. I am reminded of Kerr's perceptive insight (1986: p. 162):

Religion … has to do with something deep and sinister in us. Its power
is not ended by refutations of arguments for the existence of the deity.
Religions are an expression of human nature long before they give rise
to reflections about the divine. Certain modern reflective procedures tempt
us to forget that. Objective study of primitive religion gets in the way of
our seeing how savage our own religion is. We prefer a certain interpretation of other people's behaviour to understanding what is deep and
sinister in ourselves — and thus we do not have much understanding of
the savages either.

That considering the execution of an innocent man is a more promising starting
point for sustaining Christian theology than proving that God exists might be one
unsurprising conclusion.

Conclusion: roots in action

My previous subheading was "In the beginning is the deed". This is to make the
central point of my thesis, that the natural, instinctive human reactions, gestures,
movements, in a social setting, are the roots of concepts. I use the present tense
to reflect the significance of my use of the term "roots" (rather than, for instance,
"foundations"): for the more sophisticated developments of verbal language, arts,
and other social institutions, have their character only because of the way in which
they are embedded in natural responses.

As we have seen, verbal language could not have been invented: it evolved
from natural reactions. It could not have developed unless there were some basis
of sense on which it depended. To put the point another way, there had, and there
have, to be social practices to which ultimate appeal of meaning could, and can,
be made[4].

Coda: dance qualifications

I have tried to suggest a way in which Joan Russell's claims for the basic
importance of dance might be reformulated in a more sustainable way. We still
need to qualify her conclusion that dance is the most important art form. For the
roots-level to which I have been appealing will include, inextricably interwoven
with it, rhythm, music, mime, and play-acting, through which, even before verbal
language, stories will be told, sharing and passing on the heritage of myths and
legends which so largely contribute to the thinking, feeling, identity of a society
and therefore the individuals within it.

Last waltz

In the beginning is the deed.

Action as part of the common life of human beings is the root, the precondition of the thought given by verbal language. It is what ultimately gives sense to personal identity and individuality.

Suitably reformulated then, I submit that there may be a sound basis for the claims made by Joan Russell and the other pioneers of dance and movement. There is substance in referring to the dance that, at base, we are.

Notes

1 I offered a more careful critique of Howard Gardner's theories, and, more important, by contrast, what I believe to be a more coherent conception, in a keynote address first delivered at a National Conference on the Arts in Stavanger, Norway. I have subsequently been invited to present it elsewhere.

2 I am greatly indebted, in what follows, to Fergus Kerr's profoundly thought-provoking book (1986).

3 My description of Candomblé is undoubtedly deficient, (a) because since my experience occurred years ago, I cannot accurately remember details; and (b) more important, because of the impossibility adequately to describe in the terms of my cultural understanding an event deeply ingrained in such a very different culture. Moreover, this example illustrates my central thesis of a root-understanding which could not be captured in verbal description. It is reported that this religion is now spreading into North America, which seems to be surprising since it appears deeply entrenched within this culture of Salvador Bahia.

4 I was very interested and grateful to learn, from Kuni Jenkins and Hariata Pohatu, of the Departments of Maori Education, and Maori Studies, respectively, of the University of Auckland, that in Maori language, unlike English, the verb comes first. I hesitate to guess what this says about the Maori character, but it certainly reflects my main emphasis on *action* as the root of thinking.

Acknowledgements

My thanks are due to Graham McFee for kindly inviting me to contribute to this book, and for his long-standing interest in my work.

I am indebted to Dr David Cockburn, of University of Wales, Lampeter, for helpful comments and suggestions.

I wish to record my thanks to the many people, in many countries, perhaps especially in Canada, for their enduring interest in, appreciation of, and support for, the work I have done as a contribution to raising the academic status of the study of dance. They have greatly contributed to my understanding of the art form of dance, and its educational potential. In this respect, I am particularly grateful to Hilary Corlett and Sheila Griffiths.

References

Beardsmore, R W. (1973) 'Two trends in contemporary aesthetics', *British Journal of Aesthetics* Vol.12, No. 4: p. 346–366.

Best, D. (1974) *Expression in movement and the arts*. London: Lepus Books, Henry Kimpton Ltd.

—— (1978) *Philosophy and human movement*, London, Boston, Sydney: George Allen & Unwin.

—— (1985) *Feeling and reason in the arts*. London, Boston, Sydney: George Allen & Unwin.

—— (1993) *The rationality of feeling*. London, Washington DC: Falmer Press.

Eisner, E. (1981) 'The role of the arts in cognition and curriculum', *Report of INSEA World Congress, Rotterdam*. Amsterdam: De Trommel, pp. 17–23.

Gardner, H. (1973) *The arts and human development*. New York: John Wiley & Sons.

—— (1991) *The unschooled mind*. USA: Fontana Press.

Kerr, F. (1986) *Theology after Wittgenstein*. Oxford, Blackwell.

Marett, R. R. (1914) *The threshold of religion*. London: Macmillan.

Mounce, H. O. (1980), 'Art and real life', *Philosophy*, Vol. 55, No. 212: pp. 183–192. April.

Nussbaum, M. (1985) 'Finely aware and richly responsible: Moral attention and the moral task of literature', *The Journal of Philosophy*, Vol. 82 (October): pp. 516–529.

Phillips, D. Z. (1970) *Death and immortality*. London: Macmillan.

―――― (1983) *Primitive reactions and the reactions of primitives*. Oxford: Exeter College.

Russell, J. (1969) *Creative dance in the secondary school*. London: Macdonald and Evans.

Ryle, G. (1949) *The concept of mind*. London: Hutchinson & Co Ltd.

Wittgenstein, L. (1967) *Zettel*. Oxford: Blackwell.

―――― (1953) *Philosophical investigations*. Oxford: Blackwell.

―――― (1976) 'Cause and effect: intuitive awareness', *Philosophia*, Vol. 6, Nos. 3-4: pp. 391–445.

FURTHER REFLECTIONS ON PRACTICAL KNOWLEDGE AND DANCE A DECADE ON

David Carr

Introduction

In 1987, my *British Journal of Aesthetics* paper 'Thought and action in the art of dance' (Carr, 1987) brought to culmination a body of philosophical and educational enquiry into the epistemological and educational status of practical knowledge which had already run its course to the tune of more than a dozen papers in a variety of philosophical and educational journals (see, for example, Carr, 1978; Carr, 1979; Carr, 1981a; Carr, 1981b). Most of this work fell — to borrow a turn of phrase from David Hume — 'stillborn from the press', and much of it now seems to its author to have been less than completely philosophically successful. For all that, however, there may be something to be learned from post mortem examination of its failures — and it is my aim in this paper to explore what may well have been one of these.

Dance and the problem of practical knowledge

As an educational philosopher interested in the teaching of arts and other practical school subjects, my interest in the topic of practical knowledge was initially prompted by the short educational shrift which appeared to have been given to these curriculum areas by such post-war British pioneers of analytical philosophy of education as Richard Peters and Paul Hirst (see Peters, 1966; Hirst, 1974). Indeed, it was not just that Peters, Hirst and others ushered in a new orthodoxy of liberal traditionalism in which the theoretical or academic seemed to be accorded educational primacy over the practical — but that they threw the educational value of practical activities into question *tout court*; since Peters generally held the educational significance of a subject to consist in its rational

123

or intellectual character — and skills were for him mere 'knacks' of little or no 'cognitive' content — there was on his view relatively little to be educationally said on behalf of any practical skills-based activity (Peters, 1966: p. 159). On the face of it, however, there seemed to be something counterintuitive about any conception of skilled performance which could find no rational or educational worth in such complex artistic or other forms of expertise as playing the violin or engaging in forms of dance — except insofar as such activities might yield theoretical or academic knowledge or understanding.

All the same, given that there also appeared to be something correct about the liberal educational conception of education as a matter of initiation into rational modes of human enquiry and activity, it even then seemed clear enough that the way to an adequate philosophical defence of the educational value of practical activities would have to lie, in part at least, in showing how reason is implicated no less in skilled conduct than in theoretical or academic enquiry; more particularly, it seemed that specific attention to a usage honoured distinction between *knowing that* and *knowing how* might constitute a useful point of departure for recognising, in addition to theoretical knowledge, an educationally significant notion of *practical knowledge*. Furthermore, when I began to be interested in the problem of practical knowledge all those years ago, educational philosophers — particularly those anxious to oppose the marked intellectual emphasis of contemporary curriculum theory — took their cue from Gilbert Ryle's alleged demonstration of the primacy of knowing how over knowing that in his seminal work *The Concept of Mind* (Ryle, 1949). All the same, as someone with a more particular interest in the nature of practical teaching and learning, I found Ryle's dispositional account of practical knowledge from the outset less than helpful.

The trouble seemed to be that Ryle successfully disposed of the 'intellectualist legend' (that in order for practice to be intelligent it has to be preceded by an episode of 'theorising') only by construing practical knowledge as essentially a concept of *power* or *ability* — more a function of practical or experiential engagement than of any grasp of principle; in short, in the attempt to provide some sense of what it is for practical knowledge to be *practical*, Ryle left somewhat obscure the sense in which it is proper to regard it as *knowledge*. With hindsight, moreover, it is possible to speculate on some of the influences which may have led Ryle in this direction — for, though Ryle undoubtedly stood in an analytical philosophical tradition and was on occasions highly critical of the obscurantism of much continental phenomenology and existentialism, there can also be little doubt of the general impact on his thought, and on his account of knowing how in particular, of the notion that authentic existential engagement with experience must always evade capture in the stale intellectual categories of theoretical reason. But as this notion is not particularly helpful to any account of how practical activities might be learned via explicit teaching, the need for further illumination of the respects in which practical knowledge and skill are rational and principled — without, however, returning Descartes' intellectual ghost to the machine — seemed still pressing.

It was just such an account — at once avoiding the intellectualist legend and restoring the rationality of practice — which seemed to be promised via the modern revival by Elizabeth Anscombe (1957) and others of Aristotle's distinction between *theoretical* and *practical reasoning*. Moreover, the formal work on the logic of practical inference of such philosophers as von Wright (1971), Geach (1972) and Kenny (1975) promised a pedagogically valuable way of identifying the patterns of procedural reasoning inherent in practices, crafts and skills — which did not implausibly need to be taken as psychologically descriptive of the conscious processes of agents on each and every occasion of agency. In the light of such views, therefore, I formerly aspired to construe practical knowledge as the grasp of inferentially valid patterns of practical reasoning for the mastery of practical skills of some level of complexity; indeed, I took it as a key role of prac-tical reasoning to show how the performance of complex skills might be con-structed from an agent's repertoire of *basic actions* (construed precisely as those powers or abilities which a normal agent should not need the assistance of practical reason to exercise) in a rationally coherent way (Carr, 1980; Carr, 1981b).

On this view, the grasp by an agent of a pattern of practical reasoning (in deed if not in word) would constitute a *necessary* condition of being said to *know how* to do something — for, in the event that someone was able to do something without having had to acquire anything much in the way of technique, what was to that extent unlearned could hardly be called practical *knowledge*. However, as the account also left open the possibility of attributing practical knowledge to someone with a mental grasp of procedural knowledge, but no ability to perform a given task, the capacity to reason practically could also be considered a *sufficient* condition of knowing how — though not of the mastery of skill. Furthermore, as already indicated, as well as deploying this understanding of practical knowledge or knowing how for the purpose of constructing a general account of skill acquisition, I sought to apply it in particular to understanding the acquisition of dance technique. All the same, this account now seems to me to be immensely problematic and to fail to do anything like full justice to the range of qualities we should want to associate with intelligent human practice — especially in such a complex realm of human activity as dance.

The perils of practical reason

First, the above account is at best a partial characterization of the nature of practical knowledge which — in focusing exclusively on the normative dimensions of practical engagement — readily accommodates only the more generalizable aspects of skilled practice. In this respect, it is significant that the main focus of my earlier essay on knowledge in dance was purely on the acquisition of fairly rout*ine* or habitual techniques — staying well clear of the less predictable creative and imaginative aspects of dance practice. However, to the extent that my earlier enquiries focused exclusively on the normative they aspired to an account of practical knowledge in terms only of that mode of rationality which Aristotle characterises as *techne*. But whilst, on the face of it, Aristotle himself suggests that *techne* — 'a state of making, involving a true course of reasoning' (Aristotle, 1925: p.142) — is the *characteristic* mode of enquiry of arts and crafts, it should be clear that only the most limited forms of human productivity can be explained exclusively in terms of *techne* and that any reflective, creative or imaginative practical knowledge must be more than technical knowledge. Moreover, Aristotle himself elsewhere suggests that there are important contexts of human deliberation in which technical reasoning — operating in some abstraction from an appropriate value base — can be no more than mere 'cleverness', (Aristotle 1925, p.157) and is clearly inclined to hold that in the absence of other qualities and sensibilities *techne* can fall well short of the wisdom he would more generally regard as presupposed to genuine practical knowledge. But now, the point is not just that an account of practical reflection couched excessively in terms of *techne* is only a *partial* account of practical knowledge — but, more strongly, that any such account could not but offer a somewhat *distorted* view of the place of even technical deliberation in the general economy of practical knowledge.

Clearly we are here confronted with a peculiar and familiar worry about education in the arts — insofar as it is proper to regard education as a matter of *knowledge acquisition*. On the one hand, we are drawn to regard the arts — no less than other areas of human endeavour — as implicated in normative considerations and appraisals; it seems to make sense to characterise artistic works and performances as good or bad, well or poorly performed. But insofar as it may appear proper to make sense of knowledge in terms of an either/or recognition of propositions as true or false, or in terms of the observance of exceptionless theoretical or procedural rules or principles, it also seems inappropriate to regard the creative works or performances of artists or the appreciative capacities of connoisseurs of art in such terms. Thus — though I will acquire a reputation as a creative dancer by virtue of performing *well* what others regard as *good* or even *true*, or come to be heeded as a dance critic on the grounds that I seem able to tell what is good from what is bad — it seems bizarre to suppose that such accomplishments follow from the mastery of true propositions or mechanical rules or principles of artistic or other kinds. In the event, then, my paper on procedural knowledge in dance of ten years ago seemed to be somewhat vulnerable to the kinds of criticisms of skilled-based teaching of dance which I had already aired in an earlier paper on the perils of dance education (Carr 1984). Having accused some teachers of physical education of failing to distinguish clearly enough between the expressive movements of dance and the functional skills of hockey, I now seemed to be laying myself open to some blurring of that distinction of my own.

In my own defence, it had been my purpose in the dance and practical knowledge paper only to examine an aspect of the problem of dance knowledge and I was even then aware that there was much more to such knowledge than technical reasoning. It now seems to me, however, that the decisive (and fatal) move in the conjuring trick (in a colourful image of Wittgenstein [1953]), the one which seemed so innocent, had already been made in supposing practical knowledge in dance to be 'technical' in the commonly understood sense of this term; once, in short, dance knowledge had been analysed as part technical, all the king's horses and all the king's men could not put that part back together with the other parts I supposed to be untechnical. And, in fact, this problem shows up very clearly in another article on dance of that same period in which I was pre-cisely concerned to provide a fuller epistemological picture of dance knowledge. Thus, in 'Reason and inspiration in dance and choreography' (Carr, 1986) — a paper concerned to explore the problematic relationship of the normative to the creative or interpretative in dance creation and appreciation — I appear to have responded to a question about the basis of dance skill or technique with a rather odd taxonomy of different kinds of dance-artistic knowledge. In addition to the procedural knowledge of dance technique, then, I supposed that dancers and other artists would need to be guided in their artistic practice by two other sorts of knowledge: first, a knowledge of the conventions of a particular artistic genre; second, a grasp of more objective naturalistically grounded rules of aesthetic-affective association — a kind of universal grammar of aesthetic assent.

But what, one might well ask, could have suggested the need for any such conceptual apparatus — or, to put it another way, what could have been the question or problem to which I supposed this taxonomy to be a reasonable response? As far as I can now tell, the idea seems to have been that if the creation of dances is (at least in part) a rational enterprise — exhibited at the level of performance in the mastery of a kind of procedural knowledge — dance performance could only be rational in virtue of the prior observance of intellectual or theoretical knowledge of an aesthetic-artistic kind. But this is precisely to place a quite bizarre rationalist or technicist construction on the rationality of dance performance. It is as though in creating a choreography, one begins with an idea (I seem to have left this small role to 'inspiration'), one interprets the idea within the terms of a particular set of conventions (is this to be classical ballet, jazz or contemporary?), one checks the performance against a list of general aesthetic criteria (the music is not too dissonant for pastorale or the costumes too gay for requiem) — finally devising a repertoire of movement appropriately expressive of the theme. In short, having supposed myself to have progressed beyond the Rylean critique of the intellectualist myth (that in order for intelligent practice to be intelligent it needs prior acts of theorising) to a concept of practical reasoning which shows how practice can be rational in and of itself without reference to theoretical reasoning, I seem to have smuggled in artistic-aesthetic knowledge to perform in relation to dance precisely that theoretical role repudiated by Ryle.

I should emphasise here that I do not think that any such role for theory in relation to practice is always to be ruled out; on the contrary, it seems to me that technical enterprises are precisely cases of practice which crucially depend on prior theorising. What I am concerned to question is the idea that artistic creativity could be a case of this kind: that, in short, there might be the relations of dependence suggested in my earlier work between the procedural knowledge of dance performance and knowledge of an aesthetic-artistic kind. We may recall, with regard to this, two further thoughts and a questionable inference in earlier work on the relationship between reason and inspiration in dance: first, the thought that this knowledge must be part conventional — to observe proper rational continuity with a genre or tradition; second, the thought that if the knowledge is to be really objective — more than subjective opinion or relative belief — it must be grounded in something more basic than convention; third, the inference that these two considerations are liable for independent specification. In fact, the third move here has over the years come to me to seem more and more dubious — and it may be illuminating to explore the reasons for this a little further via attention to a different but not unrelated idea in the work of David Best.

The artistic and the aesthetic

David Best's distinction between the artistic and the aesthetic (Best, 1985) should by now be reasonably familiar to all those interested in arts education in general and dance education in particular. In the first place, Best employs the distinction for the extremely useful purpose of distinguishing the arts — in particular performance arts — from what he is inclined to characterise as *aesthetic* activities. Moreover, I have no wish to question Best's use of it for this purpose; on the contrary, insofar as it helps to debunk certain claims confusedly made on behalf of the artistic status of such sports as gymnastics or swimming, I think that it is for the most part pure gain. Indeed, though some might fear that Best's distinction sets up a false dichotomy between kinds of activities which might significantly overlap, I doubt that this devalues the distinction as such — for it is difficult to see how the problem cases might be coherently evaluated without it. What seems rather more problematic is the fault line which the distinction opens up for our understanding of artistic activities in *both* artistic *and* aesthetic terms. Again, this distinction is explored by Best via an example from the world of dance — an example frequently cited by the many modern theorists of aesthetic and artistic education influenced by Best — and briefly it turns on Best's claim that, on an occasion of attending a dance performance by a celebrated Indian dancer, he was able to appreciate the dance *aesthetically*, but not (because he lacked the necessary knowledge of Indian dance conventions) *artistically* (Best, 1985).

On this account, then, aesthetic and artistic understanding seem to have come apart in a manner which may give rise to some worries. In the first place, for example, while the aesthetic-artistic distinction accounts for artistic appreciation essentially in terms of a grasp of received artistic conventions, it appears — by the same token — to leave the nature of aesthetic appreciation quite unexplained. Indeed, secondly, insofar as the distinction appears to depend upon a contrast between artistic understanding as a rational grasp of conventions and an aesthetic appreciation which appears to require no such grasp, it is not *inconsistent* with the idea that aesthetic appreciation is a non-rational process for which there are *no* objective standards of value. To be sure, one cannot regard any such conclusion as logically *entailed* by Best's arguments, and — given his reputation as a writer popularly associated with a defence of aesthetic objectivity — there are substantial grounds for doubting whether he would accept it. Still, despite what he has written about the objectivity of artistic appreciation and judgement, there seems surprisingly little in his work to substantiate an objective conception of *aesthetic* appreciation by *contrast with* artistic appreciation; moreover, Best actually says at one point that it is possible to enjoy music aesthetically — as a pleasing succession of sounds' — without *understanding* it at all (Best, 1985).

However, the trouble is now that a rather cultural *relativist* conception of artistic judgement and appreciation might be held to follow from (i) the separation of aesthetic appreciation from more local understanding of artistic conventions, and (ii) the absence of any substantial account of objective aesthetic appreciation (not to mention the suggestion that artistic appreciation need not require understanding); since artistic understanding depends only on acquaintance with local cultural conventions, and conventions differ from one location to another, there would be some reason to deny that artistic judgements are expressive of universal truth or bearers of objective value. Again, I have no wish to associate Best with any of these agnostic or sceptical positions — and some cause to doubt whether he would subscribe to *any* of them; I am concerned only to indicate that an otherwise useful distinction between the artistic and the aesthetic is not unproblematic — and I was no doubt persuaded all those years ago by some such consideration to postulate a universal grammar of aesthetic judgement above or behind any local artistic appraisal. At all events, to whatever extent Best's distinction amply demonstrates that aesthetic appreciation is not *sufficient* for artistic appreciation (since the former can occur in non-artistic contexts), and also implies that artistic appreciation can occur in contexts of experience we should not readily regard as having an aesthetic dimension, it does not readily explain how what can *sometimes* come apart — aesthetic experience and artistic judgement — appear often enough to be related.

Indeed, although it is clear enough from recent discussions with Best that he is committed to a fairly strong version of such dissociation of the artistic from the aesthetic, I think that this view is nevertheless both counterintuitive and problematic. Aside from the already mentioned problematic implications for the subjectivity of aesthetic appraisals and the relativism of artistic judgements of Best's own version of this thesis, I think that there is a large and important kernel of truth in a common understanding of art (shared by many of the distinguished philosophers Best charges with gross confusion) as fundamentally concerned with aesthetic appreciation. To be sure, as Best argues, since artistic and aesthetic appreciation and evaluation *are* distinguishable, aesthetic appreciation is therefore not in any sense *sufficient* for artistic appreciation. Again, since there can be artistic appreciation which is not in the least implicated in aesthetic experience or enjoyment (as, for example, in the case of conceptual art), such experience is not even *necessary* for artistic appreciation; hence, it would be greatly overstating the case to characterise art as primarily concerned with the creation of aesthetic objects. But the fact that relations between art and the aesthetic resist any formal characterization in terms of necessary and sufficient conditionship should not be allowed to obscure the still important if somewhat looser conceptual relations suggested by our pre-theoretical assumptions concerning the sensual and affective bases and associations of art. From this point of view, although we may certainly acknowledge with Best the validity of artistic judgements which are not in the least addressed to the aesthetic features of an artwork, it is less easy to envisage some possible world in which there was not and had never been any artistic judgement which was so implicated.

What is clearly needed, it seems to me, is a concept of practical artistic reason and understanding other than the rational-technical one to which I was at one time drawn in the interests of explicating the notion of skill — into which a rather different concept of aesthetic judgement and sensibility from those of enlighten-ment inheritance might be comfortably fitted. For, by and large, the rationalism of modernity has inclined to deal with artistic and aesthetic judgements in one or the other of two unsatisfactory ways. On the one hand, emotivist and projectivist advocates of the fact-value distinction have assigned judgements to the effect that this object or work of art is good, pleasing or beautiful to the realm of 'non-cognitive' response; as mere expressions of subjective taste or liking, such judgements do not in any way refer to the world as it is in itself and they cannot therefore be true or false. However, the problem about such a view is that it renders the idea of aesthetic (or artistic) *education* well nigh unintelligible. On the other hand, aesthetic realists or objectivists *are* inclined to regard judgements about what is tasteful, beautiful or whatever as descriptive of external rather than merely subjective correlates of our experience — and as therefore capable of truth value — but the trouble with this view is that it does not seem to do justice to the sense in which our aesthetic and artistic judgements can be personal and individual to the point of flat disagreement.

Indeed, on perhaps the most plausible 'linguistic' version of aesthetic objectivism, the acquisition of artistic or aesthetic knowledge and understanding would appear to be a matter of more or less exclusive *rational* initiation into a form of discourse with its own particular logical grammar and vocabulary — the mastery of, as it were, some language game of aesthetic description and appraisal. But this 'externalization' of aesthetic experience and understanding renders the personal or 'agent-relative' element of true aesthetic engagement all but incomprehensible. It is surely clear that someone might have mastered a given language game of aesthetic description and appraisal to a fine degree — whilst at the same time remaining incapable of any 'authentic' aesthetic response or artistic appreciation; thus, it is not inconceivable (however unlikely) that a dance critic could be highly skilled at offering sane and sensible judgements of dance performances without ever having been affected or 'moved' by one. Hence, in the next section, I want to sketch the outlines of a more promising account of the relationship of practical artistic reason to aesthetic sensibility — and then, in the concluding section, to explore briefly some of the implications of this account for dance.

Art and the practical wisdom of 'phronesis'

Earlier I acknowledged Aristotle's notion of *techne* as the source of my erstwhile account of practical reason. However, in Aristotle's *Nicomachean Ethics*, *techne* is contrasted not only — as one sort of *practical* capacity — with theoretical knowledge, but with another form of practical understanding — to which Aristotle gives the name *phronesis* or practical wisdom (Aristotle, 1925: section 6). What distinguishes *phronesis* as a form of rationality from *episteme*, and at least some construals of *techne*, is its essential inextricability from the *particularities* of practical experience; whereas theoretical and technical knowledge are above all concerned with the framing of general laws or principles which are applicable to any conceivable empirical experience irrespective of time or place, the knowledge entrained by *phronesis* is unsusceptible of such generalization and existentially tied to specific circumstances. It is essentially

Aristotle's complaint against Plato's form of the good that formal concepts of justice and welfare, for example, are too vague and open-ended to be of much practical use in sub-lunar human affairs and only make real sense as applied to particular circumstances.

Phronesis is thus more a matter of experiential cultivation of a repertoire of situation-specific sensibilities, than of skill acquisition; such sensibilities, the values they entrain and any understanding to which they give rise are not just resistant to codification in the manner of *episteme* and *techne* but also crucially constitutive of personal identity via the cultivation of moral virtues. But, to that extent, the moral deliverences of *phronesis* are highly *agent-relative* — and, the more finely a given virtue or moral sensibility is tuned to the particularities of a specific moral occasion, the more morally *accurate* it is likely to be. Moral *objectivity* is therefore, however odd it may seem, a function of *particularity* more than generality: the more I know about someone and their difficulties, the more appropriately I can respond to them; the more I generalize about them the less morally appropriate my responses are likely to be. But it also follows that I cannot acquire someone else's moral knowledge — at second hand, as it were — as I can acquire their mathematical or scientific knowledge; there is something quite ineradicably personal about the moral knowledge which *phronesis* entrains.

However, it would appear that Aristotle's distinction of *phronesis* from other modes of knowledge in the *Nicomachean Ethics* is more or less tantamount to a distinction between *forms* of knowledge, activity or endeavour; on the face of it, *phronesis* stands to moral understanding as *episteme* stands to scientific enquiry and *techne* stands to artistic creation or production. But if we take the basic logic of human action to be exhibited in the idea of taking means to ends, it is clear that *any* exercise of practical knowledge is liable for appraisal in two ways — either in terms of the *effectiveness* of the means or the *value* of the ends — and this is suggestive of a more general account of *practical knowledge* as a matter of some interplay between *phronesis* and *techne*. That said, there would be no more reason why *phronesis*, construed as a mode of knowledge, should be tied to moral experience as such, than there is for supposing that *episteme* ought to be tied exclusively to one science — say physics — or that *techne* should be linked only to car-maintenance. Moreover, the implications for professional educational and other practice of the more complex relations between evaluative and technical deliberation actually suggested by Aristotle's account have been recently explored by such philosophers as Joseph Dunne (1993).

Indeed, I have elsewhere tried to show — via critical attention to Joseph Dunne's magisterial *Back to the Rough Ground* — that Aristotle's Eudemian analysis of *phronesis* as a mode of knowledge seems to apply just as well to artistic appreciation and creation as it does to the cultivation of moral virtue (Carr 1999). Thus, although we must here be brief with what is explored more fully elsewhere, five general features of similarity between moral and artistic engagement may be observed: (i) artistic endeavour is — like moral conduct — focused on *practice* and *knowing how* more than theory; (ii) there would seem to be a broadly analogous 'phronetic' focus on *experiential particularity* in the case of artistic appreciation and creation; (iii) just as moral knowledge and virtue seems to be concerned with the proper expression and articulation of *feeling*, so artistic involvement with experience seems to have a similar intimate concern with feeling; (iv) artistic appreciation and knowledge can be said to have, as in the case of moral virtue, a significant effect on personal formation; (v) moral and artistic knowledge and understanding appear notably isomorphic with regard to the broadly similar relationships of virtue to moral experience and of art to aesthetic experience: the cultivation of aesthetic experience seems *necessary* for the promotion of artistic appreciation or creativity, just as the cultivation of moral experience is *necessary* for the promotion of moral virtue.

This last point, moreover, takes us to the heart of the matter. For the relationship of the artistic to the aesthetic may be conceived precisely along the lines of the Aristotelian conception of the 'phronetic' relationship of virtue to natural moral response. Once again, this relationship is best understood by reference to Aristotle's view of the relationship of virtue to moral experience. For Aristotle, the raw material out of which *phronesis* attempts to construct the virtues is the everyday rough and tumble of interpersonal association; nature has equipped us with a repertoire of sensory and affective responses to the world — pleasures, pains, love, fear, anger and so on — which it the task of nurture (in the form of parents and teachers) to order in line with some defensible conception of individual and social flourishing. However, the Aristotelian shaping of nature in accordance with virtue ought not to be construed in terms of instruction in truths or precepts of moral life, but rather more in those of the encouragement and refinement of some responses and dispositions and the discouragement — if not extinction — of others. Thus, the aim of early moral education is not so much the inculcation of a body of received opinion about the nature of moral life — though this is by no means an unimportant part of moral education and training — but the fostering of a range of sensibilities and sensitivities to the feelings and needs of others, the reinforcement of positive attitudes and attachments to others and the basic control of more potentially destructive selfish and anti-social tendencies.

Likewise, however, education in artistic creativity or appreciation will depend upon the prior cultivation of an aesthetic responsiveness to experience best regarded in terms of the cultivation and refinement of certain human pre-dispositions, sensibilities and sensitivities to the sensory qualities of experience. A parent interested in the aesthetic development of a child will generally proceed not by *telling* him or her that this or that is beautiful or ugly, but by training powers of sensory perception and discrimination. Thus, just as it is a necessary — though not a sufficient — condition of moral educatedness that one has acquired certain practical powers of sympathy and empathy for others, it is a necessary — though not a sufficient — condition of artistic educatedness that one has acquired a certain reper-toire of sensitivities to the richness of sensory and aesthetic experience. Moreover, on this view of aesthetic knowledge as essentially a form of practical knowledge — expressible dispositionally or aptitudinally more than propositionally — Best's distinction between artistic and aesthetic appreciation becomes rather clearer.

For first, it is clear how someone might have real appreciation of a dance which is aesthetic but not artistic — without having to suppose this to be a matter either of purely subjective pleasurable feelings or the entertainment of non-artistic propositions; an aesthetically aware or knowlegeable person is not one who has registered a set of propositions about the beautiful or even — as some latter day theorists of art and aesthetic education seem to have supposed (Hirst, 1974) — of the grammar and semantics of a given form of aesthetic discourse, but someone to whom we are able to attribute a high level of responsiveness to sensory particularity. Moreover, although any such appreciation would certainly consist in feelings of enjoyment, these would be consequent upon the exercise of *objective* powers of discrimination rather than acquaintance with sub-artistic propositions. Secondly, however, it also explains the respects in which powers of aesthetic discrimination are necessarily presupposed to any effective artistic appreciation or creativity; if we understand artistic engagement as the 'phronetic' organization of experience in accordance with a particular vision or ideal of beauty, form or expression, then powers of aesthetic discrimination may be construed as the raw materials upon which such organization goes to work. So, on the face of it, the idea of artistic knowledge and appreciation as a form of *phronesis* reasonably well captures an earlier suspicion that, even if there can sometimes be aesthetic appreciation without artistic judgement, the two operations are all the same *conceptually* rather than contingently connected.

It follows from this that the capacities for sensory discrimination which lie at the heart of aesthetic appreciation are not sufficient for artistic knowledge and understanding precisely insofar as they are not organized in accordance with any particular artistic vision — and may well be, in another sense of discrimination, quite indiscriminate. Thus, what is precisely needed to acquire capacities for artistic appreciation and creativity is an initiation into one or more *traditions* of artistic enquiry and endeavour which have sought to make human meaning of the particulars of aesthetic experience and sensibility. But, understood in terms of the mode of knowledge Aristotle calls *phronesis*, the realms of the moral and the artistic seem of a similar order: just as it is the role of *phronesis* in the moral sphere to forge virtue from the raw materials of pre-moral human interpersonal response, so its task in the artistic sphere is to forge artistic expertise, taste and discretion from the raw materials of aesthetic sensibility.

Dance and the primacy of practice

If anyone should still have doubts about my present extension of the notion of phr*onesis* or practical wisdom to the sphere of artistic and aesthetic endeavour — a notion apparently developed by Aristotle to contrast moral judgement with the more technical reasoning he associates with the arts — it is worth noting that in his important recent critique of post-modernism, Michael Luntley (1995) actually deploys an example of learning in the sphere of the arts in order to explicate and 'de-relativize' the new communitarian idea of practical moral reasoning. It is a problem of contemporary moral and social theory that in order to critique the emotionally and socio-culturally dislocated concept of moral reason characteristic of enlightenment ethics, so-called communitarian philosophers (see, for example, MacIntyre, 1981; Taylor, 1989) have developed neo-Aristotelian conceptions of *phronesis* which seem rather relativistically tied to the contingencies of particular social conditions and circumstances. Luntley quite convincingly shows, via reflection upon what is involved in developing the sensibilities and skills of a jazz pianist, that non-relativistic judgements about the artistic goodness or badness of particular artists, their works and performances is not precluded by our recognising that particular artistic works and performances are quite socio-historically conditioned responses to problems and challenges of local artistic traditions at specific times and places.

But Luntley's choice of example here may be even richer and more telling in the present context than even he appears to appreciate. For jazz is arguably more than a music; it is in itself a human culture. To be more accurate, jazz draws resources from very many of the immigrant musical traditions of North America, but few would dispute its spiritual and cultural heartland in Afro-American folk forms, particularly the 'blues' tradition. However, the blues is not just a music of social bonding and entertainment — it was and is, for black communities long oppressed by appalling injustice and social privation, an emotional outlet and the embodiment of a peculiar stoic morality which sought to rise above suffering with remarkable honesty and integrity. But consequently it is difficult if not impossible to disentangle a particular conception of experience or vision of the world from the often very unorthodox musical techniques in which it came to be expressed. Jazz undoubtedly derives much of its musical vitality, integrity and veracity form the blues, and the music of even the most sophisticated and well musically educated of modern jazz musicians will invariably contain folk elements — for example, the use of quarter tones and slurs — which are often against the grain of a classical music training; consequently, primers of jazz and blues piano will warn the classically trained that they may find the often 'unnotatable' demands of jazz timing, phrasing and fingering fairly alien or unnatural.

There can be little doubt, of course, that one does not need to be descended from a black American slave to appreciate jazz and blues. As far as jazz goes, though it draws on blues roots, it does not exclusively do so, and musicians from a wide range of American immigrant backgrounds — Afro-American, Jewish, Italian, Irish, even native American — were involved in its creation from the outset. However, it is probably impossible to understand jazz fully — or folk-blues at all — without some understanding of the socio-cultural conditions in which it was formed. Likewise, since jazz is as much a product of white as of black musical inspiration, colour is clearly no bar to playing it. Folk blues may be different matter; for, since it was clearly forged in social circumstances which were the unfortunate predicament of a particular black community, there is something peculiarly inauthentic or dishonest about middle class white youths from Surrey singing chain gang songs. But there can be no doubt at all that learning to play jazz involves the cultivation of an entirely different range of musical habits responses and sensibilities from the learning of other musical forms — which makes it difficult if not impossible for a musician to be equally fluent in, say, the languages of classical and jazz piano; indeed, musicians who attempt to 'cross-over' are invariably and conspicuously less successful in one sphere than the other.

The point is that any understanding of moral and artistic practical knowledge (and I believe that these are interestingly connected) in terms of *phronesis* — particularly of the rich interplay of the social, the cognitive and the affective, culture, reason and sensibility in such knowledge — must I think show us the final bankruptcy of any notions of universal *episteme* or *techne* in either morality or the arts. Moral and artistic knowledge — however much we take that knowledge to express objective truths with which we would have all human beings acquainted — are nonetheless the deliverences of experience in its fine-grained particularity; moreover, far from there being any opposition between experiential particularity and objective truth, I may only come to full understanding of the appalling truth expressed in a Billie Holiday song insofar as I am able to enter imaginatively or empathetically into the human particularities, including the expressive musical and other cultural resources, which occasioned that song. But, since we are here in the realms of practical knowledge, what goes for understanding and appreciation must apply all the more to the acquisition of moral virtue and artistic expertise. Different instances of that rich interplay of cognition and affect which is great art are liable to have roots in diverse culturally indexed traditions of expression which may share little, if anything, in the way of a common technical grammar or vocabulary. Indeed, what more than likely inclines us to deny the label of great art to the stylistic playfulness of much 'postmodern' art is the mistaking of eclecticism for originality, the apparent lack of integrity of what is merely eclectic and the shallowness of what is short on integrity.

Be that as it may, it should be clear that the particular routes through experience created or provided by the performance and other arts are liable — even if we want to claim neo-Hegelianly that they are all partial glimpses of on*e* truth — to some inconsistency of practical realization. Here, it is not just that there is no a common set of rules or techniques of pianistic engagement which might be given here a classical and there a jazz application; it is rather more seriously that — insofar as an artistic response is one which by definition goes beyond mere rule following — the development of artistic expertise is not at all well modelled on the idea following rules. In learning to play jazz, then, it is not that one learns certain techniques and in due course comes to experience the feel of jazz, but that cultivation of a particular range of aesthetic and emotional sensibilities — the feeling for jazz gained through listening, understanding and appreciation —

determines what shall count as appropriate technical responses. Moreover, as we have already noted, what we are here calling "jazz technique" — that range of conventional and personal responses to the needs of the music expressive of jazz feeling — must come to be indelibly printed upon the agency of the performer in such a way that playing in another musical style would require conscious re-adjustment if not actual physical reconditioning. But what is true for a perform-ance art like jazz here can only be exponentially so for an art like dance in which the body is itself the instrument of performance. If practical dance expertise is a matter of physical adjustment to the requirements of dance meaning, and the creation of dance meaning is a matter of personal-cum-conventional organization of aesthetic sensibilities and responses in the light of particular movement possibilities, then the physical adjustments required to realise some possibilities may well conflict with those required to realise others; the route back from dance meaning — classical ballet, contemporary or jazz — to dance capability will surely reach back beneath the skin to affect the very anatomical structure and muscle organization of the dancer.

Thus, though we might want to insist that there is basic piano technique — mastery of scales, piano harmony and simple co-ordination — which are likely to be required by any pianist, jazz or classical, it is not clear how there can be anything precisely analogous in the case of dance. To be sure, the techniques of classical ballet have sometimes been regarded in this way — but, as the contribution of Chris Challis (Chapter Nine) to this volume so vividly shows, this is an assumption which seems to be long overdue serious artistic questioning. Indeed, we need to appreciate with Challis that there are potentially two mistakes here about the terpsichorical centrality of classical ballet — and it is possible that many who have emancipated themselves from the one may yet be held captive by the other. At the political level, then, one may well have come to appreciate that classical ballet is only one part of the greater dance vision which has to take its place alongside other alternative but equally culturally valid dance forms — just as a classical musician may have come to recognise the alternative musical validity of jazz. But, despite this, one might still continue to hold that there is a universal physical grammar of dance movement which is best exemplified in the techniques of classical ballet — and which must thereby constitute correct dance training for any sort of dance whatsoever. My best current guess, however, is that such a belief could follow only from the myth of a universal dance-artistic *techne* — against which, in my theoretically fumbling way, I have been inveighing in this chapter.

References

Anscombe, G. E. M. (1957) *Intention.* Oxford: Blackwell.

Aristotle (1925) *The Nicomachean ethics.* Oxford: Oxford University Press.

Best, D. (1985) *Feeling and reason in the arts.* London: Allen and Unwin.

Carr, D. (1978) 'Practical reasoning and knowing how', *Journal of Human Movement Studies* Vol. 4: pp. 3–20.

—— (1979) 'The logic of knowing how and ability', *Mind* Vol. 88: pp. 394–409.

—— (1980) 'What place has the notion of a basic action in the theory of action ?', *Ratio* Vol. 22: pp. 39–51.

—— (1981a) 'Knowledge in practice', *American Philosophical Quarterly* Vol. 18: pp. 53–61.

—— (1981b) 'On mastering a skill', *Journal of Philosophy of Education* Vol. 15: pp. 87–96.

—— (1984) 'Dance education, skill and behavioural objectives', *Journal of Aesthetic Education* Vol. 18: pp. 67–76.

—— (1986) 'Reason and inspiration in dance and choreography', in J. Adshead (ed) *Choreography, principles and practice.* University of Surrey: National Resource Centre for Dance, pp. 40–50.

—— (1987) 'Thought and action in the art of dance', *British Journal of Aesthetics* Vol. 27, pp. 345–357

—— (1999) 'Art, practical knowledge and aesthetic objectivity', Ratio Vol. 12, No. 3: forthcoming.

Dunne, J. (1993) *Back to the rough ground: 'phronesis' and 'techne' in modern philosophy and in Aristotle.* Notre Dame: University of Notre Dame Press.

Geach, P. T. (1972) *Logic matters.* Oxford: Blackwell

Hirst, P. H. (1974) 'Liberal education and the nature of knowledge', in his *Knowledge and the curriculum.* London: Routledge and Kegan Paul, pp. 30–53.

Kenny, A. (1975) *Will, freedom and power.* Oxford: Blackwell.

Luntley, M. (1995) *Reason, truth and self: The postmodern reconditioned.* London: Routledge.

MacIntyre, A. C. (1981) *After virtue.* Notre Dame: Notre Dame Press.

Peters, R. S. (1966) *Ethics and education.* London: George Allen and Unwin.

Ryle, G. (1949) *The concept of mind.* London: Hutchinson.

Taylor, C. (1989) *Sources of the self: The making of the modern identity*. Cambridge: Cambridge University Press.

von Wright, G. H. (1971) *Explanation and understanding*. London: Routledge and Kegan Paul.

Wittgenstein, L. (1953) *Philosophical investigations*. Oxford: Blackwell.

DANCING BODIES: CAN THE ART OF DANCE BE RESTORED TO DANCE STUDIES?

Chris Challis

Introduction

The fashionable idea in dance writing in the past decade has been to locate dance meaning within what Crowther (1997: p.1) terms "semiotic idealism"; that is to say, that the art object is not seen as an aesthetic object, but as a site for interpretation in terms of race, gender, sexuality and class. On this account, meaning in dance is conferred only by its contexts, and social theorists become the "managers of meaning" (Crowther, 1997: p. 2). Whilst it is clear that contextual issues can and do offer important insights into dance works, when they do so without taking into account the internal relations within an individual work, and the connectedness between works in an historical continuum, they distort or even deny the possibilities of meaning of dances as works of art: these internal relationships, it will be argued, are not merely formal, they are also the particular means of expression which allow choreographers to make their ideas visible. I take these, the internal relationships, to be the aesthetic dimension of dance as art, and I argue here that a reductionist view of dance which permits only a contingent connection between the dance movement and its expressive possibilities is mistaken. If a dance is to be seen as meaning-bearing, then the ability to understand it pre-supposes the recognition at the very least that the choreographer meant it to be the way it is. This is not to fix the dance within a time warp; changes can and do take place, but they are subject to the same scrutiny in that they are also seen as deliberate acts by those who cooperate in the collaborative venture of making and performing works of art: a ballet sub-titled *Makarova after Petipa* serves not only to link the two choreographers, but to see the one work within the context of the other.

143

Dancers too are intrinsic to this collaborative venture, dance meaning is not generated by choreographers alone: choreographers make their work on dancers, dancers bring to it knowledge and experience of interpretative practices, and their ability to give believable performances is important to dance identity and existence. David Carr sums it up:

> Dance is not merely a sum of text and performing it but an artistic whole in which performance is not incidental to content but intrinsic to it. (Carr, 1997: p. 353)

The understanding of dance works on this account is a matter of viewers coming to see what different meanings different dancers bring to the work on different occasions; the audience is the third active participant in the enterprise.

This paper does not directly confront existing philosophical theories in dance concerning identity or ontology[1] of dance works but it attempts to open up the debate by offering an alternative account. At the centre of the argument is the question of what dance theorists and practitioners think they are doing when they make, remake and perform dance works.

The paper is in three sections, the first consideration is the relationship between technique and performance; the second is an examination of the relationship between choreographers and dancers; the third is a discussion of the relationship between dance works, culturally engendered meanings, and what other writers have called "life-issues" (Best, 1992: p. 173; McFee, 1992: pp. 173-179).

Dance technique and performance

McFee (1992: p. 202) argues the inter-relationship of technique and meaning. He quotes Marcia Seigel in claiming that technique is not two things, a method of training the body and a systematic approach to the whole process of moving, but rather having consequences for our understanding of artworks composed using that technique.

There is a widely held belief in dance that ballet is not only superior to other dance forms as a body discipline, but is the root from which all other art dance forms grow. Many professional schools which do not have ballet performance as an end product have a daily ballet class for all students: so-called modern dance companies such as *D.V.8* and *Mark Morris Dancers* endorse this through their daily class, although it will be suggested later that the classification 'modern dance' does not help to explain the ballet material in the works of these two companies.

It is clear that the systematic structure of ballet can provide a framework for developing bodily facility, but it is questionable that it provides the best way to train all dancers where different outcomes are preferred; if McFee and Seigel are right, then the bodies which result from ballet training do not necessarily make better jazz dancers. Ballet training specifies a 'ballet body' which is different in shape and musculature to a 'jazz' one. Thus the traditional view of dance training conceals many misunderstandings. Firstly, it assumes a commonality of dance forms which can be traced back to ballet; secondly, it assumes that if dancers can perform ballet, then they can perform any dance form, a principle which underlies the mistaken assumption of a hierarchy of dance with ballet taking precedence; thirdly, it assumes an incorrect relationship between technique and performance. The argument in this paper is that technique is not a system of training, but a system of education through which a dancer acquires not only bodily shape and facility but also learns the traditions, conventions and values which underpin the concept of dance being taught: the artistic body is thus skillful, intelligent and expressive of that form. If it is the case that there are no general principles of moving as claimed above, then the claim of ballet to be a superior system of training needs to be questioned. The ability to perform a double turn in ballet is not the same as being able to do it in jazz: in this sense, there is no "it" here. That the two share the idea of turning twice in the air does not pre-suppose a commonality of all features; that the former is performed with the body held with the emphasis on the verticality upwards, while the latter performed on a bent knee with the body moving into the ground, is indicative of two different systems. A double turn in ballet has both a technical and expressive dimension, and is not learned outside ballet — the rules and conventions of ballet are embedded in it; similarly for jazz.

Moreover, ballet is not a single system of training but many; there are similarities between systems, but each is codified in particular ways, and the rules for the arrangement of units or meaningful phrases of action depends on the system in question. By "system" I mean those identifying features of a method of training such as the 'Vaganova method' which underpin a whole way of working: they are not just the 'style' features, but the 'grammar'[2] of dance; and those who use the system take for granted its implicit rules and conventions in much the same way as those using language. Thus meanings in particular ballets made in particular systems depend on understanding the system which constitutes the work.

A comparison of short sections from two dance works will illustrate the point. At the end of the male solo from the *pas de deux* in *Le Corsaire* (after Petipa, 1899), there is a spectacular double turn in the air, the dancer finishes on one knee, arm raised in the heroic manner, a celebration of the bravura of the male dancer in classical dance; that he dances it in a particular way is due to dancer/company style, that he dances those steps in that particular relationship with the music is a display of technical and expressive mastery. The idea here is that the accomplished performer underlines the difficulty of the dance by demonstrating the ease with which he performs it.

The second case is from *New Love Song Waltzes* (Mark Morris, 1982), which I argue can also be classified as a ballet for just the reason that makes it a suitable example here. The female dancer begins the work with a double turn in the air, her arms and torso are then flung from side to side and she finishes the sequence on a cartwheel with bent knees. Rather than displaying the technique, the dance makes light of it; it looks as if anyone can perform this sequence, and yet the body has to be completely centred in order to accomplish it successfully; it is a case of disguising the effort, rather than displaying it. The idea here is that Mark Morris' dancers can do any thing and make it look easy and throwaway. In these examples, not only is there a different concept of technique at work, but a different concept of a dancer. Both dancers make clear the artistic concerns of their dance form and the values and concepts which underpin them. That the Mark Morris Company have a daily ballet class is quite clear in his choreography; there is unmistakable ballet material in it but in his work he both subverts the ballet tradition and honours it.

If meaning is tied in this logical way to the grammatical features of the system, then impairment or deletion of these features calls into question the possibilities of understanding both the system and the dance works it engenders. The system is both philosophical and conventional. It is philosophical in that its main features are ordered and classified by those who interpret the medium according to the theoretical concerns of what they take dance to be, and conventional in that any new system manipulates or questions previous ones. When learning such a system, dancers typically 'take on' all the features of it: dance academies and colleges teach systems; and through, for example, 'the Cunningham class' students are initiated into appropriate responses by experienced practitioners in the field. Dance companies continue the practice as part of the compulsory daily routine.

Daily class is one of the places where a dancer learns the skills, conventions and traditions of the whole enterprise of dancing; it is not an end in itself, but neither is it a rehearsal for something else; the performance demands on the dancers invests the movement with expressive potential, dancers do not merely mark the steps, they dance them: not dance movement, but dance action (Carr, 1987: p. 352). When class and choreography are mismatched, then there is a major difficulty to be resolved; Geraldine Morris[3] argues that the 'Ashton body' is no longer within the technical scope of the present Royal Ballet Company. This means that when an Ashton work is revived, Ashton material is either cut or replaced. How much this can be done and the ballet remain an Ashton work is a serious consideration which will be discussed in the next section. A major question occurs: What is it that the dancers of the Royal Ballet think they are doing when they are performing a work attributed to Ashton? Well, they are not performing 'Ashton', as we have seen; and what they are performing, how to identify it, and to what body of work we make reference when we attempt to understand it remain problematical, as we shall go on to see.

Choreographers and dancers

If the above is plausible, then there is problem for repertory companies who have the work of many very different choreographers in their repertoire. If the basic technical principles of ballet cannot be taken for granted, then the differences based in the traditions, training and conventions of ballet systems need to be accounted for in the acquisition of works made on one company and danced by another. The Royal Ballet dance works by Balanchine; their ability to do so rests on the assumption that they *understand* a Balanchine work — it is not just the case of the adaptation of ballet technique, but learning a different way of moving: a change in body concept, line, spatial orientation, speed and musicality.

It was suggested above that the present company has similar problems in dancing 'Ashton': it is questionable that the company, ten years after his death, can dance an Ashton work, taking into account the changes of style and training which have taken place. It is interesting that the reconstruction (in 1997) of *Cinderella* [Ashton (1948)] is described in the publicity leaflets as follows:

> [the] tale is told in a brilliant sequence of dances which combine the formal precision of the Russian classical tradition with the emotional depth of the English style.

This is straightforwardly a contradiction: and one which the previous section attempts to question; the two features of the claim, "formal precision" and "emotional depth", illustrate the misconceptions concerning the relationships between technical requirements and choreographic meaning. Firstly, and following from the argument above, it is dualistic to suggest to that the same movement can be harnessed to different emotional features in the same work, and for it to remain the 'same work'. At the risk of repetition, the expression is constitutive of the action and the action 'represents' the expression; to look for separate features is to be mistaken in how dance works have meaning. This is not to say that they have only one meaning; dance features can be construed in many different ways, but not in any way.

Secondly, to dance an Ashton work with "Russian formal precision" is to dance it inappropriately. Ashton's choreography is not amenable to Russian interpretation in this way, based as it is in a different philosophical tradition, a different cultural tradition, and a different historical context — clearly there are implications for meaning and thus the understanding of the work. The distinctive characteristics of Ashton cannot be grafted onto the Russian ones if decipherability (Wollheim, 1979: p. 133) or comprehensibility (Wollheim. 1993: p. 174) is to be possible.

A conflict of meaning which is at issue here is compounded when a dance work attempts to cross the boundaries between two dance forms. In November 1997, Angela Kane and Susan Mcguire gave a paper to the conference *Preservation Politics*, at the Roehampton Institute. They argued that the works of Paul Taylor which were danced by ballet companies such as American Ballet Theatre were misunderstood. The companies had bought works such as *Auriole* (1962) and *Airs* from Taylor because these works looked classical to them. Kane (1999), in her paper for the forthcoming book, quotes Taylor as saying, "I think they get lyricism and ballet mixed up together". She goes on to develop the argument,

> although the shaping of the upper body is similar to classical ballet's port de bras, the degree of torso bend, and the use of gravity undoubtedly are not. For example the classical allonge is extended to the extreme often with the torso inclined from the vertical and this can be seen most clearly in the fifth movement of Airs. Also in Taylor's work. transference of body weight is accomplished through undercurve… Significantly, the *plié* is initiated by a soft torso contraction, and the *relevé* by a release. From my own interviews with Taylor, he can be quite querulous about the use of

contraction in his work. Clearly he wants to avoid any comparison with Martha Graham,... and I would argue that the Taylor contraction is different from Graham's. The contraction is seldom used as a dramatic statement in itself, more often it initiates a sustained larger movement of the whole torso, thus producing a concave body shape in which the neck and shoulders form part of the upper curve — unlike a Graham contraction where the upper and middle spine create a counter tension. (Kane, 1999)

The contraction and spiral are fundamental to Taylor's style, and together with a sense of weight and undercurve are the least understood movements in the restaging of his work. Kane claims that Taylor's musicality in cross-phrasing several bars of music is very difficult for a ballet dancer because of the tendency of such a dancer to move in evenly metred phrases, and to emphasise certain positions on route. She thus argues that the restaging of Taylor's work is a question not of what is danced but how.

If the use of the legs and spine is alien to the ballet dancer who has not developed the bodily shape or skill to perform the actions, and if the flow of the movement is changed from continuous to positional, with consequent changing of accent and phrasing of the work, then it is not just the 'how' of the work which is lost, but its expressive potentiality: what is missing here is not just the spirit of the work, but the *concept* of it, rooted as it is in the artistic bodies of the Taylor school. Every Taylor work is concerned with the nature of the expressivity of dance for Taylor; it is the very core of his choreography. The features which Kane describes questions the possibility of translatability from one dance form to another, important decisions as to what counts as a Taylor work, and which features if any, can be discounted.

A post-modern view might question the importance of such an analysis: the ballet interpretation could add richness to a Taylor work. Against this, another question needs to be posed: What is it that is being made here? There seems to be an irony in that a ballet company buys a *Taylor* work, and dances it as something else. There is a logical relationship between the choreographers concept of a dance and the dancers' interpretation of it: the artistic ideas of the choreographer are realised only in the technical, intellectual, and expressive abilities of the dancers. These artistic ideas cannot be construed in any way, but in and through the conventions, rules and practices as they are seen in individual works by particular choreographers. These parameters matter if interpretative practices are to be acknowledged, this does not to stifle interpretation, rather to suggest that it takes place within a range of tolerance.

If this is correct then it has implications for ontology, authenticity and identification of dances. The reconstruction of dance works, particularly those which have not been seen for many years, is not purely an empirical matter. A checklist of steps, music, costume will not do until the conceptual issues (concerning what the collaborators in the reconstruction take that task to be) are addressed. It is a prior and pressing consideration concerning the total contextualisation of the work. The notated score, important though it is, is not sufficient on its own to warrant a claim of authenticity, if indeed a claim is possible at all. On this explanation, there is no sense to the idea that a reconstruction is sixty per cent accurate!

The idea of dance as art

The above attempts an explanation of dance as a co-operative enterprise in which the distinctive ways in which a choreographer uses dance material are made clear. The dances display the choreographer's concepts of the dancer, the major concerns of what s/he takes dance to be, and therefore possibilities of meaning. Interpretative practices suggest that the choreographer neither closes down the possibilities of meaning, nor has the priority in deciding meaning. Interpretation is opened up through the use and manipulation of all the resources; dancers, and audiences alike understand that the same work is never exactly the 'same' in any subsequent performance, and yet it can be recognised 'as the same work' and be discussed accordingly. A dance work makes visible all the conditions of its existence.

Where the subject matter of the art work is dance itself [for example *Points in Space*, Cunningham (1986); "They All Laughed" in *Shall We Dance*, Fred Astaire (1936), *Made in the USA*, David Gordon (1987)], the focus is on the materials of the dance and the inherent expressiveness of those materials. Where it represents some other subject matter, it can only do so through the materials of the dance, the means by which it represents. Thus, where it expresses life-issues, 'real world' meanings are recognised, but they are rooted in 'the art world': the dancers' bodies in dance are first and foremost artistic bodies through which social or political messages are understood. The naturalistic gestures in the work of Lea Anderson may be recognisable from real contexts, but within the art of dance they become part of the artistic vocabulary of the artist; a hand-washing motif which is immediately discernible loses its literal meaning and may take on many symbolic meanings as part of the interpretative possibilities of the dance. If there is a failure to recognise this idea, then dancing-bodies are not distinguished from real bodies, and reality and the imaginary are conflated and confused. Thus the social dance in a Jane Austin novel projects a social situation which embodies the conventions and values of the society in which it exists; bodily proximity, sexual roles, gaze, social relationships are governed by these conventions and are prescribed for this and all other social activities. In 'art' dance, the rules of the social situation are held in abeyance, the artistic conventions prevail; proximity, eye contact, touching in a Cunningham dance are all aspects of his work, but do not denote sexual encounter, though they do display a respect for persons.

Where real life situations are projected, they conform to social rules, though we do not mistake them for 'real': an example from the fictional world of Cranko's ballet *Onegin* (1965) illustrates the point. The ballroom scene in act 2 reflects the social scene of the 18th century, the dancers enact the rituals which are publicly acceptable; Onegin offends social codes in tearing up Tatiana's private letter in a public place and by flirting with his friend's fiancé. In the two *pas de deux* in the same work however, the idea of love projected and rejected is not the only subject matter: of equal importance is the dance material itself, and the ability of the choreographer and dancers to extend the boundaries of the classical duet in order to express other ideas in the dance. Cranko challenges the conventions of the medium by, firstly, expanding the formal structure of the *pas de deux* and, secondly, through the introduction of 'public' and 'private spaces. In the public places, the garden or the ballroom, the social rules of society are projected; breaking the rules, as in the example above, underlines their importance. In the private spaces, the bedroom and Tatiana's sitting room, intimate bodily contact, lifting and supporting can be explored, and do not offend social acceptability by public displays of intimacy. Thus the internal rules of the dance are clearly set out; where choreographers do break social conventions, they do so knowingly. What is being suggested is that a dance work calls attention to the means by which it comes into being: what is represented and how it is represented are inextricable. When the choreographer shows us a view of the world which deepens or challenges our understanding of it then this is only possible if we understand what dance is and can do: this is the way in which *dance* means.

Further

There is a short post-script to the above. If dance both displays itself and the world, under what conditions does the significance of dance as art over ride other meanings? It is one thing to claim the primacy of dance as art and another to ignore ideological conflict which the dance may project. But, if the emphasis shifts from the internal cohesion of the work to the message it conveys, if the 'art' of dance is seen as secondary to the covert narrative, then our attention shifts from 'art' to 'social issues'; and dance as 'art' becomes indistinguishable from any other narrative. In this way, the art of dance becomes contingent to the message, and its study subsumed under the heading of 'Cultural Studies'. It is therefore incumbent on the dance community to make clear the means by which particular dance works have significance, so that the legitimate concerns of 'Cultural Studies' are considered against the background of the 'art' of dance, and only then can the debate begin. As Amy Koritz (1996, p.91) argues:

> Dance scholars' tools for analysing and communicating about bodies might help feminists and those working in cultural studies clarify and understand cultural uses of bodies in a variety of contexts. Dance historians from this perspective have much to contribute to the worthwhile goal of keeping cultural studies honest in its invocations of the body.

Notes

1 See for example Goodman (1968: pp. 64–65; 121–122; 211–218); McFee (1992: pp. 88–111).
2 I am indebted to David Carr for this suggestion, any mistakes in its applicability are mine.
3 Geraldine Morris, a former dancer with the *Royal Ballet* is researching the work of Ashton. This point was made in the context of a lecture on Ashton to the MA Ballet Studies, November 1998.

References

Best, D. (1992) *The rationality of feeling*. London: Falmer Press.

Carr, D. (1987) 'Thought and action in the art of dance', *British Journal of Aesthetics* Vol. 27, No. 4: pp. 345-357.

——— (1997) 'Meaning in dance', *British Journal of Aesthetics* Vol. 37, No. 4: pp. 349-366.

Crowther, P. (1997) *Language of twentieth century art.* London: Yale University Press.

Goodman, N. (1976) *Languages of art.* Indianapolis: Hackett.

Kane, A. (1999) 'Issues of authenticity and identity in the restaging of Paul Taylor's Airs', in S. Jordan and A. Grau (eds) *Preservation politics*, London: Dance Books Ltd. [forthcoming].

Koritz, A. (1996) 'Re/Moving Boundaries: From Dance History to Cultural Studies' in G. Morris (ed) *Moving words re-writing dance.* London: Routledge: pp. 88-103

McFee, G. (1972) *Understanding dance.* London: Routledge.

Wollheim, R. (1979) 'Pictorial art: two views' in B. Lang (ed) *The concept of style.* Philadelphia: University of Pennnsylvanis Press: pp. 128-145.

Wollheim, R. (1993) 'Pictorial Sytle: two views' in his *The mind and its depths.* Cambridge, MA: Harvard University Press: pp. 171-184.

TECHNICALITY, PHILOSOPHY
AND DANCE-STUDY

Graham Mcfee

Introduction

This chapter's concerns are shaped by three ideas which — although I have been committed to some version of them for a considerable time — I have had occasion to revisit recently, ideas central to the thrust of this book (and of the conference at which this material was first presented):

- first, the centrality (for dance studies) of philosophy. The recent reprinting (Mcfee, 1997a) of a paper first presented in 1992 reminded me of my forceful claim *there* that an honourable dance studies — one that was more than a collection of the history of dance, the sociology of dance, the anthropology of dance, etc. — would need a centre based in philosophy.

- second, the need for any philosophical investigations here to be consistent with, and to derive from, other philosophical commitment (since, as David Best [1974: p. xi] put it, "[p]hilosophy is one subject").

- third, the need to preserve *roughly* the same account of dance as its practitioners give — that philosophy here should not be radically revisionary [that it "… leaves everything as it is" (PI § 124[1]) in this sense].

These last two ideas — which guide *my* search for the distinctiveness of dance from among the arts — may be identified through a contrast with Peter Kivy's recent urging of the philosophical value in "looking for differences among the arts rather than finding them accidentally in flawed definitions" (Kivy 1997: p. 218). I do not wish to dissent from this (except perhaps to take a stronger — and more Wittgensteinian — line than Kivy against putative definitions). And I certainly applaud its implicit commitment to *dance the artform*.

The difficulty I see results from an implicit tension here between, on the one hand, the claims of philosophy — its integrity, methodological structures, etc. — respected in the second idea and, on the other, the claim of dance studies (at least in this aspect) neither to collapse into 'philosophy of dance', one of the dreaded '-ologies' feared in the first idea, nor to be *swamped* by philosophy, so that the practical concerns of dance-professionals are left behind (third idea).

These thoughts came to a head partly because, in the last few years, I have been thinking about the nature of the philosophical enterprise; partly because I asserted that (once its ethical questions are omitted) 'philosophy of sport' will, and perhaps should, become an '-ology' (McFee, 1998); and partly because a recent paper by David Carr (1997), offering a mild attack on ideas of David Best and myself, includes a suggestion that one of my tools for discussing dance — the type/token distinction — was not consistent (or not wholly consistent) with my more general philosophical frame: or, to put that more bluntly, that it was un-Wittgensteinian, perhaps even anti-Wittgensteinian.

Now, I can reasonably comment on this section of Carr's paper since it applies only to me (most sections relate to ideas David Best and I share, and over which he might plausibly be thought to have propriatorial interest); also, it actually raises problems for *both* my principles since (in addition to Carr's explicit target, a conflict between my general philosophical concerns and my specific 'gadgets'), *one* further issue here must be the degree to which this 'gadget' from philosophical logic, the type/token distinction, is an intrusion into the world of dance, having nothing to do with the concerns of its practitioners.

With these points in mind, I first sketch the nature of philosophy as I conceive it the first section, then lay-out my use of the type/token distinction in this dance context (second section), before briefly meeting Carr's objections (third to fifth sections), and seeing where that leaves us for the philosophy of dance (sixth section). Before concluding, I offer some general reflections on the place of the philosophical in dance studies (seventh section).

The project of philosophy

Put bluntly, and following Wittgenstein, I endorse a *therapeutic* conception of philosophy — showing particular flies the way out of specific fly-bottles (PI §309: see McFee, 1996; Baker, 1986). So the philosophical puzzlement comes about because it is *very easy* to slide into (or be lured into) ways of thinking that confuse or mislead ... by leading us to ask questions like, "But what *is* consciousness?",

"Why are thoughts 'inner'?" — crazy questions, since in *one* sense we have all the answer we need; in another, *no* answer is possible.for instance, Deborah Hay (quoted Foster 1986: p. 6) says that "Everyday the whole day from the minute you get up is potentially a dance". Of course, it isn't that all of her life *is* a dance, but that any of her movements *could be* (part of) a dance — yet, given the way *she* puts it, others might think (under-rating the word "potentially") that all of her life could actually be a dance, and so raise the *crazy* questions.

In this way, we are granting that Hay's remarks might confuse/mislead. But is the mere *possibility* of such misunderstanding a genuine worry? To see that it is not, imagine that I am talking about sunrise; say, in the context of having seen a beautiful sunrise, or of sunrise being a good time to view such-and-such a species of bird. I see no reason to take issue with this kind of talk, even though I don't believe in sunrises (any more than the rest of you) since I take us to live in the *solar* system. So it would be misguided of some 'philosopher', hearing my remark, to conclude, "McFee operates with a pre-Copernican cosmology!". To repeat, it is important to reject the kind of literalism much beloved by some philosophers with analytic training who, finding a way to 'read' a sentence *as* misleading, take it to have misled. Rather, ascription of misunderstanding must be based on *evidence* of misunderstanding — that is, evidence of *genuine* misunderstanding, not the mere *possibility* of misunderstanding. This would typically take the form of some inference drawn. In my sunrise case, someone might, for instance, argue that, since there are sunrises, it *follows* that the sun is moving and hence that God could cause the sun to stand still. Further, this point might be used as part of a proof about the nature or existence of a deity, perhaps. Such a person is *misunderstanding*: none of that does follow from what I'd said! So it is *possible* to be misled by this form of words. But that possibility does not lead me to demand that talk of sunrises be banned!

Of course, some *implications* which might be drawn from certain ways of putting a point must be rejected — just as we reject any move from the possibility of sunrise to the fact of the sun's movement. (This is of a piece with Wittgenstein's insistence that the search for essence and the programme of analysis[2] must be abandoned: belief that there *must be* some underlying structure is unwarranted.)

Wittgenstein wrote next to nothing on aesthetics as such, although (a) he did write stuff on the arts which might be *taken* as a contribution to aesthetics, and (b) he did use arts examples for *other* purposes (where the assumption is that the aesthetic case is transparent).

Types, tokens and multiples

Let us now consider the way of talking about multiple arts that I employed in *Understanding Dance* (McFee, 1992 cited throughout as "UD") — this way of talking having implications for our study of works of art themselves, implications not always recognised (Redfern, 1983: p. 19). And, although it may be well known, I will briefly rehearse the position. The technical device used was the distinction between types and tokens, where the token is the specific object in front of me and the type is the general object (UD: pp. 90-93). For example, in the case of the Union Jack flag, the *token* is a piece of cloth that I am holding. But this is no more, and no less, the Union Jack than, say, the one on The Palace of Westminster. The Union Jack (in the type-sense) is an abstract object.

This type/token language provides us with a clear way of talking about works of art that are multiples. We can have a discussion of one sort about *Swan Lake* — the dance in the abstract, as it were — and another discussion about a particular performance (a token of that type).

At least two important features from the type/token distinction will carry over to the discussion of multiples, were that way of talking used. First, the type is an abstract object — one never confronts the type directly. Second, all tokens are equally important, all equally the type. Thus, for example, no individual text of Joyce's *Ulysses* is uniquely the novel itself. Each is as much (or as little) the work of art as any other. In particular, the novel is not uniquely instantiated in the version that Joyce himself wrote by hand (supposing that he did this). Each token is equally a token: the hand-written token no more so than the printed ones. Those not prepared to regard the work in this way cannot use the type/token contrast to characterise it. To apply, using the type/token analysis will preclude thinking that a particular performance — say, that staged by the choreographer — is somehow more central than any other performance[3].

Of course, performances will differ in detail. So its being *the very same artwork* cannot require indistinguishability. In this way, focus on *Swan Lake* (rather than on a particular performance) recognises certain features of the work as under-determined — not all the features of a particular performance will be *required* by the dance itself: so performances could differ in these respects without becoming tokens of a different type. Since there can be these differences between performances, and yet they still be performances of that very same dancework, the work itself cannot be determinate on whatever are those 'changeable' features.

In this way, and for roughly these reasons, in *Understanding Dance* I had therefore urged the employment of Peirce's *type/token* distinction, with performances as *tokens* of a dancework *type* (UD: pp. 90-97)[4].

Versions, interpretations and performances of dance

Now let us turn to David Carr's recently published criticism of my views on this matter (Carr 1997 — cited as "Carr"). Although it may seem slighly laborious to do so, it is worth considering in some detail a number of Carr's points here (and therefore rehearsing some of his presentations of them) since the objections turn on the specificity of my Wittgensteinianism, its internal coherence, and the like. Further, Carr implicitly raises a criticism of another 'term of art' from my account of dance.

Carr's position is that, methodologically, I have "failed to be Wittgensteinian enough" (Carr: p. 358), and have therefore ended-up with a position "uncharacteristically un-Wittgensteinian" (Carr: p. 362), contrary to the second idea mentioned initially. His reason is that the type/token analysis as a way of characterising the relationship between the work (as multiple) and the performance is "realist or essentialist" (Carr: p. 354) — but in what sense? *Roughly* in the sense of presupposing some 'Platonic fiction' of a dancework (the type), which is then subject to *interpretation*. Carr (rightly) objects to such Platonism: it is incompatible with my Wittgensteinianism — and it is not aiming to answer any genuine questions. So, with Carr, I accept that *this* will not do as a doctrine.

Luckily, it is not mine. There is no need to think of the type/token contrast as *essentially* Platonistic, as we will see. And our central argument here will concern the *function* of the type: Carr thinks of it as an *ideal* to which performances approximate, while 'partaking' in it — a sort of Form of the Good Dance! In contrast (and as Carr notes), I recognise that the type under-determines performances: any performance makes concrete (and thus fixes) what is colourless/unfixed in the type. So talking of *the type* is really no more than talking of what performances *of that dancework* share.

For Carr, one part of my problem is that I regard performances as *interpretations*. Now, in Carr's view, there are interpretive arts alright: like drama, where "acting might be regarded as a mode of interpretation of some pre-existently meaningful poetic or dramatic text or narrative" (Carr: p. 352). But dance, it is supposed, is not like this, since we cannot encounter the dance *itself*, divorced from some particular performance (which I had spoken of as a "performer's interpretation"). In this vein, Carr writes:

> ... McFee might be better to conclude from his difficulties in applying the type-token distinction to dance that dance is not in the relevant sense an interpretive art ... (Carr: p. 353)

Indeed, for Carr, this emphasis on interpretation motives my use of the type/token contrast. He writes:

> ... the only possible art-theoretical significance of the type-token distinction is to explicate the idea of artistic interpretation. (Carr: p. 353)

Now, Carr cannot mean that *because* it is not interpreted (assuming him to be right about this), dance is not to be treated in a type/token way. For novel, poems and sculptures, for instance, are (arguably) type/token without, in themselves, requiring interpretation for their existence, or to bring them into being — even if appreciating them is interpretive.

Still, if we take Carr to mean this to be the only rationale for using the type/token contrast *in this context*, I would still disagree. For my use relates only to the unity-in-difference idea, rather than to the specifics of interpretation. And even if the type/token language does permit us to say that the token, the performance, is an interpretation of the work itself, the type, this would be a *performers' interpretation*, such that the performance itself instantiates that interpretation.

Carr is rightly concerned to reject any assimilation of understanding (or meaning) to *interpretation*: and this is a good Wittgensteinian point (PI §201 [c][5]). But, as we will see, this provides no reason to reject discusion of dance performances in terms of "performer's interpretation".

Here one of Carr's own problems raises the issues of this paper in another form: he imports (or seems to import) a [metaphysical?] thesis about the nature (or role) of *interpretation*; namely, "that a rule determines an action as being in accord with it *only* in virtue of an interpretation" (Baker and Hacker, 1985b: p. 20, my emphasis). It is precisely because the 'interpretation' of the performers in a dance work is *not* of this sort that Carr castigates me for using the term "interpretation" in this context (Carr: p. 353).

But this is misguided in two ways: first (not considered here, but see Baker and Hacker 1985b), it is false as a thesis about interpretation — or so I would urge. Yet, second and more centrally here, it is simply irrelevant to the kind of interpretation at issue: namely, performer's interpretation. First, there *is* a clear sense of the term "interpretation" here — it is explained by pointing to the difference between *this* performance and another performance of *the very same dancework*. Granting that this is indeed the very same work (numerical identity) brings out the *difference* (identity-in-difference, of course) that justifies describing these different performances as instantiating different performer's interpretations. Second, using the term "interpretation" here is not assumed — as interpreting a literary text might be — to involve some uninterpreted 'object': indeed, an idea Carr and I share is that one can only genuinely confront a dancework by confronting a performance of it; and — for me — that will always be a performer's interpretation in this sense.

Carr does not see it this way, partly (no doubt) because he is unhappy about the sense in which performers' interpretations are rightly called *interpretations*. Later he speaks of my:

> … false assimilation of the idea of a different *version* to that of a different interpretation. (Carr: p. 354)

For the idea of X as an *interpretation* seems to imply that there is something interpreted (in these various ways). So Carr is urging that a more profitable idea might be that of a *version*, which lacks this implication. As he notes:

> Horticulturalists can produce different versions of a given beetroot species without having to suppose they are interpretations of a particular type to which particular instances do or do not correspond; there is no universal Platonic beetroot of which particular roots are only imperfect realisations … (Carr: p. 354)

Investigating this comparison further shows its limitations: for, while these 'new' beetroots are members of the one species, they are essentially *different* beetroots. By contrast, as we shall see, the performances of *Swan Lake* are performances of the *very same* dance, the *very same* artwork. Although Carr (p. 354) seems to acknowledge this point, he thinks its recognition cannot be accomplished through the use of the type/token contrast. Yet that contrast *precisely* does give one a way of talking about *unity-within-diversity*. In this sense, I take it that Carr (rather than myself) is making "heavy weather" (Carr: p. 353) of this topic.

There are really two aspects to the response here: first, that talk of a *version* (as Carr understands it) will not do the job, since we need (in addition to commenting on *this* performance) to discuss/criticise/applaud what the performances are 'versions' *of*: namely, the dancework. So some structure which allows us to refer to *the artwork itself*, rather than just to 'versions', is required. And, as we have seen, it is unclear that the idea of a *version* can support the identity-judgements crucial here: that it is *that very dance* (say, *Swan Lake*) that I go to see — although what I see is always some performance of that dance.

Second, there is something to be said for the term "interpretation" here — since we naturally talk of performers' interpretations (and this language is in the literature; see Carr: p. 354, where the performer's 'contribution' to a dance performance is spoken of as a "mode of interpretation") while acknowledging that these are not *interpretations of* (something) ... in the sense in which *critic's interpretations* are: these second are interpretations *of the artwork*. And such interpretations typically include strings of words (although they may include, say, gestures too; UD: pp. 122). By contrast, a performer's interpretation brings into being that in which the ('witnessable'; Urmson 1976: p. 243) work consists. So, of course, to call it 'an interpretation' could be misleading (although those familiar with the topic won't be misled; see B&H 2: p. 47 note, quoted later — the idea that we know what the problem is ...). Yet recognition of this point is fundamental to our understanding of (in this case) *dance* as a performing art.

For — in an idealised case — what the performer does is to bring that dancework to completeness by *performing* it: but this performance will inevitably differ from others, not least because (typically) he/she gives the work a personal 'twist', emphasising (slightly) different aspects of it. Recognition that there is an *it* here, distinct from any performance, is crucial for the idea of performing art. Therefore, if we consider a dance performed on Tuesday and on Wednesday, there will be differences: and *some* of theses differences will be differences in what I have called *performer's interpretation*.

In the case under consideration, the performance on Tuesday night and that on Wednesday night are — essentially? — performances of the same work: that is not the issue here. Now I am recognising three (related) situations: first, that some (practical) cases *will be* performances of such-and-such a work — say, *Swan Lake*. I take this to be agreed on all sides: and it is these *I* am calling tokens of the same type. Second, some cases clearly *will not* be the same work (despite similarities: Mats Ek uses the music and a *version* of the story). Third, some cases will be border-line or contentious: what do we make of Nureyev's re-staging (McFee, 1994b: pp. 30-31) — is it re-choreography? And what about Matthew Bourne's *Swan Lake* with "a radical gender twist" (Mackrell, 1997: p. 32)? Is the performances of either of these really *Swan Lake*? There need be no answers to such questions, apart from that given (implicitly or explicitly) by the practices of the Republic of Dance (UD: pp. 71-74); and therefore as mutable as such things are. (Indeed, we could usefully consider when such an issue might arise.) Certainly, we should not assume/expect that there *must* be such an answer: and I take *that* to have been the essentialist view here. For saying that two performances of the same dancework have *something* — the type — *in common* need be nothing more than a manner of speaking (*a façon de parler*): as we might note that all games are games, to use Wittgenstein's famous example — nothing need turn on this.

Afterall, there is no suggestion here that all *dances* have something in common — that is, it is not the claim that the term "dance" could be defined, or that there are necessary and sufficient conditions of dance-hood. So the debate is unlike one where, say, it is asked what all tables have in common. Instead, the claim is a much weaker one: that not *anything* could count as a performance of *Swan Lake*, even if we cannot say precisely what would and what would not (in the abstract) — that (concrete) performances are 'constrained' by the (abstract) *type*.

The argument *for* some sort of 'constraint' here really has three motivations (already sketched). First, and negatively, it is a rejection of the 'anything goes' of subjectivism — the thought (to which I will return shortly) is that not just *anything* could count as a performance of *Swan Lake*. Second, this is a case of *unity-and-difference*: that there is one specific artwork, *Swan Lake*, here — in the jargon (Scruton 1997: p. 101), this is a discussion of *numerical identity*[6]. So the case differs from, say, that of tables, where each is a table (of the same kind) *without* the implication of there being only *one* table: at best, this discussion of tables would turn on qualitative identity. (And the same is true of our different beetroots [Carr's example].) Here, in the important case where *this* performance differs from *that* one, both are performances *of the same work* — this point must surely be granted (indeed recognised to occur very regularly) by any who accept the possibility of performing arts, where the artform is a multiple (UD: pp. 88-90). So granting that they are the same work does not imply that they do not differ. Thus there is a reason to refer, at least sometimes, to the work 'underlying' various performances (of it): hence, to refer to the *type*-artwork. And if we rehearse on Monday and perform on Tuesday and Wednesday, for *which* performance was the Monday event a rehearsal? If we answer "both" (as we must) we highlight the sense in which there is just *one* artwork here (UD: p. 93) — one rehearsal can (simultaneously?) be a rehearsal for more than one performance.

Third, the 'constraint' referred to above is not a *practical* one: it means only that if someone wants to stage *Swan Lake*, the resulting performance will be constrained. In effect, this recognises the difference between *re-staging* (which gives a performance of the *same* dancework, tokens of the *same* type: arguably, Nureyev's *Swan Lake*) and *re-choreography* (which gives performances of a *different* dance work, tokens of a different type: say, Mats Ek's *Swan Lake*). Of course, the details of this boundary will be contestable. As earlier, what are we to make of Matthew Bourne's all-male *Swan Lake*, with its "radical gender twist" (Mackrell, 1997: p. 32)? A *critical* debate (as I think of it [UD: pp. 71-74], a debate *within* the Republic of Dance) might be located around just this point. But, in recognising it, we acknowledge the (possible) distinction between two dances, both called "Swan Lake", with (largely) the same music and similarities of story-line, and so on: all we dispute is *where* this boundary falls in practice, one group arguing that Bourne's is a work *different* from the Ivanov and Petipa (a token of a *different* type) while the others dispute this claim.

Next, notice that no-one ever suggested that just *anything* could count as a performance of *Swan Lake*: typical suggestions for constraints would be provided by its having to be a *movement-sequence*; its having to be a *dance*; its employing *certain music*, and perhaps a certain *narrative thrust*. Any of these might be missing or attenuated in a particular case (within [arguably] limits of re-staging, short of re-choreography), but an 'object', even an art-object, which lacked *them all* would not be *Swan Lake* — indeed, it would not even be a dance! (Lest this seem too prescriptive, we might additionally concede that a choreographer might even succeed in getting round these constraints — but it would require a complex critical story, drawing on yet other features of dances valued by the Republic of Dance.)

The type/token contrast is centrally a *way of talking* about artworks that are multiples, a way which permits us to *distinguish* talk about the art-object from talk about 'its' performances (or instantiations)[7] . Of course, first (as we have seen above, and recognised; UD: pp. 90-92), this jargon has certain implications: for instance, that the type is an abstract object, and that all tokens of that type are *equally* tokens (there are no privileged tokens). The suitability of such implications to the analysis of dance must be investigated. And, if these implications did not hold for dance works, this would be an inappropriate way to talk about them. Second, it is a highly *abstract* way of characterising the relation between dancework and performance — as such, it is hard to see its 'teeth'. For this reason, any *practical* implications to this way of talking (beyond those, noted above, that attend this way of *conceptualising* danceworks) must be located by finding a *practical correlate* of the type: this is what my *Thesis of Notationality* (UD: pp. 97-98) is designed to do. I will return to this point.

Finally, the considerations given above suggest that — if the *type/token* language is rejected — some *alternative* must be proposed (UD: pp. 98-99) since we will continue to treat dance as a *multiple* artform; and that any alternative too would have implications, which must then be analysed. Equally, any practical problems it posed, or practicalities it suggested, would need investigation. So, at the least, there is a useable insight here in identifying *the need* for some descriptive framework, since issues about the relation of performance to dancework arise regularly.Thus — to return to the topic — one needs *something* here, and any candidate 'something' is likely to be *some* kind of 'gadget'. Further, the issue being approached is not as isolated from the professional practice of dance as might be thought.

Misguided particularism?

However, this has not taken us to the root problem (or problems) that Carr discerns in my use of the type/token contrast. Carr seems to have two (related) worries of relevance here, one metaphysical, one practical. The metaphysical worry is that the type/token distinction is *inherently* Platonistic (also Kivy, 1993: pp. 35-36; p. 59; p. 75), and hence un-Wittgensteinian. But, as I have suggested, this is not so. Indeed, the type/token contrast merely highlights some (candidate) features of the *unity-within-difference* for danceworks; and might be rejected if danceworks do not possess these features. Further, as we have seen, Carr's counter-suggestions (in terms of *versions*) fare less well. So there is no reason to consider the view un-Wittgensteinian: at least, once Wittgenstein's *therapeutic* conception of philosophy is acknowledged.

The basis of Carr's practical worry is that — by assuming some *type* to which performances must *correspond* (his word; Carr: p. 354) — my suggestion *too tightly* constrains what can count as a performance of, say, *Swan Lake*: the only alternative being a misguided *particularism* on which "each dance performance is uniquely what it is and not another thing" (Carr: p. 254; compare UD: p. 118; McFee, 1994a: pp. 22-24). Perhaps, though, each of us is here stressing — perhaps *over-stressing*? — one aspect of what is required, without (I suspect) intending to deny the other. For my worry thus far is that *enough* constraint be ensured — and, as flagged earlier, my device is *The Thesis of Notationality*. By recognising the *flexibility* of its constraints (and its *responsiveness* to institutional factors; UD: pp. 71-74; 76-86) we shall see that it does no more than — on reconsideration — Carr should want.

At present, dances are very often, perhaps even always, made by making a particular token. That fact is uninformative concerning the nature of dances. By contrast, the possibility of making the type by making the score offers a useful insight into the character of performing arts by suggesting a relationship between the type and the notated score.

Of course, the Thesis of Notationality does not give us a way of determining absolutely whether or not a particular performance is a token of the same type as another performance. The notation is only a movement notation, after all. But that Thesis does offer us a (defeasible) necessary condition for dance-identity, when we have the notated score. That we often lack such scores is one reason why the Thesis of Notationality cannot always offer practical help. In such cases, we might hope for a (future) score, or see such a score as an idealisation — catching the contraints of the type[8].

We acknowledge that *the dance itself* (*Swan Lake*) is not identical with any particular spatio-temporal event — any particular 'object'. The temptation then is to see it as identical with a non-spatio-temporal 'object': that is, an abstract object[9]. And, effectively, the type/token language adopts this strategy. Such a move is not wrong but has the possibility of misleading us (as, perhaps, it misled Carr: see earlier). For we may (mistakenly) *imagine* either that there is some 'ideal' to be matched here[10] or that there is a *direct* 'access' to the dance itself, contrasted with the *indirect* one through its performances.

Suppose, in one hundred years time, a complete Labanotation score (including Effort notation) were found for some contemporary dancework — say, Christopher Bruce's *Swan Song* (1987) — that had long disappeared from the dance repertoire. Now *Swan Song* can be performed, although for the previous one hundred years that was (in practice) impossible. Of course (one of Wittgenstein's insights here) this would not be possible unless a whole background of dance understanding (LC I §20 [p. 6]; I §26 [p. 8]) — what Wittgenstein calls a "special conceptual world" (Z § 165) — were already in place: one could not reconstitute dance from this score alone, or even (perhaps) the dance-manner appropriate to dance of Christopher Bruce. My example is only that *this particular* dance is lost and then, as it were, found. Now, has the dance existed all that time (as the language of 'lost' and 'found' suggests)? Neither saying that it has nor that it has not seems satisfactory: but why must we decide? As Baker and Hacker respond to a similar point, "[t]he question is misleading, but the facts are clear" (B&H 2: p. 47 note, cited earlier). For there is no substantial question here that we cannot answer. So we need not be misled if we *refer* to "the dance itself", the *type*, here: such reference need have no further implications.

It is in *this* sense that a concern with the *practicalities* of staging dances is detached from the concern with the type/token character of (most) danceworks. If we look for the constraints provided by the type, we must look to something practically available: in this vein, I offer the *Thesis of Notationality*, which both *idealises* what might be a quite general constraint and *models* what such a constraint might achieve.

So, what *can't* one do as a performer of such-and-such a work? The difficulty here — according to me — is to be given an *institutional* answer: the Republic of Dance decides (UD: pp. 72-74; 80-81). And this I take to be in line with Wittgenstein's thinking. Indeed, all of the *determining* features of institutional accounts (as I understand them) are to be found in what Wittgenstein says about the arts. For, first, there is in Wittgenstein no general answer about what are aesthetic (artistic) possibilities, but only an answer at a particular time (and place?): an answer to a particular question (PI: p. 184 [b]). Second, there is an "authoritative body" (B&H 1: pp. 272-273) in respect to art-status and art-understanding: there are *real* 'cultivated/cultured tastes' here, as well as what might be *called* cultured tastes (LC I §29 [p. 9]. [Also, in LC I §12 [p. 4], we can learn to appreciate poems by being shown revealing (right?) ways to read them — which supports the idea of an authoritative body, but also the idea of (possible) misperception.] Third, while art-status is not merely a matter of whim, neither is it just a matter of *finding* the work *art* (in UD: p. 72, I treat this in terms of the need, within the institutional account, for both *other-acclaimation* and *self-election*). Fourth, art-status (like appreciation) is a *rational*, rather than a causal, matter (seen most clearly in LC[11]). Although these are not how Dickie (1974: pp. 33-49; 1984: pp. 80-82; 1993) understands institutional accounts of art (or even how others reconstruct such accounts from Danto's writings: see Danto 1981), they constitute *my* constraints for such accounts. (Moreover, these seem to me to replicate, at least broadly, the conditions T. S. Kuhn identifies for science: and his account of science is institutional in just this sense [McFee, 1993: p. 183].)

Of course, Wittgenstein would not have thought of it in this way — he would have denied having any 'theory' of art in this sense. But what I offer is not a *theory* in any complete sense. In part, I am offering a set of remarks which I hope will be generally revealing about aesthetics or art-appreciation: I do not think of them as revealing in all circumstances; but, still, as generally helpful. My aims for aesthetics include making remarks *generally* helpful in understanding art and artistic experience. This involves addressing perplexities which regularly arise (as one might know from contact with artists, students and others); and doing so in ways which *suggest* strategies even to those whose *precise* perplexities are not thereby addressed. These seem legitimate *aims*, however well realised. At the least, anyone with a commitment to philosophical aesthetics should be sympathetic to them. And an institutional account of art (of the kind sketched here) seems to me to consolidate some of Wittgenstein's insights into art.

Therefore, this is *one* way to make-out the *practical credentials* of this account of art: while it does not provide details, it offers the logical or explanatory framework 'behind' our discussion of the arts (and especially the performing arts). Accepting such an account would tie-in the philosophical material — even the type/token 'gadget' — with the practical concerns of dancers, stagers and choreographers. So that there is no *general* difficulty here, no *in principle* conflict between the philosophy and the artistic practice. In this way, we have answered the criticisms I found in Carr; and, in passing, illustrated the *value* of thinking in these (or *broadly* these) ways on these issues.

So, thus far, I have endeavoured to emphasise both the unity of views here, despite superficial dissimilarities (using my own view as an example), and the contribution of philosophy to getting clear our key questions.

'Meaning' and art-status

Carr might reply, though, that my method here is suspect: my response thus far has imported, and relied on, the contrast between our response to apporopriate artworks as artworks (*artistic* judgement, appreciation, etc.) and our response to all the other things in which we take an aesthetic interest (*aesthetic* judgement, appreciation, etc.). And has been explicit in doing so (UD: pp. 38-44). But the way I make-out this contrast, by pointing to the meaningful-ness of art (in contrast to the [merely] aesthetic: UD Chapter 8) draws on an unexplained, and inexplicable, notion — that of *life-issues* or *life-situations* (two expressions I treat as equivalent in this context).

For Carr's primary target in his article is the account of *meaning in dance* which I (broadly: UD: pp. 179-182) share with David Best. So there are two specific aspects of Carr's discussion on which it seems appropriate to comment, given my earlier points. The first asks whether the notion *meaning* is at best inappropriately applied to dance at all — and connects with Carr's reservations about the sense in which dance is an interpretive art. The second involves the usefulness (perhaps even the coherence) of ideas that, following Best, I had used both to explicate the artistic/aesthetic contrast and to characterise a crucial aspect of artistic meaning — as above, the idea of life-issues (or life situations).

Recall, though, that my interest here is only in these issues as they bear on the more general questions of complexity, technicality and relevance. So here I will merely sketch replies, taking them in reverse order. Yet there is a more general point, for this chapter's theme: that the artistic/aesthetic contrast represents another technicality — although one of a different sort!

With respect to the artistic/aesthetic contrast, my typical strategy has been, first, to locate the *whole* of this contrast within the 'aesthetic' side of the purposive/aesthetic contrast (UD: pp. 39-42) and then to characterise differences between artistic judgement etc. and (merely) aesthetic judgement etc. via two quotations from David Best[12], the first identifying the crucial *point* of artworks (namely, their role in emotional education: UD: p. 169), the second characterising *art* in terms of this achievement (UD: p. 174): and then I have seen the *overall* basis for the distinction in the (twin) ideas that artworks were (and mere aesthetic objects were not) *meaning-bearing*, where a characteristic of meaning-bearing in this sense was the 'life-issues' connection (to put the point with suitable vagueness).

Surely some such distinction is uncontentious, especially for those committed to aesthetic education, or the educational relevance of the arts (as Carr clearly is). Consider, say, our appreciation of a great painting and of the wallpaper of the wall on which it hangs: my point is just that these are very different, although both a within the 'bigger aesthetic' — that is, not purposive and concerned with line, grace, etc. In thinking that there is, for instance, *more to say* about the painting (and especially about the *value* of the painting) we are recognising the artistic/aesthetic distinction.

To fill-in this contrast, we might notice the ways our judgements of artworks (artistic judgements) differ from at least three cases[13]:

(i)   natural beauty (the waterfall, or the sunset) — which is not intended and has no meaning;

(ii)   an object designed for purely aesthetic purposes (the wallpaper) — which is not intended in the way art is intended and (therefore?) has no meaning;

(iii) a functional aesthetic object (the Ferrari) — which still has some residual means/ends concerns, and no meaning.

If we grant these three broad classes as the first 'stab' at a framework, contrasting these cases with art, we are acknowledging the artistic/aesthetic contrast. If we deny their contrast with art, it is hard to see that we have the concept "art" at all — philistines (McFee, 1994a: p. 115) would, of course, deny just these contrasts! So, there does seem *some* point in giving *some* weight to *some* notion of meaning in drawing the artistic/aesthetic distinction — and hence in applying it to dance.

But, if we are to get less programmatic, we must recognise the importance of specificity about the notion of *meaning* — contrasting it with *significance*, *association*, and the like — explained by thinking about, say, Picasso's *Guernica*: it has a social 'meaning' by virtue of being the mural planned for *that* wall, in *that* pavilion, as part of the Republican exhibition at *that* event. But that 'meaning' (which I would not call "meaning" but rather "association") is independent of the paintings *specific* features — for instance, of whether or not it is a good painting — since a bad painting could have that same social *association*. So, in this way, the *meaning* here is not a matter of what, say, the painting tells us about 20th century capitalism, unless that is part of the painting's topic.

A parallel here: if I learn, from your 'body language', that you are nervous or bored, this may well be the very last thing you wanted me to find out — hence, the last thing you were *communicating* — even though I *did* find it out by watching your behaviour (see Best, 1978: pp. 132-168; UD: pp. 243-244). In just this way, artworks might *reveal* something about, say, the socio-economic conditions of their production but, since this would apply to poor as well to great art (and also to non-art artifacts), it cannot be part of what makes *this* the artwork it is — cannot be part of *its* meaning, or how it is appropriately understood.

To summarise, then: if (a) we grant the artistic/aesthetic *contrast*, recognised from the examples — at least, grant it as a starting point for more detailed consideration — and (b) we concede that this distinction has a bearing on our *valuing* of the objects that are or are not art[14] , then we begin from a position where this distinction (*if* we can sustain it) must explain a *something* on the art side of the artistic/aesthetic distinction (not on the other side) which connects with human thought and feeling; and of a kind the history of art has made familiar[15]. It is this "something" for which I have 'appropriated' (as placeholders) Best's terms "life-issues" and "life situations"[16].

There is a *mild* cognitivism implicit in this artistic/aesthetic contrast: for instance, the painting differs from the wallpaper in being an object embodying intentions differently — as we might say, the painting has meaning in the *strict* sense in which linguistic items might: so that this is not just *significance* or *association*. And, of course, our heart-felt response to the *beauty* of either is beside this point. Peter Kivy's (1993: p. 371) claim against the art-status of *music alone* is precisely this: that *music alone* is not meaning-bearing in this (relevant) sense. His position illustrates the connection of art-status to meaning-bearing: that is, endorses our (mild) cognitivism. (Even though Kivy is wrong about the outcome of applying this test to music — or so I claim [McFee 1997b] — the test itself seems sound.) So, I suggest, any good answer to questions about the *difference* between a typical painting that is an artwork and typical wallpaper must sustain this mild cognitivism — although of a kind far less appropriately embraced by the cognitive/affective contrast[17]. But even that shows why a discussion of this topic is simultaneously a discussion of artistic meaning.

I am here urging four points about the idea of 'life-issues' in respect to artistic meaning: first, I recognise this 'life-issues' connection (as many others do[18]) *independently* of the term "life-issues" — so using this term is introducing a *placeholder* for an idea that (frankly) I see only 'in the distance', and have (yet?) no better account of (although see UD Chapter 8). Second, I concede that this term is indeed a *placeholder* when it occurs: of course, it may turn out that nothing *more* can usefully be said *in the abstract* — so that, as long as philosophical aesthetics operates at a certain level of abstraction, no more comprehensive *general* account is possible. Even if this were so, the addressing of the *specific* perplexities of particular individuals ("shewing particular flies the way of specific fly-bottles") could still take place within a *framework* suggested by the idea of 'life-issues': that is, in the context of human thought and feeling. Indeed, it is hard to see how *valuing* some objects as we value art would be explicable in any other way. Third, insisting on the idea of a 'life-issues' connection is insisting on art's connection (of the kind noted above) to human thought and feeling. So that if I claim — as I do (UD: p. 181) — that a work might 'satisfy' this 'requirement' by being in *explicit* contravention of it, my thought is that, since such a work might be important in the 'construction' of a history of art (in that form), it might *shape* the kinds of connection to human thoughts and feelings characteristic of art: if this is so, it seems churlish (or pedantic) to deny it *a* connection to human thought and feeling. Fourth, it seems right to think of this *placeholder* as having an important *relation* to meaning-bearing: artworks (i) have this 'life-issues' connection and (ii) are meaning-bearing, while (mere) aesthetic objects lack both.

Why should Carr dispute this? I suggest two reasons: first, for him, the issue is 'all-or-nothing' in ways it is not for me — I am happy that *how* the placeholder is redeemed might differ *radically* across cases, so that there is no one thing (nor set of things) that the term "life-issues" identifies (although I agree with Carr that spelling-out some of these, in their contexts, is work I should do). And my commitment to this strategy is a part of my Wittgensteinianism. Second, Carr (rightly) is struggling to make sense of what motivates the *mild* cognitivism inherent in (at least) *my* account of meaning for danceworks: he ends up discussing it by reference to what *he* concedes (Carr: p. 365) is a more extreme — and unsuitable? — cognitivism (namely, that of Paul Hirst). Read *my* way, these are questions more easily answered. And these answers illustrate how *this* aspect of my position in philosophical aesthetics depends on my other commitments.

The danger here, to return to an earlier point, is that we could undermine *all* of the argument for the educational value of the arts by *not* sustaining the distinction between the artistic and the aesthetic: indeed, that we are bound to do so — since a commitment to the distinctive educational place of the arts must be a commitment to some mildly cognitive value to the arts (McFee, 1994a: pp. 1-2). So, as with the type/token contrast, my argument here is that some useful point *to think about* is identified: not some solution to all our problems, it is true, but perhaps a way of getting clearer what some of those problems sometimes are.

The nature of aesthetics?

An important *general* question (which our cases bring to our attention) concerns — roughly — the point of philosophical aesthetics: for instance, this type/token discussion can seem too abstract, too divorced from the practicalities of art-making and art-understanding. The danger is that it becomes nothing but what Wittgenstein called, dismissively, "academic chat" (see Monk, 1990: p. 431) — philosophical aesthetics can (and has[19]) been appropriately criticised in just this way. For art can clearly be central to *some* lives. As Colin Lyas puts it:

> ... we know that our encounters with art ... go not merely wide but also deep, and, moreover, go as deep as anything in our lives can. (Lyas 1997: p. 2)

But aesthetics can fail to bring out this depth. Indeed, John Wisdom's diagnosis of how aesthetics could be a waste of time focused precisely on its attempts to give some 'logical framework' for artistic value with no connection to this value

as such (Wisdom, 1953: p. 222). Here Lyas reminds us of the student moved by
a work of literature who:

> ... is told instead to attend to some hocus-pocus involving such barbarisms
> as 'signifier' and 'metonymy'. (Lyas, 1997: p. 5)

The implication is that such discussions are fruitless (and, perhaps, fruitless because
footling — as ornithology might be to birds: see O'Neill, 1992: p. 247). But is
this because *these* terms are inappropriate (say, embodying a misconceived view
of meaning: contrast Travis 1996; Travis 1997), or because *all* terms possible for
such discussions are? Authors of books on aesthetics — such as Lyas — might
seem committed to the first option: for clearly they take their own contributions
to be exempt from this criticism (at least in principle). In fact, the response to this
objection might be a more *subtle* one: that this sort of 'aesthetic' discussion is flawed
by its introduction of *unwarranted* complexities, complexities not *supporting* 'our'
appreciation of the artworks. To put it bluntly: that the discussion introduces 'gadgets'
from philosophy which, whatever their general merits, shed no light on the
experience of art; and hence have no *real* place in philosophical aesthetics.
[I have read David Carr's comments on my 'technical expressions' as subtending
this point: note that the type/token contrast is from the lexicon of Peirce's
philosophical logic.]

In reply, it would be attractive to have a general answer, vindicating an activity
I have given a deal of time to[20]. But such a general vindication is neither available
nor (properly understood) desirable. It is not available for two obvious(-ish) reasons:
first, this is a case-by-case matter — we cannot conclude that because *one* discussion
employing tools (or 'gadgets') from, say, philosophical logic is unrewarding or
unenlightening that *all* are[21]. And here some usefulness for the type/token contrast
has been illustrated. (This point is even sharper if seen in reverse: being willing
to grant *something* from philosophical logic cannot possibly saddle the aesthetician
with the whole paraphernalia — even assuming [counterfactually!] that there were
just *one* such paraphernalia.)

Second, the usefulness of any such 'gadget' depends on the issue it is supposed
to address: someone who finds illuminating talk of what follows for the play *Hamlet*
from Shakespeare's having made the eponymous hero more forceful, say, may
still feel that this discussion is not *aided* by the introduction of, for example, a
possible-worlds semantics for counterfactuals. Yet such a person might recognise
that something must be said about how one's concern for *Swan Lake* (and perhaps

for Nureyev's *Swan Lake*) relates to one's concern for Tuesday evening's performance. Hence the point of using the type/token contrast might be clear.

Of course, *some* sets of arguments seem more generally crucial; and are ignored at one's (aesthetic) peril. A central example for me would be the neglect — bordering on ignorance — which Wittgenstein's 'private language' considerations receive (in philosophy of mind as well as aesthetics). But, as here, any such arguments must be understood aright — mere lip-service to them is not sufficient. Further (again, as here), such arguments typically have a *strategic purpose*, rather than being wholly general considerations.

This thought introduces the second claim made earlier: that a *general* vindication of aesthetics is not desirable. For here we should remind ourselves that Wittgenstein's account of philosophy was as *therapeutic* (PI §309), directed at the specific puzzlement of some particular person. So the aim is not to produces answers to perennial problems, nor to analyse concepts in ways that preclude future misunderstanding: indeed, both these targets are illusory since, first, sources of misunderstanding appear and disappear — for example, from the activities of scientists (see below). And, second, the question addressed is always contextual: the form of words in which you articulate your precise problems might ask something different in someone else's mouth. Further, drawing on some of the points about rules, one cannot preclude *all possible misunderstanding*, since there is no finite totality of possible misunderstandings, no sense to the word 'all' here.

So philosophy typically consists in identifying how puzzlements arise either because some peculiar (and unwarranted) inference is being drawn — as before, you hear me talk about sunrise, and infer that I have a pre-Copernican cosmology — or some piece of jargon has been misunderstood. For instance, talk of Chaos Theory leads someone to think that scientists now think of the world as chaotic: but, of course, Chaos Theory is fully deterministic, as is demonstrated by the facts that the Chaos Theorists preferred research tool is the computer! What is need here is to get a clear view of one's (mis)understanding: then it will (eventually) go away — one will be misled nolonger. But this is difficult both because of the difficulty of finding the "magic word" (or "liberating word"; PO: p. 165) here — the one that makes the matter clear to you — *and* because we regularly acquire misleading ideas. As Wittgenstein (PO: p.185) put it:

> Teaching philosophy involves the same immense difficulty as instruction
> in geography would if a pupil brought with him a mass of false and falsely
> simplified ideas about the course of rivers and mountain chains.

Faced with philosophical problems, then, one has to try to get a clear view of what it is that is misleading you since, if it is a *philosophical* problem (and not one in, say, natural science, where empirical investigation might help) this is the only way to move forward. And one might be helped here: for example, in by far its best moment, the Derek Jarman film *Wittgenstein* has two students asserting that the reason 'people' typically believed that the sun went round the earth was that it *looked* as though it did — then Wittgenstein asks how it would *look* if the earth went round the sun. It takes a moment for them to realise that, since that *is* what happens, it must look like this! The scales fall from their eyes.

Such a conception of philosophy is directed fundamentally against the assumption that there is always and everywhere *one* question/issue for us all. Rather, *your* perplexity may differ from mine, even if they are expressed in the same words: we cannot assume in advance of investigation that one-and-the-same puzzlement is shared (although *some* human commonalities might speak in its favour — as some differences speak against!). What is clear is that, for many humans, art is important in their lives, and that this importance is deep-seated[22]. But it is a mistake to place too much emphasis on this fact. For art does not *necessarily* serve one purpose only: nor should we think that it does. In particular, it is a mistake to think its deep-seatedness gives art *experience* some (logical) priority over the careful analysis of artworks and their importances (of the kind philosophical aesthetics offers).

One point (with a certain Wittgensteinian tinge) is that asking about *priorities* is often exposing an issue where more than one *purpose* is at work. But, then, such uses are not (obviously) in competition. So that asking if a theory of art might rest upon a theory of interpretation (Dworkin, 1985: p. 153) makes sense in a context where (or so it seems) *either* one's judgements about art are certain — and hence prior to any remarks about interpretation (and, as noted initially, this seems to be Wittgenstein's assumption in some of his arguments) — *or* one's judgements about interpretation seem firm enough to ground the "wavering and deceptive stuff"[23] of one's judgements of art. This can then *seem* like a dispute about logical priority.

But are we sure that the very same question is at issue between those who stress one and those who stress the other? For might there not be issues where we could take the artwork for granted, to discuss its interpretation, and different issues where we could take for granted some interpretive theory, asking where it left the artwork under consideration? For instance, my reflections on how I should direct *Hamlet* take for granted both its (general) art-status and the need for that status to be preserved in my production: this is why — for example — I decline to do it without the Prince of Denmark (although I know that other directors 'leave out' sections of dialogue as long as all Hamlet's speeches, from whatever is the longest text of the play: probably a combination of passages from the first Folio and second Quarto.). Here the issue is (roughly) *how* to instruct others so as to produce what must satisfy two conditions: it must be (a) a vivid *performers' interpretation*, and (b) of that play.

Equally, faced with a vivid performance *of something*, critics might dispute whether or not it was *Hamlet*; and (also?) whether it was *art* — with the implication that giving a "yes" answer on the first issue settled the second, while a "no" answer there left it open. (This might be *another* artwork, a token of a *different* type: like the Mats Ek *Swan Lake*.)

But both these cases represent someone's worrying about how to stage *Hamlet*: of course, they differ in what is taken to be problematic. Yet surely they both represent legitimate worries, illuminating that one can have these different concerns.

If the dispute were one about logical priority, then — as Lyas emphasises — humankind's deep responses to art ("as deep as anything in our lives can be": Lyas: p. 2) would seem to settle the matter: art comes first. But this is misguided in two ways. First, the matter is one of chicken-and-egg, a matter where *one's concerns* are to the fore. For the question asked is not one which *interrogates* logical priorities, but one which *assumes* a certain priority — it reflects the questioner's own puzzlement in the light of what he/she takes for granted. That the same form of words in the mouth of another might ask a different question is neither here not there. Second, this contrast assumes (mistakenly) that one could have art *without* such interpretation: for these artworks are, at least in some weak sense, Danto's *transfigured objects* (from Danto, 1981), transfigured by human 'interpretation' — that is, by human thought and action. For, in becoming dance, the sweeping movements, say, cease to be (mere) sweeping (UD: pp. 51-52) — they are transformed. In this sense, although sections of some danceworks might be *mistaken* for everyday movements (as some of Danto's artworks might be *mistaken* for his "real things"; Danto, 1981: p. 1), they are centrally different from the everyday.

Yet this is not to say that artworks are essentially detached from (the rest of) human life. As we have seen, integral to Wittgenstein's general conception of the place of the arts is a dependance (among other things) on the fact that humans have the capacity to *react* to artworks (CV: p. 71); but also on the "conceptual world" (Z §165) within which this takes place. And doing so is locating artistic value within what is valuable to humans[24]. As Wittgenstein urged in the case of the 'signs' of mathematics:

...it is essential to mathematics that its signs are also employed *in mufti*. (RFM V §2: p. 257)

The thought is that the 'life' of such a 'sign' depends on the fact that it "enters into our lives" (Beardsmore, 1971: p. 49): that not *all* the uses of mathematical concepts are the one circumscribed by the conventions and rules of the discipline of mathematics.

But then our *experience* of these objects must be *appropriate* experience: struck by the gracefulness of certain lines or the elegance of certain gestures, I am doubtless entranced by the *aesthetic* dimension of each. Yet if these are artworks, my experience involves *misperception* (as we have seen), no matter how heart-felt it is. Of course, I may be happy to continue to misperceive the object: "I know what I like". Doing so only precludes my finding whatever that object's *transfigured* status — that is, its status *as art* — has to offer. If I am (in general) interested in *art*, that concern should drive me towards regarding the 'object' as *centrally* 'interpretated' ...

Consider the idea of beauty in this context: to see aright the logical priorities here, one must recognise the possibility of *misperception* — so that (a) I do regard X as beautiful, and (b) it is beautiful. Now recall (from the previous section) our distinction between the *artistic* and the *aesthetic* : here, the concern with *beauty* is (merely) aesthetic. I am being struck by its line, grace, colour-combinations and the like: however, I do not regard it as an artwork — perhaps (being from Mars) I even lack the concept *art*. Still (being otherwise like earthly humanity) I am struck by the object's beauty. But X *is* an artwork; and, since my perception of it is not *under* ('mediated by') the appropriate artistic concepts, I am misperceiving X. Of course, even if this is pointed out to me, I will still continue to see it *as beautiful*. So this must indicate a *certain* lack of univocality to the concept *beauty*[25]. Indeed, one might conclude that terms occuring in both artistic and aesthetic judgements[26] are *systematically ambiguous* in just this way. In effect, this is an argument that the philosophy of art has *problems of its own*, which need not (and should not) be confused with those concerning aesthetic experience. Certainly the idea of a *unified* aesthetic experience — covering art, nature and (say) Ferraris — is to be rejected. If this is granted, it follows that one cannot usefully assign logical priorities here — although the thought[27] that we could not come to learn artistic concepts without a (prior) *human capacity* to be interested in grace, beauty and the like (and their opposites?) might well be conceded.

Of course, this is just to restate (from the previous section) the artistic/aesthetic distinction. Doing so allows us to make two points:

• As we saw, the artistic/aesthetic contrast is rooted in our practice — we do distinguish our valuing of the painting from (say) our valuing of the wallpaper on the wall that it hangs on (although both might be beautiful).

• This way of *drawing* the distinction is *technical*, since the words are not used in this way in English: indeed, both words are used on each side of the distinction — we both talk of *art* when we do not intend artistic appreciation ('the womanly art of breast-feeding') and ascribe aesthetic properties to artworks (without noting that to do so is precisely not to regard them as artworks). So *reserving* the terms solely for one side of this contrast is treating them as technical: as 'terms of art of the aesthetician. Thus this contrast is in line with the need for technicality of sorts.

Once we take seriously this need to recognise as *technical* some of the expressions used in describing and appreciating artworks — in our case, dances — we also see the need to investigate such technicalities, and to gauge their usefulness for, and relevance to, practitioners of dance.

How to study dance

One way to introduce a more general discussion of the nature of dance-study: by asking if I have left out something (crucial) by not talking (enough?) about the *performance* itself? One response is considered by Paul Thom (1993:: p. 27)[28] who — after quoting Aristotle on tragedy (*Poetics* 1450b) — remarks that on this view:

> … staging is a dispensable accessory to tragedy: for if the tragedy is the poem, then staging is indeed incidental to it. The tragic effect is possible without the staging …

We readily see the thought here: that the *central* artwork is the poem, rather than the performance. But could this be *the same* tragic effect in both cases? More exactly, what could count as a criterion of its being *the same*? For the 'intentional object' (Kivy, 1990: p. 121; McFee, 1997b: p. 37; Scruton, 1997: pp. 232–234) of that effect is the artwork itself: yet this is the artwork *as we confront it* — and if we confront it *in performance*, then that is indeed the *it* here.

[The point is, of course, even sharper for dances — here, there *could not* be a confrontation with the artwork that was not a confrontation with a performance of it. This is important when we reflect that the 'perceptual mode' appropriate to the artistic appreciation of dance is indeed primarily a visual one — we *watch* dances — even if it includes, say, auditory aspects. (And this is one worrying feature of the tendency to talk of *reading* dances {Foster, 1986 and Mackrell, 1997}.)]

Now this discussion has a distinct bearing on two central questions: first, can one engage with a work of performing art *other than* by seeing performances? Here, the implied answer is, "no" — at the least, engagement with the *text* (either the literary text or the notated score) is not *the same* as engagement with the work in performance. So, for example, one might distinguish, within dramatic art, between its text-led and its performance-led aspects. Second, and relatedly, the thought of just *one* object of (artistic) appreciation is a confusing one for the performing arts — even when we have put aside obvious ways of generating difference of meaning for the same work: different performer's interpretations and differences in particular performances of the *same* performer's interpretation, as well as acknowledging the variety of (acceptable) critic's interpretations. For there is clearly *some* sense in which these texts can be appreciated artistically — at least, by those who can make sense of them. But that is not everyone[29]. This last point is important since some theorists are keen to emphasise the *performer's* role here. While this role may be overemphasised (UD: pp. 273-276), it cannot safely be ignored across the board: even if, with Wittgenstein (CV: p. 51[30]), we recognise that *for some purposes* listening with understanding (for music) or watching with understanding (for dance) have a good deal in common with — and hence can revealingly be compared with — *performing* with understanding.

Yet, if we grant the *force* of Wittgenstein's slogan that *In the beginning was the deed*, what *explanatory power* then resides in talking about the performance *from the performers' viewpoint*? Rather, we seem committed to the insight that performers *just do it* — no doubt, based on their knowledge, training and the like, and on the input from both choreographer and stager (where these differ). Indeed, it is the capacity to do *this* that marks one out as a (suitable) performer in this sense or for these purposes. So there is nothing (distinctive) that, in constituting or instantiating the work, the performer *does* — except what any of us do in being *agents* in the world. For there are no specifically artistic 'acts of will' or 'intentions' on the part of performers, which constitute their actions being *that* artwork. They are simply performing the actions sensitively or expressively; where the terms "sensitively", "expressively" pick-out qualities of the movements. And, of course, they are doing so *in contexts* where this amounts to instantiating the dancework. [There is a connection here to visual arts: also — and by the same token — there is nothing the painter or the sculptor *does*, beyond being an agent (UD: p. 281). These artists are distinguished from the rest of us, of course, by the ranges of their actions. But if we want to explain these actions — say, by reference to intention or to genius or some such — we must recognise that such explanations are typically 'after the fact': that they describe the event *as explained* rather than describing the (causal?) motivation of the event. And the same ideas apply for performances also.] Yet, if there is little mileage in describing the performance from the *performer's* viewpoint, this does not leave us with *no* questions to address — but what remains relates closely to what *counts* as a performance of the work in question (say, *Swan Lake*). And this is the issue I took to be central, and addressed, in my discussion in *Understanding Dance*.

Conclusion

The overall morals, then, — which I have tried to illustrate from my own case — include these:

(a) the importance of a conception of philosophy *behind* philosophical dance-study, for this is necessary to meet objections. In that sense, the topic is *genuinely* philosophical. It also implies that one cannot do this work knowing *only* dance-aesthetics;

(b) the need to make the philosophy consonant with the requirements of dance-practitioners — not to invent issues that do not ever 'bite' on them; but …

(c) not to 'take the practitioner's word for it' either: not all puzzlements will be resolved through the resources of, say, ordinary ways of talking — we may need 'gadgets' from (say) philosophical logic, used judiciously. For even when it is forms of words that generate the confusions (as often), the remedy may be effected from elsewhere;

(d) that even contrasts which we draw in practice (such as the artistic/aesthetic contrast) may need to be marked in a technical way;

(e) that a comparison with other arts, and especially other performing arts, *may* be revealing: equally, it may not.

This may seem a pretty small haul from this debate. No doubt it illustrates other points too. But these conclusions amount to rather more that it appears, for they suggest purposes (and techniques?) for a respectable philosophical contribution to dance studies.

More specifically, I have met Carr's charge of inconsistency by showing both that Wittgensteinian considerations do not militate against using the type/token contrast (that there was no *essential* essentialism there) and that such technical expressions might be required to make sense of the complexity of our experience of danceworks (at least, to make sense of it for the purposes of dance studies) — a project central to any dance study worth of the name. And this is consistent with how practitioners in dance think about their own activity, even though not (typically) reflecting their words about it. Further, I have briefly sketched how my concern with meaning in dance might be vindicated: how it might be of a piece with a plausible commonsense account of artistic value. If all of these are central to dance studies — as I urge — the centrality (for dance studies) of philosophy is ensured.

Of course, this returns us to the three ideas from which this chapter began. For I have tried to stress how each of the elements discussed flow from others — how a consistent view of philosophy is presupposed, as well as a consistent picture of the value (especially the educational value) of dance, and of the study of dance. I have ilustrated how my *technicalities* might be justified; and how they might reflect *real* issues for practitioners. I have here neither argued nor insisted that my views are *right*: but my point has been to use these views to expose to public scrutiny a vein of ore within dance-studies, that others might profitably mine.

Notes

1   References to works of Wittgenstein are:
    Wittgenstein 1953 — cited as "PI"
    Wittgenstein 1966 — cited as "LC"
    Wittgenstein 1967 — cited as "Z"
    Wittgenstein 1978 — cited as "RFM"
    Wittgenstein 1980 — cited as "CV"
    Wittgenstein 1993 — cited as "PO"

2   Strawson (1956: p. 108) speaks of one important species of philosophy as "therapeutic analysis": the 'analysis' part of this title is what might be queried here.

3   The point is to see that, if we think of all the performances as tokens, we are precluded from treating them as an engineer might treat a model. For a fuller

consideration, see Baker and Hacker (1980 — cited as 'B&H 1': pp. 284–296) on exemplars: and my notion of "a temporary paradigm" in McFee, 1978: pp.67–68.

⁴ See later (third section), and Aaron Meskin's Chapter in this volume, for some reservations about my entitlement to this combination of type/token and numerical identity.

⁵ As Wittgenstein says (PI: §201 [b]):

What this shews is that there is a way of grasping a rule which is *not an interpretation*, but which is exhibited in what we call 'obeying the rule' and 'going against it' in actual cases.

⁶ Note that talk of "numerically identical persons" amounts to there being only *one* person in the story: but the what is true of that person may differ at different times — *was* cheerful, short, hairy; *is* morose, tall, bald etc.

⁷ A problem raised by Sharpe (1979): not enough terms, with just "type" and "token", to cover the cases of abstract object, performers interpretation and particular performance. See McFee, 1994b: pp. 36–37.

⁸ A complexity of the Thesis of Notationality is that it places weight on the particular notation system in question (UD: pp. 105–106). A different notation system would have taken as crucial different features of the dance, so that movements which satisfy a Benesh score might not satisfy a Labanotation score, and vice versa. In response, we can only urge that reputable notation systems alone count here: that those who are knowledgeable about the art form decide what is and what is not reputable.

⁹ Consider the idea of the *abstract* [from Baker and Hacker 1985a — cited as "B&H 2"]: rules as abstract and rule-formulations as concrete — one part of the problem is (like?) the fluctuation of criteria and symptoms (PI: §354) etc.: such-and-such is a *rule* viewed this way, a *rule-formulation* viewed that way (different questions go with each; B&H 2: p. 41).

¹⁰ The type cannot be an ideal, since many of its features are *essentially* under-determined, to be realised in any performance: indeed, even the Union Jack, our specimen *type*, will leave *some* features (for example, size, material) under-determined. Whatever is specified here in the casae of dance, there will always be some features left unspecified — since there is no finite totality of such features. Thus the token will always be underdetermined.

¹¹ LC III note 5 [p. 28]: "The puzzles which arise in aesthetics, which are puzzles arising from the effects the arts have, are not puzzles about how these things

are caused". Indeed, such puzzles "are answered in an entirely different way" (LC II §36 [p. 17]). Again, LC IV note 3 [p. 29], with an implied 'no' answer: "Would a syringe which produces these effects on you do just as well as the picture?". Similarly, LC IV §9 [p. 34] emphasises the lack of 'detachability' of the work of art from its impact:

> You could select either of two poems to remind you of death, say. But supposing you had read a poem and admired it, could you say: 'Oh, read the other it will do the same'?

And, LC II §38 [p. 18]: "You could say: 'An aesthetic explanation is not a causal explanation'". Presumably, this means that, for some purposes, you could also say the opposite?

[12] These quotations are, respectively:

> ... in exploring and learning new forms of expression, we are gaining and refining the capacity for experiencing new feelings. (Best, 1974: p. 159)
> ... it is intrinsic to an artform that there should be the possibility of the expression of a concep[tion of life issues. (Best, 1992: p. 173)

[13] I have discussed these cases in two papers presently unpublished: 'Art, beauty and the ethical', presented to a conference 'Beauty and Ugliness', Antwerp, September 1996; and 'The artistic and the aesthetic', presented to national conference of British Society for Aesthetics, Oxford September 1998.

[14] A similar idea: that the effect on one's judgement of a painting of discovering that it is by a chimpanzee (say) is to remove from that categories of artistic appraisal — the net effect will alter one's judgement by "knocking it sideways" (Wollheim, 1993: p. 174). So the issue is not 'better or worse' exactly — more like 'meaning-bearing or not?'.

[15] See here McFee, 1997b: Kivy (1993: pp. 369–373) seems to grant *this* point.

[16] If this is not how Best uses the terms, I would happily treat them as reflecting *what I got* from considering Best's writings — I have some reason to think that my views here are congruent with his; at the least, this is what I think he *should* mean (whether or not he does).

[17] See Scruton's (1997: pp. 153–154) considerations against cognitivism: his argument is that either the term 'sad' applied to music is the same term as is applied to sad persons (which doesn't seem right, since "the sadness of persons is a property that only conscious organisms can possess" [p. 154]) or it is another term — but that can't be right either, since to "say that the word ascribes ... another property is to say that it has another sense — in other words that it

is used not metaphorically, but ambiguously" [p. 154]. This, Scruton thinks, cannot be an attractive line for anyone who is a realist about artistic properties. But has Scruton thought enough about (a) the variety of properties [especially including emergent properties], and (b) the variety of different contributions that might be made here? [His argument might work on some views of meaning, truth etc..; but not on mine!]

18 For example: "artworks are ... typically about something" (Danto, 1981: p. 3). Danto (1981: p. 81) writes of "'aboutness' being the crucial differentiating property' for artworks. This fact is something we learn in, roughly, learning 'how to go on' (PI: §151; §179) in art. For, as Danto (1992: p. 46) puts it:

> The artworld is the discourse of reasons institutionalised, and to be a member of the artworld is, accordingly, to have learned what it means to participate in the discourse of reasons for one's culture.

19 See Lyas, 1997: pp. 12–13: faced with only a few hours of life remaining, Colin Lyas would go to the performance rather than addressing its philosophical problems! See too his presentation to the British Society of Aesthetics national conference, Oxford 1997, where he expressly identified *philosophical logic* as one area of 'intrusion': and note that this is the area from which the type/token contrast arises.

20 I am especially sensitive to this point since I have repeatedly asserted that aestheticians cannot look *solely* at aesthetic matters if their work is to be successful: that they must look to the philosophy of mind or to philosophy of language, for example (McFee 1989). But this thought must be tempered by the recognition that these are two areas not presently conducted as I would wish! (See Travis, 1996; Travis 1997)

21 See, for example, Frege's discussion of fiction in his 'Logic' (1897) reprinted in Frege, 1979: p. 130.

22 This is what is missing in the philistine response attributed to Ryle, in Mehta, 1963: p. 67:

> Once, Ryle saw Isaiah Berlin coming from a performance of Bach's B-Minor Mass ... Berlin was totally absorbed by the moving experience he had just undergone. Ryle shouted to him across Broad Street, 'Isaiah, have you been listening to some tunes again?'

23 Carritt, "Foreword" to Carritt, 1931: p.ix:

> Its subject matter is such wavering and deceptive stuff as dreams are made of; its method is neither logical nor scientific, nor quite whole-heartedly and empirically matter of fact... Without application in practice to test it

and without an orthodox terminology to make it into an honest superstition or a thorough-going, soul-satisfying cult.

24 As above, I have used the terms "life-issues", "life situations" (both taken from David Best; UD: p. 174) as place-holders for this kind of connection; see UD: pp. 173-190.

25 Contrast Savile (1982: p. 181), who speaks of the need for "univocality" here; and earlier he comments:

> Unless the analysis I have offered [of beauty in art] can be extended to cover natural cases of beaust as well, and extended in such a way as not to import ambiguity into the concept, my proposal will have to be judged a failure. (Savile 1982: p. 176)

26 Although this points in the right direction, it (mis-)takes the thesis as one about words: better to say that using a term (say, 'gaudy') of art addresses a question different than using the term of (merely) aesthetic objects.

27 The beginning of such a thought might be found in Lyas' (1997: p. 18) remark:

> It is because we are struck by rainbows, entranced by fictions, moved by rhythms, unsettled by certain colour combinations, that we developed the words and behaviour that articulate aesthetic responses.

Of course, Lyas is here ignoring/denying the artistic/aesthetic contrast.

28 After noting this, I see that Kivy (1997: p. 68) uses the same quotation to raise a similar point: did I read it there first? I cannot now say, but would readily acknowledge the influence of this and Kivy's other writings.

29 Native speakers *can* understand words, etc.: for musical or dance works, scores only *really* make sense as recipes (Urmson 1976: pp. 244-245) — so perhaps they can only be appreciated as indicative of *structures*, etc. (that is, formally). Certainly, talk of hearing/ seeing *in one's head* must be treated as a *metaphor* for something else.

30 The passage begins: "what is it to follow a musical phrase with understanding, or to play it with understanding?". Here Wittgenstein implies that one's answers to such questions might sometimes resemble each other.

References

Baker, G. (1991) '*Philosophical Investigations* §122: neglected aspects', in R. L. Arrington and H-J. Glock (eds.) *Wittgenstein's Philosophical Investigations: text and context.* London: Routledge, pp. 35–68.

Baker, G. and Hacker, P. (1980) *Wittgenstein: understanding and meaning (volume 1 of an analytical commentary on Philosophical Investigations).* Oxford: Blackwell.

——— (1985a) *Wittgenstein: rules, grammar and necessity (volume 2 of an analytical commentary on Philosophical Investigations).* Oxford: Blackwell.

——— (1985b) *Scepticism, rules and language* Oxford: Blackwell.

Beardsmore, R. W. (1971) *Art and morality.* London: Macmillan.

Best, D. (1974) *Expression in movement and the arts.* London: Lepus.

——— (1992) *The rationality of feeling.* London: Falmer Press.

Carr, D (1997) 'Meaning in dance', *British Journal of Aesthetics.* Vol. 37 (October): pp. 349–366.

Carritt, E. F. (1931) *Philosophies of beauty* Oxford: Clarendon Press.

Danto, A. C. (1981) *The transfiguration of the commonplace.* Cambridge, MA: Harvard University Press.

——— (1992) 'The artworld revisited', in his *Beyond the brillo box.* New York: Farrar, Straus, Giroux, pp. 33–53.

Dickie, G. (1974) *Art and the aesthetic: an institutional analysis.* Ithaca, NY: Cornell University Press.

——— (1984) *The art circle.* New York: New Haven Publishers.

——— (1993) 'A tale of two artworlds', in M. Rollins (ed) *Danto and his critics.* Oxford: Blackwell, pp. 73–78.

Dworkin, R. (1985) *A matter of principle.* Cambridge, MA: Harvard University Press.

Foster, S. L. (1986) *Reading dancing: bodies and subjects in contemporary american dance.* Berkeley, CA: University of California Press.

Frege, G. (1979) *Posthumous writings* [Edited H. Hermes, F. Kambartel and F. Kaulbach]. Oxford: Blackwell.

Kivy, P. (1990) *Music alone: philosophical reflections on the purely musical experience.* Ithaca, NY: Cornell University Press.

——— (1993) *The fine art of repetition.* Cambridge: Cambridge University Press.

——— (1997) *Philosophies of art.* Cambridge: Cambridge University Press.

Lyas, C. (1997) *Aesthetics*. London: UCL Press.

McDowell, J. (1998) *Mind, value and reality*. Cambridge, MA: Harvard University Press.

Mcfee, G. (1978) *Much of Jackson Pollock is vivid wallpaper*. New York: University Press of America.

―――― (1989) 'Logic of appreciation in the republic of art', *British Journal of Aesthetics*, Vol 28: pp. 230–238

―――― (1992) *Understanding dance*. London: Routledge.

―――― (1993) 'Reflections on the nature of action-research', *Cambridge Journal of Education*. Vol 23: pp. 173–183.

―――― (1994a) *The concept of dance education*. London: Routledge.

―――― (1994b) 'Was that *Swan Lake* I saw you at last night?: dance-identity and understanding', *Dance Research* Vol. XII No. 1: pp. 20–40.

―――― (1996) 'A nasty accident with one's flies; or, life in philosophy', Inaugural Lecture as Professor of Philosophy, University of Brighton, May.

―――― (1997a) 'Education, art and the physical: the case for the academic study of dance — present and future', in G. McFee & A. Tomlinson (eds) *Education, sport and leisure: connections and controversies*. Aachen: Meyer & Meyer, pp. 103–117.

―――― (1997b) 'Meaning and the art-status of music alone', *British Journal of Aesthetics* Vol 37: pp. 31-46.

―――― (1998) 'Are there philosophical issues in respect of sport (other than ethical ones)?', in M. McNamee & J. Parry (eds) *Ethics and sport*. London: E&FN Spon/Chapman Hall, pp. 3–18.

Mackrell, J. (1997) *Reading dance*. London: Michael Joseph.

Mehta, V. (1963) *Fly and the fly-bottle*. London: Weidenfeld and Nicholson.

Monk, R. (1990) *Ludwig Wittgenstein: the duty of genius*. London: Jonathan Cape.

O'Neill, J. P. (ed) (1992) *Barnett Newman: selected writings and interviews*. Berkeley, CA: University of California Press.

Redfern, B. (1983) *Dance, art and aesthetics*. London: Dance Books.

Savile, A. (1982) *The test of time*. Oxford: Clarendon Press.

Scruton, R. (1997) *The aesthetics of music*. Oxford: Clarendon Press.

Sharpe, R. A. (1979) 'Type, token, interpretation and performance', *Mind* Vol. 86: pp. 437–440.

Strawson, P. F. (1956) 'Construction and analysis', in G. Ryle (ed) *The revolution in rhilosophy*. London: Macmillan, pp. 97–110.

Thom, P. (1993) *For an audience: a philosophy of performance*, Philadelphia, PA: Temple University Press.

Travis, C. (1996) 'Meaning's role in truth', *Mind* Vol. 105 (July): pp. 451–466.

—— (1997) 'Pragmatics', in C. Wright and B. Hale (eds) *A companion to the philosophy of language*. Oxford: Blackwell, pp. 87–107.

Urmson, J. O. (1976) 'The performing arts' in H. D. Lewis (ed) *Contemporary british philosophy* (fourth series). London: George Allen & Unwin, pp. 239–252.

Wisdom, J. (1953) *Philosophy and psycho-analysis*. Oxford: Blackwell.

Wittgenstein, L. (1953) *Philosophical investigations*. Oxford: Blackwell.

—— (1966) *Lectures and conversations on aesthetics, psychology and religious belief* [Edited C. Barrett]. Oxford: Blackwell.

—— (1967) *Zettel*. Oxford: Blackwell.

—— (1978) *Remarks on the foundations of mathematics* 3rd Edition. Oxford: Blackwell.

—— (1980) *Culture and value*. Oxford: Blackwell.

—— (1993) *Philosophical occasions 1912–1951* [Edited J. Klagge & A. Nordmann]. Indianapolis: Hackett Publishing.

Wollheim, R. (1993) *The mind and its depths*. Cambridge, MA: Harvard University Press.

Index

A

action *6, 47, 111, 113, 115, 148*
Adams, John *51*
Adshead-Lansdale, Janet *36, 37*
aesthetic *129–132*
aesthetics *171, 172*
affect *138*
affective *131, 171*
agent-relative *132, 133*
agreement *89, 92*
Ailey, Alvin *54*
'Airs' [Taylor] *148*
Albery, Tim *42*
ambiguous *37–38, 40*
American Ballet Theatre *148*
'American Elegies' [Adams] *51*
American Sign Language *25*
analysis *157*
Anderson, Lea *34, 150*
Anscombe, Elizabeth *125*
anthropomorphism *97, 98*
'Anticipation of the Night' [Brakhage] *29*
'Apollo' [Balanchine] *27*
appreciation *4, 129, 130–131, 135, 136, 167, 179*
Aristotle *16, 17, 18–19, 126–129, 132, 133, 134, 178*
artistic *129–132*
artistic/aesthetic *8, 9, 169–172, 177, 178, 180, 185*
Ashton, Frederick *46, 147*
'Auriole' [Taylor] *148*
Ayer, A. J. *3*

B

Bach, J. S. *116*
Baker, G. P. *156*
Baker, G. P. and Hacker, P. M. S. *88, 89, 90, 92, 98, 160, 166, 182*
Balanchine, George *27, 28, 147*
ballet *15, 20, 25, 54, 144, 149*
ballet body *145*
ballet pantomime *25, 26*
Batteux, Abbé Charles *17*
Beardsley, Monroe *47*
Beardsmore, R. W. *115, 177*
Beaumont, Cyril *26*
Beethoven *24, 58*
Bergner, G. and Plett, N. *39*
Best, David *6, 87, 93, 129–132, 135, 144, 155, 156, 168, 168–171, 185*
Bharata Natyam *93*
Bintley, David *97*
bodily shape *149*
body/ies *7, 104, 150*
Bourne, Matthew *34, 162*
Brakhage *28*
'Bring in 'da Noise, Bring in 'da Funk' *25*
Brown, Trisha *54*

C

Candomblé *117, 119*
'Carnation' [Childs] *91*
Carr, David *6, 7, 47, 144, 147, 152, 156, 168, 172, 173, 181*
Carritt, E. C. *184*

189

Carroll, Noël *60*
Carroll, Noël and Banes, Sally *7*
case-by-case *173*
cause *113*
Cavell, Stanley *98*
Challis, Chris *7, 139*
Chaos Theory *174*
Chomsky, Noam *68*
'Cinderella' *147*
'Cinderella' [Ashton] *46*
'Cinderella' [Orta] *51*
Clinton, Bill *50*
code *21, 25, 110, 112*
cognitivism *170–171*
Cohen, S. J. *31*
commedia dell'arte *25*
community *75, 76*
conceptual confusion *112*
concrete *46, 72*
conventions *128, 129, 151*
conversation *108–109*
"Coppélia" *39*
"Coppélia: *24*
Corneille *18*
costume *92*
Crébillon *18*
criticism *67*
Crowther, Paul *143*
cultural background *93*
culture *64, 67, 73, 77, 78, 79, 80–
    81, 83*
Cunningham, Merce *19, 146, 151*
Currie, Gregory *60*

D

dance critic *127*
dance studies *1–10*
dance-practice *71*

dancelike *66*
danceworks
    'Airs' *148*
    'American Elegies' *51*
    'Auriole' [Taylor] *148*
    'Carnation' [Childs] *91*
    'Cinderella' *147*
    'Cinderella' [Ashton] *46*
    'Cinderella' [Orta] *51*
    'Games' [McKayle's] *24*
    'Giselle' *24*
    'L'Allegro, il Penseroso e il Moderato'
        [Morris] *46*
    'Le Corsaire' [Petipa] *146*
    'Les Sylphides' *96*
    'Made in the USA' [Gordon] *150*
    'New Love Song Waltzes ' *146*
    'Night Journey' *27*
    'Onegin' [Cranko] *151*
    'Orphée et Euridice' [Noverre] *27*
    'Orpheus' [Balanchine] *27*
    'Points in Space' [Cunningham] *150*
    'Raymonda' *24*
    'Swan Lake' *96, 99, 161*
    'Swan Lake' [Bourne] *162, 164*
    'Swan Lake' [Nureyev] *174*
    'Swan Lake' [Petipa-Ivanov] *26*
    'Swan Song' [Bruce] *166*
    'The Moor's Pavane' *46*
    'Trio A' *46*
danceworld *66*
Danto, Arthur *167, 176, 184*
definition *87, 88*
Delsarte *25*
Descartes *125*
Dickie, George *82, 167*
drama *19*
dualism *148*
dualist/ism *102, 103, 107, 112, 114*

Dunne, Joseph *133–135*
D. V. 8 *144*
Dworkin, Ronald *175*

E

education 2, *7*, *8*
educational *79*, *83*, *123–139*, *172*
Eisner, Elliott *104–106*, *107*, *109*
Ek, Mats *34*, *38–41*, *42*, *162*
episteme *133*, *138*
essentialism *86*, *87–88*, *159*, *163*
essentialist *159*
examples *93*
experience *50*, *56*, *60*, *71*, *94*,
       106, *125*, *134*, *177*
explanation *7*, *80*, *97*, *180*
expression *143*

F

family resemblance *67*
Forti, Simone *27*
forward retroactivism *34–38*
Foster, Susan Leigh *43*, *157*, *179*
Frege, G. *184*

G

'Games' [McKayle] *24*
Gardner, Howard *111–112*, *113*, *119*
Geach, P. T. *125*
genre *36*, *63*, *94*, *128*
'Giselle' *24*
'Giselle' [Mats Ek] *35*, *36*, *43*, *38–41*
Glickman, Jack *59*
Goethe *4*
Goodman, Nelson *152*
Graham, Martha *27*, *54*
grammar *145*
Guernica *170*

H

Hamlet *22*, *173*, *175*, *176*
Hanna, Judith *95*
Hay, Deborah *157*
Hirst, Paul *123*, *135*, *172*
historical/histories *56*, *75*
Hodgens, Pauline *36*
Holiday, Billie *138*
Holm, Hanya *46*
'Homage to Mahler' [Holm] *46*
Hume, David *123*

I

identification *150*
identity *144*
ideology *152*
imitation *14–19*
Indian dance *25*, *63*, *93*, *129*
institutional theory of art *66*, *167*
intention *6*, *96*, *180*
intentional *85*, *95*
interpretation *6*, *35*, *37*, *41*,
       52, *53*, *58*, *159–165*, *175*
Ito, Midori *65*

J

Jarman, Derek *175*
Jaspers, Karl *83*
jazz *116*, *128*, *137*, *138*, *139*, *145*
'Jewels' [Balanchine] *28*
Jones, Sue *6*
Judson Dance Theatre *91*

K

Kane, Angela *148–149*, *149*
Kathak *93*
Kenny, A. *125*

Kerr, Fergus *108, 112, 114, 115, 117, 119*
Kivy, Peter
    31, 49, 155, 165, 171, 185
knowledge *6, 9, 24*
knowledge acquisition *126–129*
Koritz, Amy *152*
Kristeller, Paul Oskar *17*
Kuhn, T. S. *167*

L

Laban, Rudolf *101, 102*
'L'Allegro, il Penseroso e il Moderato' [Morris] *46*
language
    65, 68, 74, 78, 79, 83, 93, 103, 107, 108, 109, 113, 118
language and learning *110*
language-learning *67–68, 89, 94*
'Le Corsaire' [Petipa] *146*
learning *75*
'Les Sylphides' *96*
Levinson, André *13*
Levinson, Jerrold *45, 46, 47, 50– 55, 53, 57–58*
life-issues *144, 150, 168–171*
life-situations *168–171*
'Light' [Takei] *27*
Limón, José *27, 54*
Luntley, Michael *136, 137*
Lyas, Colin *172, 176, 184, 185*

M

MacIntyre, A. *136*
Mackrell, Judith *162, 179*
'Made in the USA' [Gordon] *150*
Marett, R. R. *113*
Mark Morris Dancers *144*

Mason, Monica *41, 42, 43*
McFee, Graham *34–38, 39, 47, 59, 86, 87, 89, 90, 99, 144, 156*
Mcguire, Susan *148*
McKayle, Donald *24*
meaning *4, 27, 34, 36, 38, 39, 42, 72, 113, 114, 115, 143, 150, 152, 160, 168–170*
medium *146*
Meskin, Aaron *6, 7–8, 182*
metaphor *74, 97, 98*
mimesis *14*
misperception *35, 177*
misunderstanding *157*
modern dance *55*
Mona Lisa *21*
Monk, Meredith *172*
Morris, Geraldine *147, 152*
Morris, Mark *34, 54*
Mounce, H. O. *116*
Movement Education *101*
Mozart *58*
multiple/s *158, 159, 165*
music *92*

N

narrative
    7, 25, 38, 39, 40, 72, 75, 152
necessary and sufficient conditions
    125, 131, 166
necessary conditions
    17, 20, 86, 87, 99
'New Love Song Waltzes' [Morris] *146*
'Night Journey' [Graham] *27*
non-cognitive *131*
normative/normativity *15, 96, 127*
notation *64, 150, 166*

Noverre, Jean-Georges *13, 14–20, 27, 30, 31*
numerical identity *161, 163, 182*
Nureyev, Rudolf *42, 43, 162*
Nussbaum, Martha *114*

O

objectivity *130, 131–132, 135*
'Onegin' [Cranko] *151*
ontology *30, 46–48, 144, 150*
original *91*
'Orphée et Euridice' [Noverre] *27*
'Orpheus' [Balanchine] *27*
Orta, Carlos *46, 51*
Ozawa, Seiji *65*

P

paradigms *98*
particularism *165–168*
particularity *138*
'Pastoral' *24*
Paul Taylor *148*
Peirce *173*
perception *70–71*
performance *6, 37, 45–58, 70, 95, 127, 128, 136, 144–146, 159–165, 161, 162, 163, 164, 165, 178, 179*
performer *95*
performer's interpretation *160, 176, 179*
personal *132*
perspectival *7, 45–58*
perspective/s *73, 95*
Peters, Richard *123, 124*
Petipa *26*
Phillips, D. Z. *108, 113*
philosophical logic *156, 173, 180*

phronesis *132–136*
Picasso *35, 36*
'Planet' [Forti] *27*
Plato *18, 47, 69, 71, 133*
'Points in Space' [Cunningham] *150*
post-modern/ist/ism *8, 20, 42, 54, 136, 138, 149*
post-structuralism *33, 34, 83*
practical *70, 124, 166, 168*
practical knowledge *7, 124, 125, 126, 127, 133, 138*
practical reason *126–128, 131*
practical wisdom *132–136*
practice *2, 16, 72, 73, 76, 77, 78, 80, 81, 109, 115, 134, 149*
practitioners *156, 181*
procedural knowledge *127, 128–129*
procedural rules *91*

R

Racine *18, 30*
'Raymonda ' *24*
reason *2, 35, 40, 116*
recipe *49, 90*
reconstruction *150*
recording *54, 64*
Redfern, Betty *158*
rehearsal *163*
relativist *130*
representation *8, 13–30, 151*
Republic of Dance *163, 164, 167*
restoring *16*
Rhees, Rush *104*
ritual *117*
Romantic *40, 41*
Rowell, Bonnie *7–8*
Royal Ballet *96, 97, 147*
rule-following *85–98*

rule-formulations *90–91*
rules *49, 127, 128, 149, 151*
Russell, Joan *102, 117, 118, 119*
Ryle, Gilbert *103, 124, 128*

S

samples *90*
Savile, A. *185*
Schier, F. *21*
Schiller *65*
Scruton, Roger *8, 163*
Seigel, Marcia *144, 144–145*
sexuality *40, 41*
Seymour, Lynn *41, 43*
Shakespeare *110*
Sharpe, R.A. *46, 59, 182*
Shawn, Ted *25*
Siegel, Marcia *38*
skill *52, 147, 149*
Smith, Adam *14*
social dancing *15*
Socratic dialogues *69*
Sparshott, Francis *5, 6, 31*
spectator *95*
St. Denis, Ruth *26*
staging *167*
standards *130*
'Still Life at the Penguin Cafe' [Bintley]
        97
student *69–70*
style *36*
sub-type *46–47*
subjectivist/ism *48, 102–*
        108, 109, 114, 163
sufficient conditions *86, 87, 130*

'Swan Lake'
        26, 47, 96, 99, 158, 161,
        162, 163, 164, 173
'Swan Lake' [Petipa-Ivanov] *26*
'Swan Lake' [Bourne] *162, 164*
'Swan Lake' [Nureyev] *174*
'Swan Song' [Bruce] *166*
symbol *103, 109, 110, 112, 113*
'Symphonie Fantastique' *24*
system *145, 146*

T

Takei, Kei *27*
Taylor, C. *136*
Taylor, Paul *148–150*
teaching *52*
techne *126–129, 132, 133, 138, 139*
technical *7, 67, 178*
technique *126, 127, 127–*
        128, 137, 139, 144–146
technologies *64*
telos *16, 19, 53*
text *29, 30*
The Concept of Mind *124*
'The Loves of Mars and Venus' [===]
        26
'The Moor's Pavane' [Limon] *46*
Thesis of Notationality *165, 166, 182*
Thom, Paul *45, 49, 178*
Thompson, R. *27*
tradition *136*
transfiguration *176–177*
Travis, Charles *9, 184*
'Trio A' [Rainer] *46*
type/token *46, 48, 49, 59, 90, 156,*
        158, 160, 161, 164, 166, 172,
        173, 181

U

Ulysses *158*
underdetermination *37*
understanding *7, 10, 69, 70–72, 72, 73, 76, 86, 88, 94, 95, 97, 107, 111, 114, 136, 174, 179*
uniqueness *91*
Urmson, J. O. *162*

V

value *2, 4, 8, 9*
Vermeer *56*
versions *159–165*
video *54, 55, 64*

Voltaire *18*
von Wright, G. H. *125*
voodoo *117*

W

Weaver, John *13, 14–20, 25*
Wisdom, John *2, 172*
Wittgenstein, Ludwig
   4, 5, 36, 67, 83, 85–86, 95, 96, 98, 110, 112, 113, 114, 115, 127, 156–157, 166, 167, 168, 174, 176, 177, 179, 181, 182, 185
Wollheim, Richard *10, 46, 148*
Worton, Michael *37*

SRC Edition

Volume 1
Tomlinson/ Fleming (eds.)

Ethics, Sport and Leisure

Crises and Critiques

This volume offers a reflective, multi-disciplinary and partly inter-disciplinary collection of complementary articles concerning ethics, sport and leisure, and how such areas are investigated, researched and understood. Its three parts deal with: I. ethical issues and ethics in sport and sports practice; II. with ethical issues in research in sports science and III. with ethical issues in research in the sociology of sport and leisure.

304 pages, paperback, 14,8 x 21 cm
ISBN 3-89124-441-X
DM 34,-/ SFr 31,60/ ÖS 248,-/ £ 14.95/ US $ 24.-/
Austr. $ 32.95/ Can $ 34.95

Volume 2
McFee/ Tomlinson (eds.)

Education, Sport and Leisure

Connections and Controversies

This volume presents topical and trenchant thinking on cultural and curricular issues in education, sport and leisure, in the light of such factors as Compulsory Competitive Tendering (CCT), Local Management of Schools (LMS) and the National Curriculum in Physical Education. It underlines the need for critical evaluation of the changing role of the teacher, of the development of a revised physical education curriculum etc.

232 pages, paperback, 14,8 x 21 cm
ISBN 3-89124-442-8
DM 29,80/ SFr 27,70/ ÖS 218,-/ £ 12.95/ US $ 17.95/
Austr.$ 29.95/ Can $ 25.95

Volume 3
Alan Tomlinson (ed.)

Gender, Sport and Leisure

Continuities and Challenges

Reporting data and case-studies – this volume is offered as a modest contribution to a continuing debate on the continuities apparent in gendered sport and leisure cultures, and the impact of some of the most notable challenges to those continuities.
The book is divided into four parts the headlines of which are:
I. Participation; II. Education; III. Popular Culture; IV. Policy and Action.

272 pages, paperback, 14,8 x 21 cm
ISBN 3-89124-443-6
DM 34,-/ SFr 31,60/ ÖS 248,-/ £ 14.95/ US $ 24.-/
Austr. $ 32.95/ Can $ 34.95

Volume 4
Sugden/ Bairner (eds.)

Sport In Divided Societies

This collection of essays looks at the importance of sport in countries which are particularly affected by social division. Sport is used as a window through wich the relationship between national identity, nationalism, ethnicity and sporting expression in diverse cultural setting is explored. Several studies of societies, in wich sport is popular and within the boundaries of wich there are a significant number of people who dissociate themselves from their goverment, seek to show how sport contributes to a social change and how easily it can be manipulated.

200 pages, figures, paperback, 14,8 x 21 cm
ISBN 3-89124-445-2
DM 29,80/ SFr 27,70/ ÖS 218,-/ £ 12.95/ US $ 17.95/
Austr. $ 29.95/ Can $ 25.95

Volume 5
Maurice Roche (ed.)

Sport, Popular Culture and Identity

This book is concerned with the relationship between sport and collective identities in contemporary societies. It looks at political and policy issues in the relationship between sport and national identities and between sport and urban/local identities. Furthermore it deals with the increasingly important sphere of "media sport" and the role of television and press in expressing and forming collective identities. The essays investigate European Football, the Olympic Games 2000 and Rugby.

200 pages, figures, paperback, 14,8 x 21 cm
ISBN 3-89124-468-1
DM 29,80/ SFr 27,70/ ÖS 218,-/ £ 12.95/ US $ 17.95/
Austr.$ 29.95/ Can $ 25.95

Volume 6
Lincoln Allison (ed.)

Taking Sport Seriously

This inter-disciplinary collection of essays seeks to define the achievement of the academic study of sport as it has developed over the past ten to twenty years.
Each essay investigates an aspect of the importance of sport as it is understood in the academic world nowadays. Essay-titles included are: „Sport and Civil Society", „Sport and History", „The Concept of Doping and the Future of Sport", „The State of Play: Sport, Capital and Happiness" and more.

204 pages, paperback, 14,8 x 21 cm,
ISBN 3-89124-479-7
DM 29,80/ SFr 27,70/ ÖS 218,-/ £ 14.95/ US $ 17.95/
Austr.$ 29.95/Can $ 25.95

MEYER & MEYER SPORT

Von-Coels-Str. 390 • D-52080 Aachen
Tel.: ++ 49 (0)2 41/ 9 58 10-0 • Fax: ++ 49 (0)2 41/ 9 58 10-10
e-mail: verlag@meyer-meyer-sports.com • http://www.meyer-meyer-sports.com